CONTENT

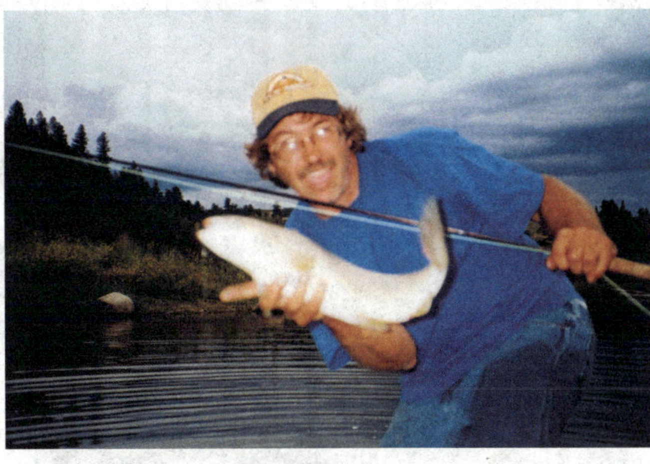

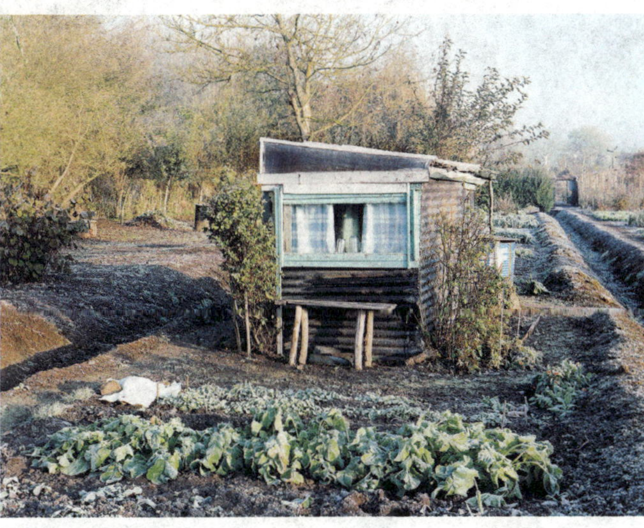

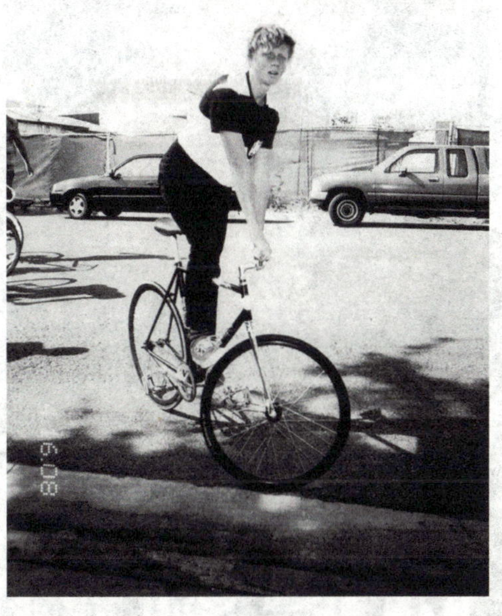

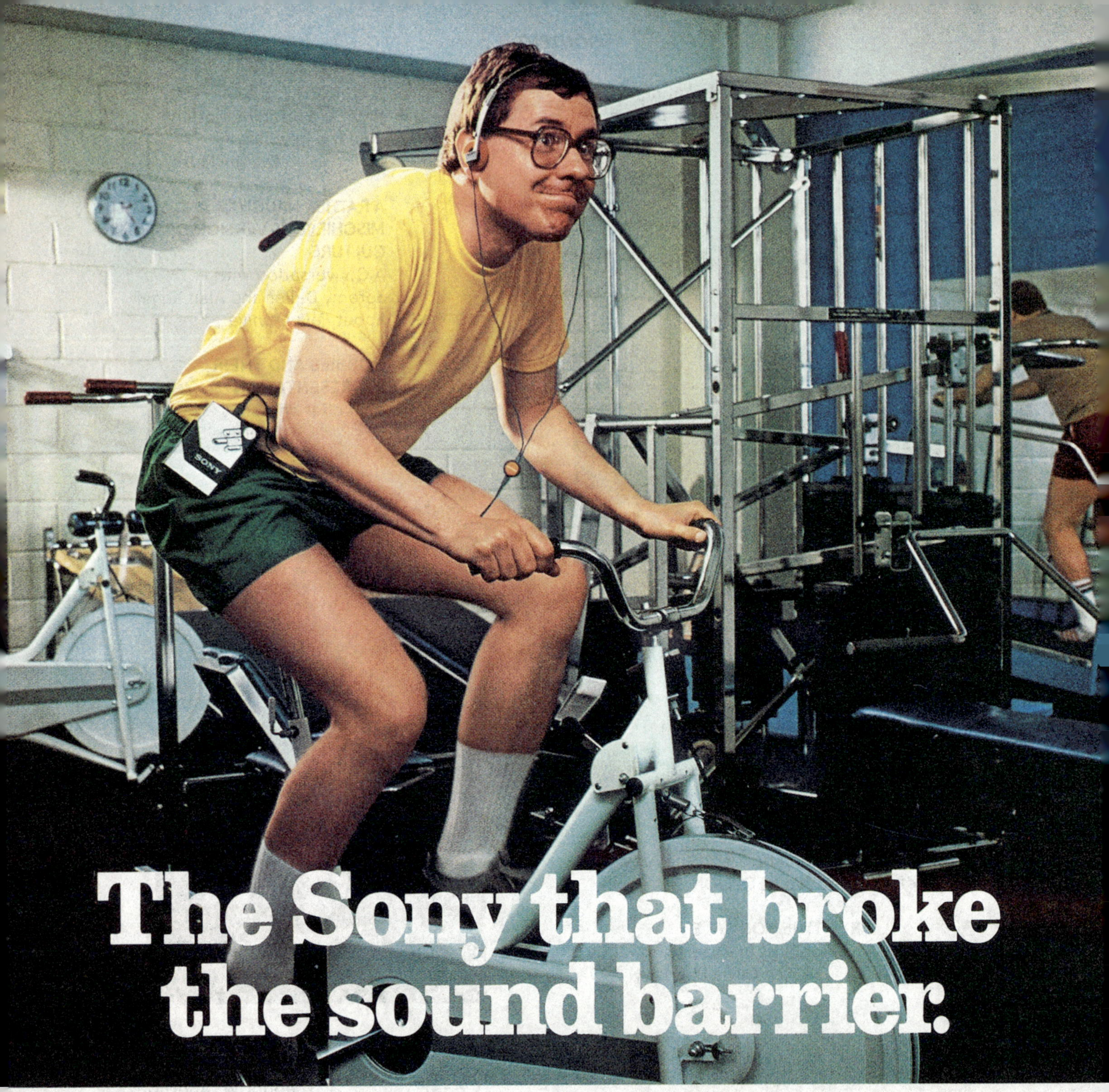

The Sony that broke the sound barrier.

Until Sony introduced the Walkman (a stereo cassette player about the size of a cassette), there was no way to hear quality sound reproduction this good unless you bought a ticket to Carnegie Hall, or sat home with an expensive component stereo.

Unfortunately, it was impossible to ski, jog, roller-skate or take a walk in a concert hall or your living room.

That is why on November 1, 1979, the Walkman took a historic step forward by combining incredible sound with total portability. What followed can only be described as a Sonic Boom.

Now people everywhere are taking their music with them, even if they're going nowhere fast. **THE WALKMAN**

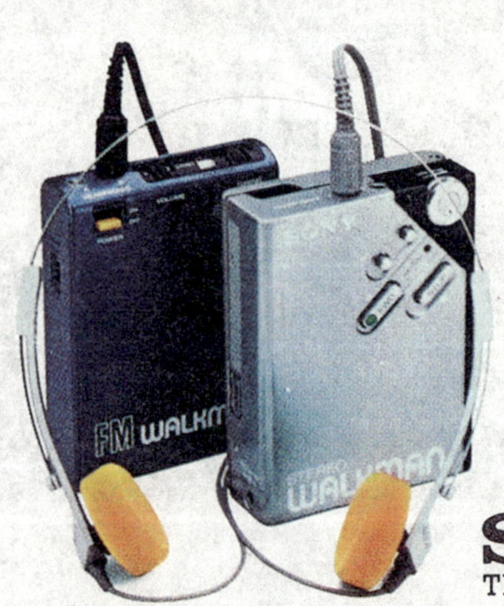

SONY®
THE ONE AND ONLY

DEAR READERS

What happens when photographers and artists incorporate hobbies in their work as a means of challenging artistic practices and hierarchies? How do hobbyists depict their passions photographically? And what might a hobby be in an age when our notions of private and social spheres have shifted due to the impact of the Internet? Has the digital era possibly conjured up the end of the hobby culture? Or have phenomena like YouTube and media-related developments in photography actually given hobbies and leisure time a new lease of life?

Against this current backdrop, *The Hobbyist* looks at the phenomenon of the hobby in an increasingly visualized and mediatized culture and reflects on its multiple layers of meaning within the contrasting spheres of leisure and work, ideology and consumerism, amateurism and professionalism. *The Hobbyist* is the first major exhibition to explore the relationship between photography and hobby culture, focussing both on the photography of hobbies and photography as a hobby.

From the hippie and avant-garde cultures of the 1960s to the DIY craze of the 1980s and today's maker movement, *The Hobbyist* explores specific places where hobbies are pursued and considers aspects of their commercialization with regard to consumerism and lifestyle. With the help of documents from the early 1970s, such as the *Whole Earth Catalog*, the exhibition looks back on the countercultures in the hippie and nascent computer communities of that era. They produced prototypical tools for the future that would, within the space of just two generations, become an integral part of daily life. The fact that the pursuit of hobbies takes on the form of a ritualized passion is illustrated by the content and scope of the photographic works whose creators often operate on the border between documentarian and hobbyist, expert and amateur, probing the ways in which photography relates to some very quirky, offbeat, and eagerly pursued hobbies.

A phenomenon as diverse and participatory as the hobby can hardly be tackled through a classical exhibition alone, which is why a comprehensive events program has been conceived to be an integral part of *The Hobbyist*. This magazine has been published to accompany the exhibition and opens up room for thought in its three sections, 'Stories,' 'Practices,' and 'Context,' which expand on the relationship between the visual and hobbyist culture.

We would like to take this opportunity to express our thanks to all participants, artists, lenders, authors, colleagues, and sponsors.

Pierre Hourquet, Anna Planas, Thomas Seelig
Exhibition Curators

The Sony for Sun-Lovers

If you're a person who hates to stay indoors watching television on a bright sunny day, we've got the perfect set for you. Because with the all-transistor Sony Sun Set, you can go outdoors and watch television on a bright sunny day.

The secret is the screen. Instead of a conventional white screen, the Sun Set has a special black screen that cuts down the glare. Which means that the picture won't fade out unless it's supposed tc And since it plays off AC current as we as rechargeable batteries, there's nothin to stop you from going indoors and watch ing the Sun Set after the sun goes dowr

The Sun Set

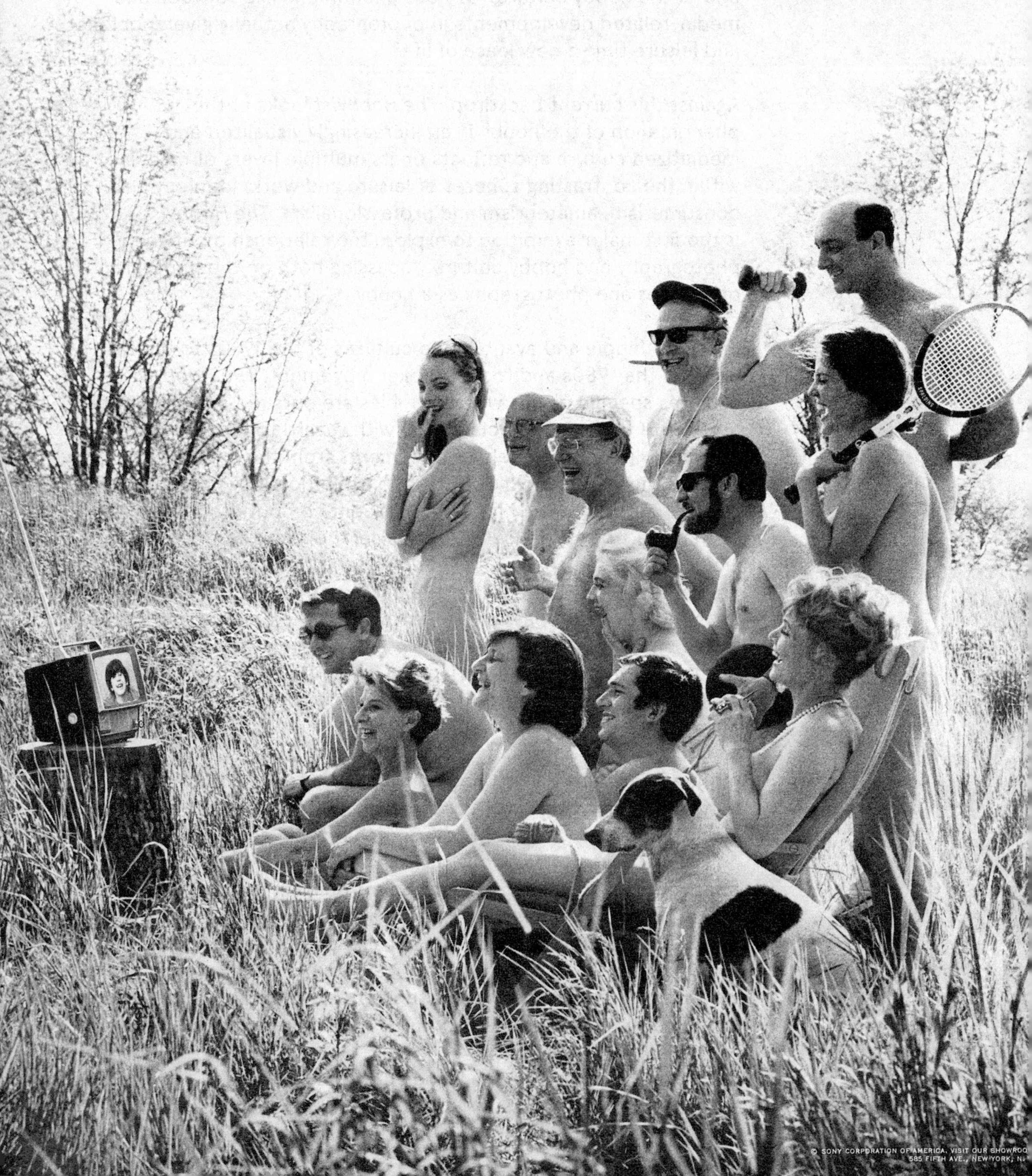

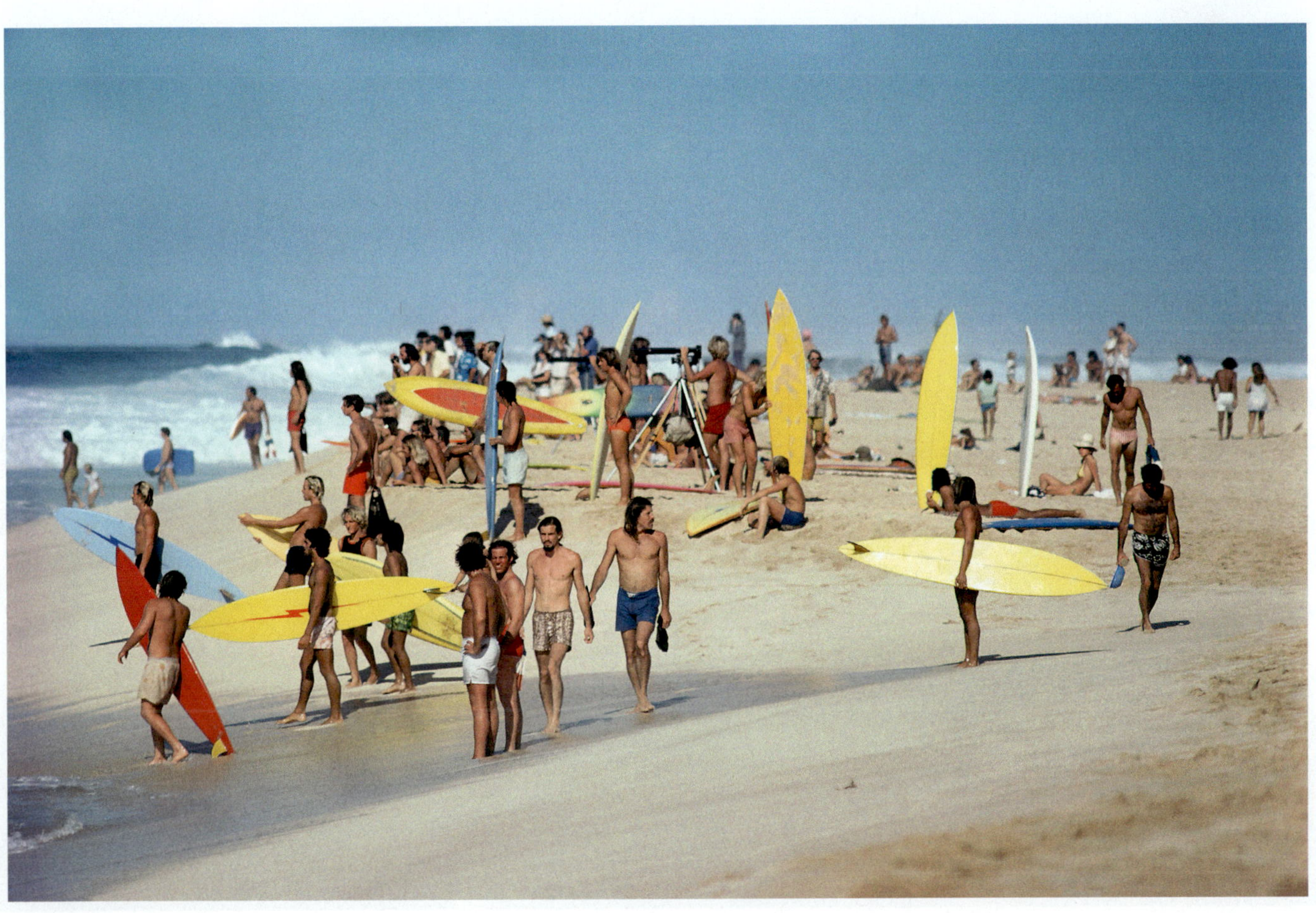

Jeff Divine, *Surfers on the Beach*, 1974

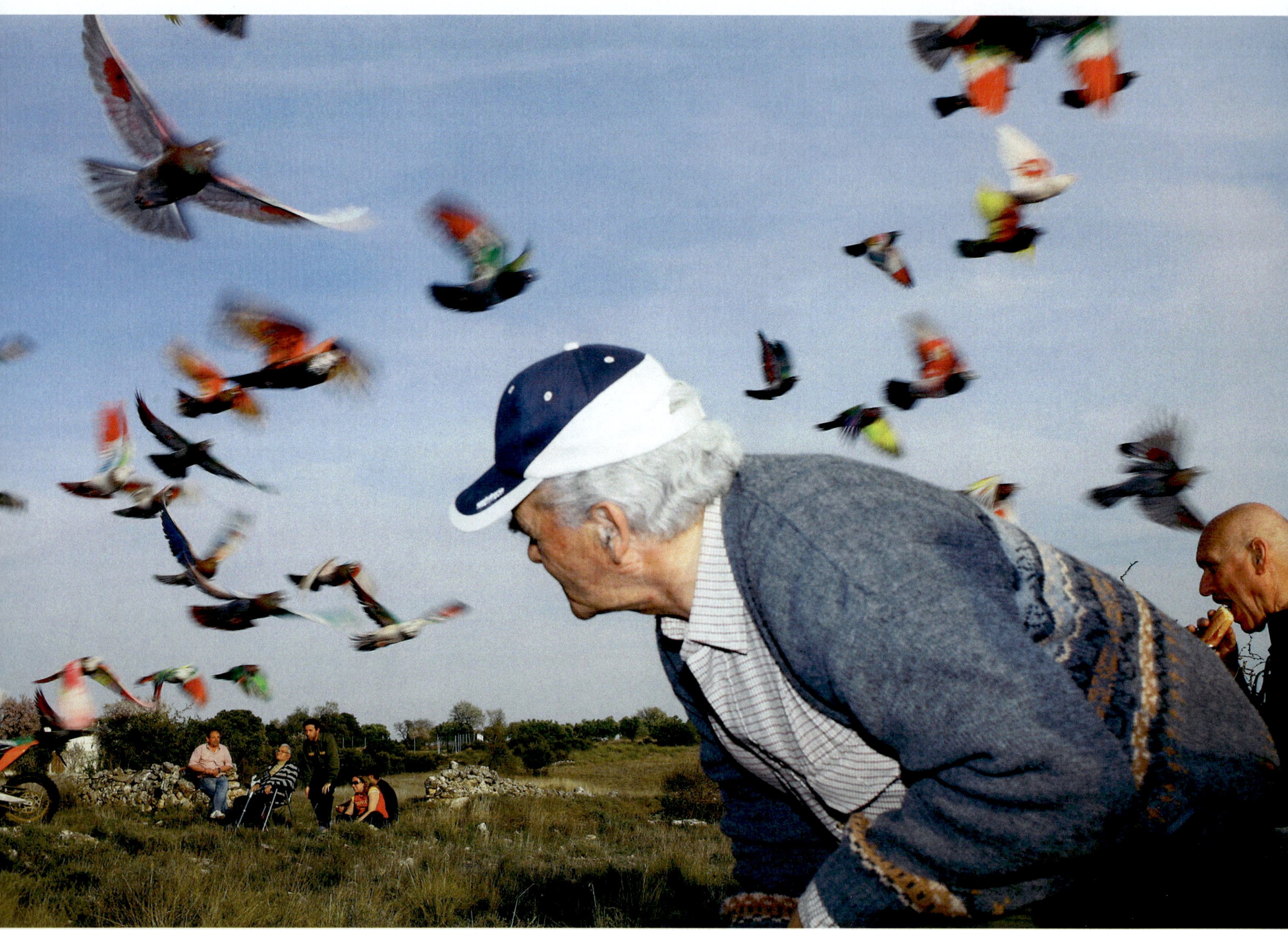

"Cocks, as you might suspect, are male birds. A young cock is any cock under the age of one. All the rest are old cocks. Female birds, or hens, are classified similarly. Reifsnyder says, 'I'd rather win with a hen than a cock because it's harder. And hens are the key to breeding anyway. Cocks just give color. Hens pass on type and power.' 'Type' is the way the carriage is formed and how the bird stands. 'Most of the points in this breed are in the nose; that's where the power is. It's like a bull's-eye area ... But the fact is, you'll never find a perfect bird."

From Andrew D. Blechman, *Pigeons,* 2007

Ricardo Cases, from *Paloma al Aire*, 2011

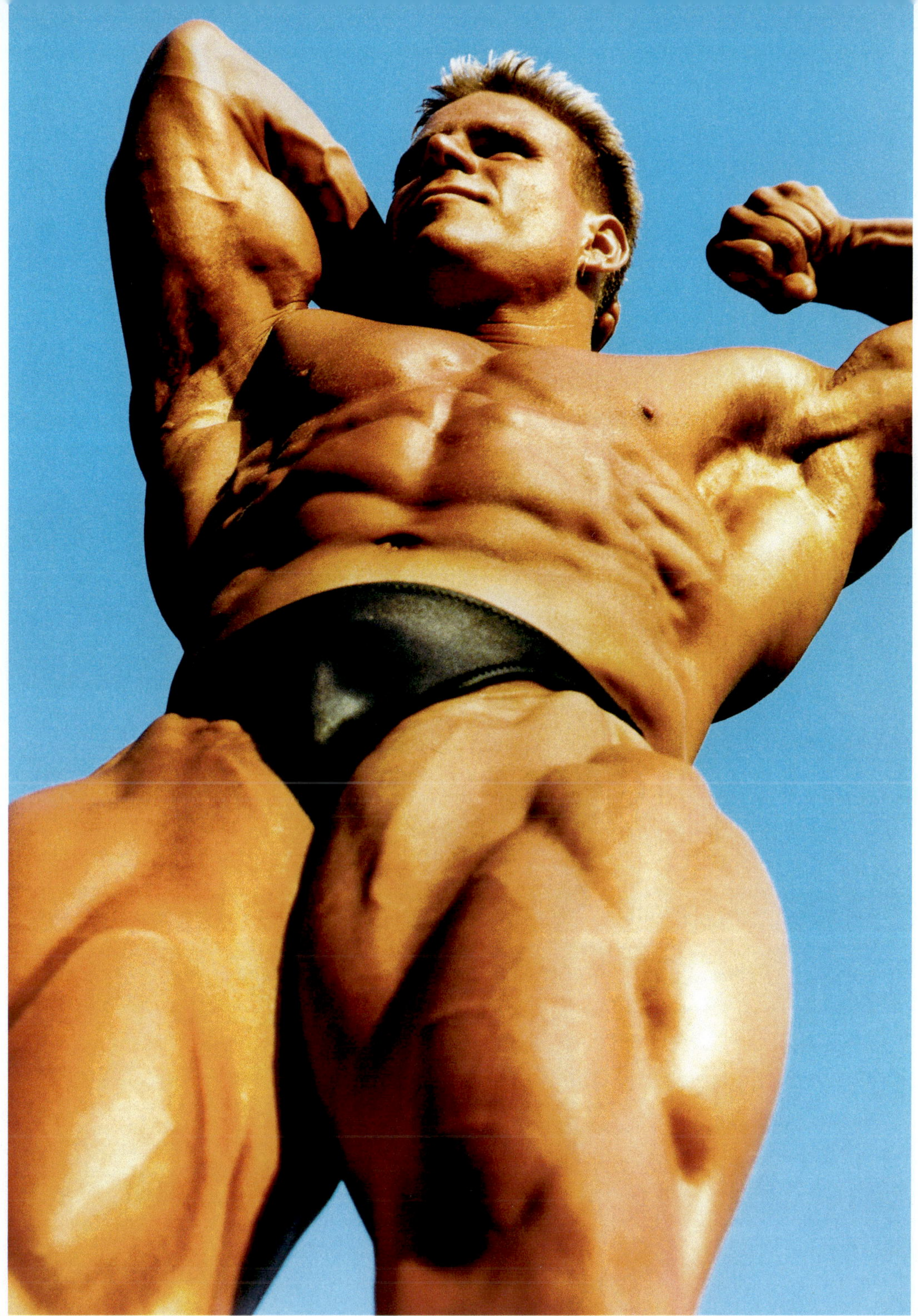

It is in no small part thanks to Arnold Schwarzenegger that bodybuilding evolved into a media-marketed pursuit. In 1967, at the age of nineteen, Schwarzenegger became the youngest ever winner of the Mr. Universe title, which he would go on to win another four times before devoting himself to a career in acting. During the first half of the twentieth century, bodybuilding was still very much a sport on the margins, but in the early 1960s it developed into a sport for men that enjoyed particular popularity on the gay scene, where eroticising the male body was celebrated as a parody of heterosexuality. Schwarzenegger's mother was so concerned by all this naked male flesh that she consulted the family doctor. "Doctor," she said, leading him through Arnie's room, "all the other boys, Arnold's friends, when I go to their homes, they have girls hanging on their walls. Posters, magazines, colored pictures of girls. And look at him. Naked men."

Quoted from Arnold Schwarzenegger, *Total Recall,* 2012

Eckhard Schaar, *Bodybuilder*, 1993

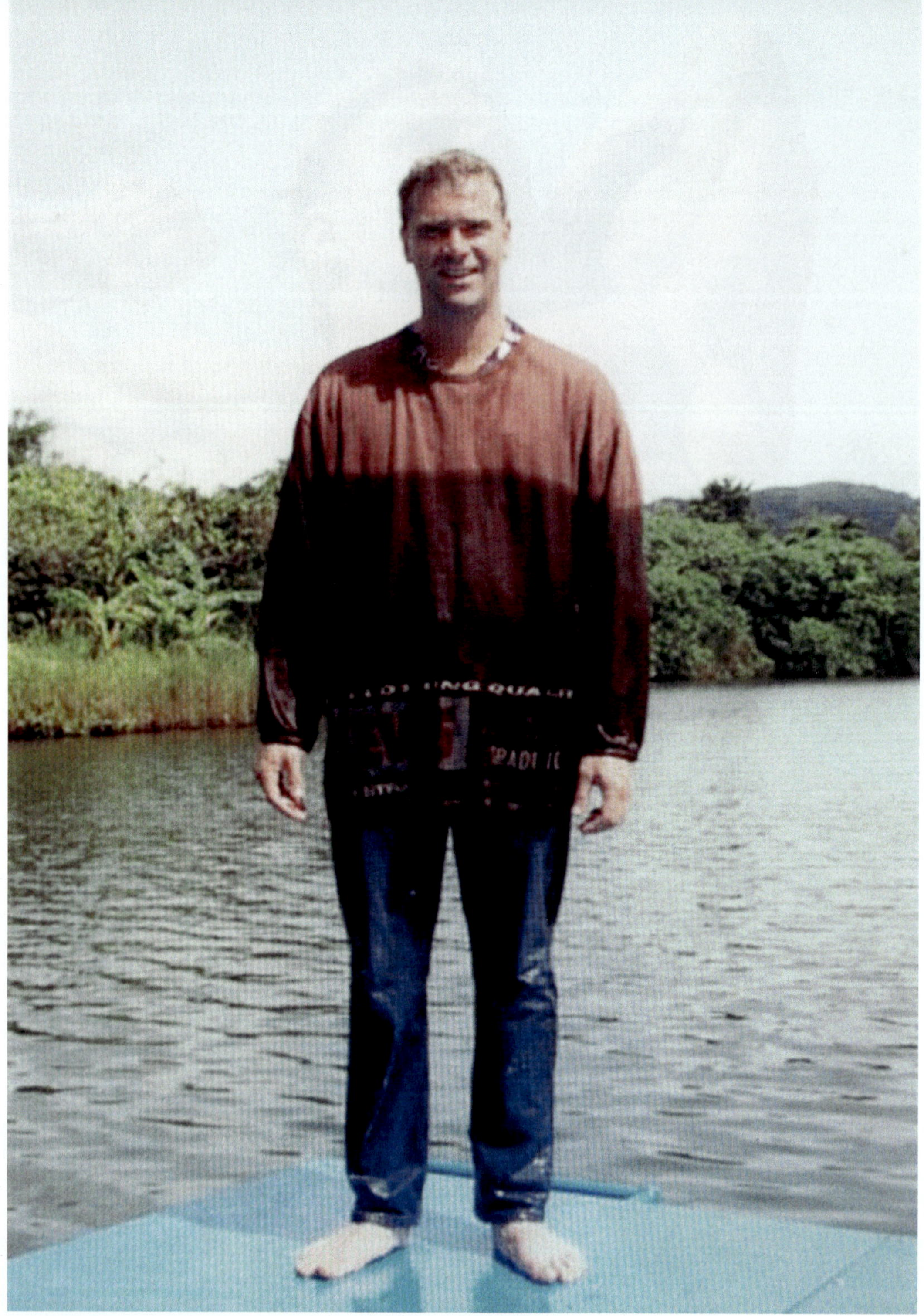

"I thought: wow, that was really great, experiencing water in your very own way." When he goes swimming, Christian just loves to keep his clothes on. He relishes the feeling of the heavy, water-soaked fabric on his body, the sight of the translucent, naked, foreign skin. A hobby, even a philosophy of life that emerged—if you believe his diary-like online posts—in childhood. Showing off, flirting, finding like-minded people—the wetlook celebrates physical freedom and sensuality within the group, and clothing that shields off the gaze is turned into an eye-catcher.

Quoted from Christian Gallati, christian.nasse-klamotten.ch

Lotte Reimann, from *Bis morgen im Nassen*, 2013

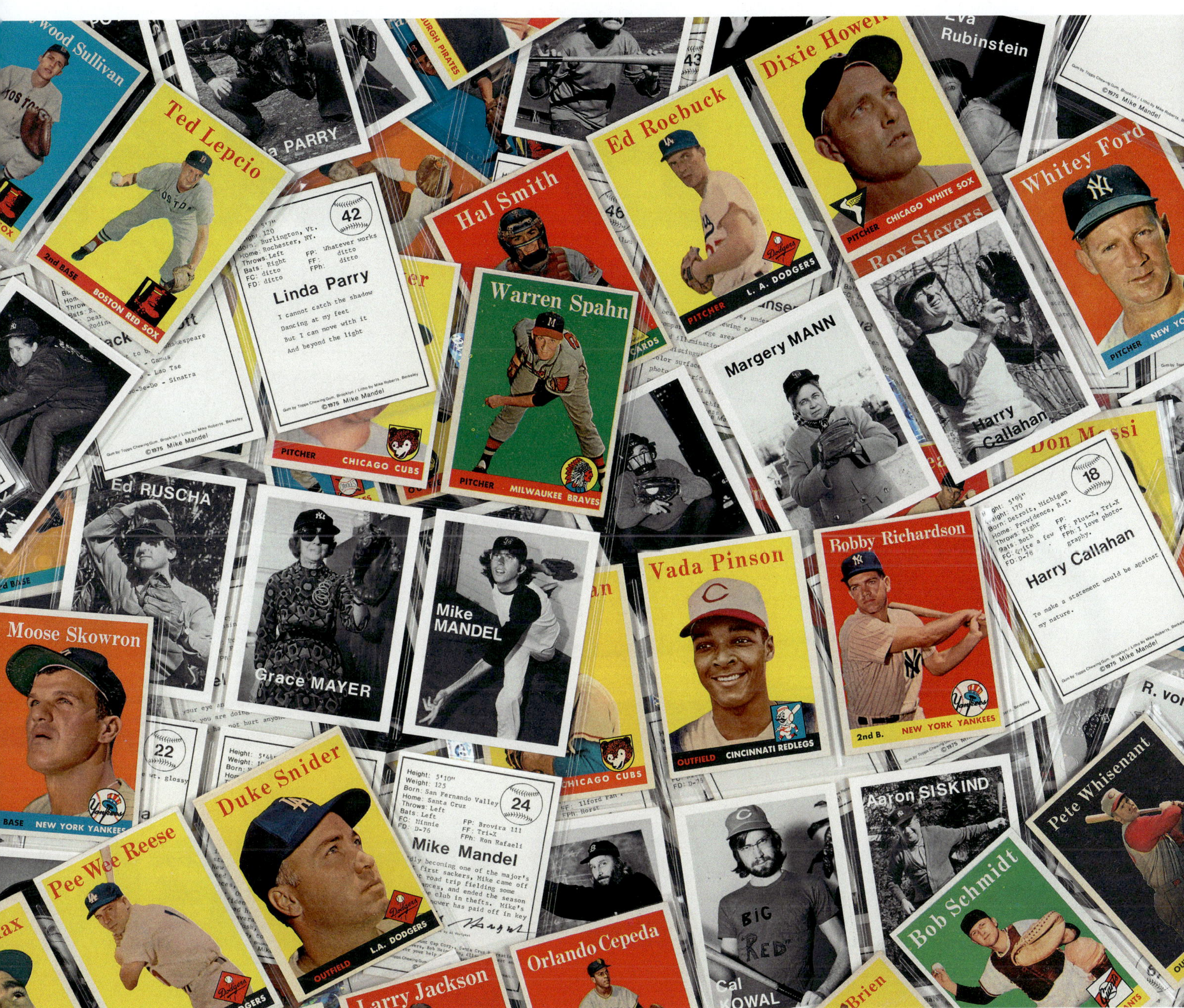

Mike Mandel

Height: 5′10″
Weight: 125
Born: San Fernando Valley
Home: Santa Cruz
Throws: Left
Bats: Left
FP: Brovira 111
FC: Minnie
FF: Tri-X
FD: D-76
Fph: Ron Rafaeli

"Rapidly becoming one of the major's finest first sackers, Mike came off the last road trip fielding some tough chances, and ended the season tops on the club in thefts. Mike's occasional power has paid off in key homers."

"Mike Mandel" trading card

Mike Mandel, Topps Baseball Trading Cards/*The Baseball-Photographer Trading Cards*, 1958/1975/2017

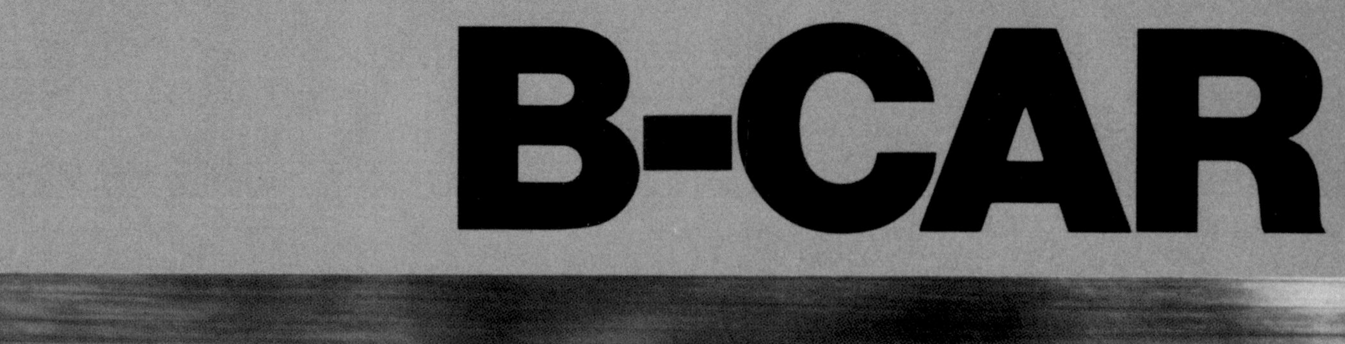

B-CAR

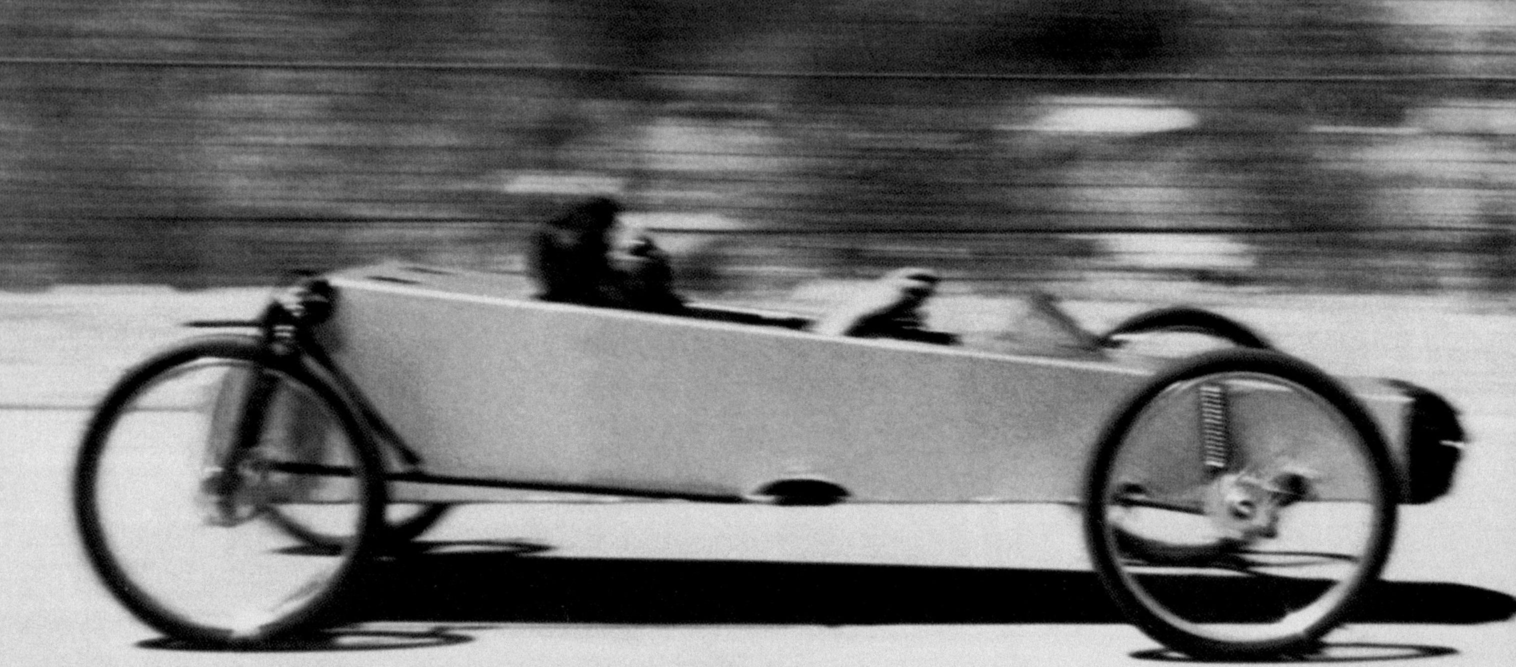

CHRIS BURDEN

"During the two-month period between August 24 and October 16, 1975, I conceived, designed, and constructed a small one-passenger automobile. My goal was to design a fully operational four-wheel vehicle which would travel 100 miles per hour and achieve 100 miles per gallon. I imagined this vehicle as extremely lightweight, streamlined, and similar in structure to both a bicycle and an airplane. Once the project was conceived, I was compelled to realize it. I set the goal of completing the car for two shows in Europe. I saw building the car as a means toward the end of driving it between galleries in Amsterdam and Paris as a performance. When I arrived in Amsterdam, I knew that the accomplishment of constructing the car had become for me the essential experience. I had already realized the most elaborate fantasy of my life. Driving the car was not important after the ordeal of bringing it into existence."

From Chris Burden, *B-Car,* 1977

Chris Burden, *B-Car*, 1977

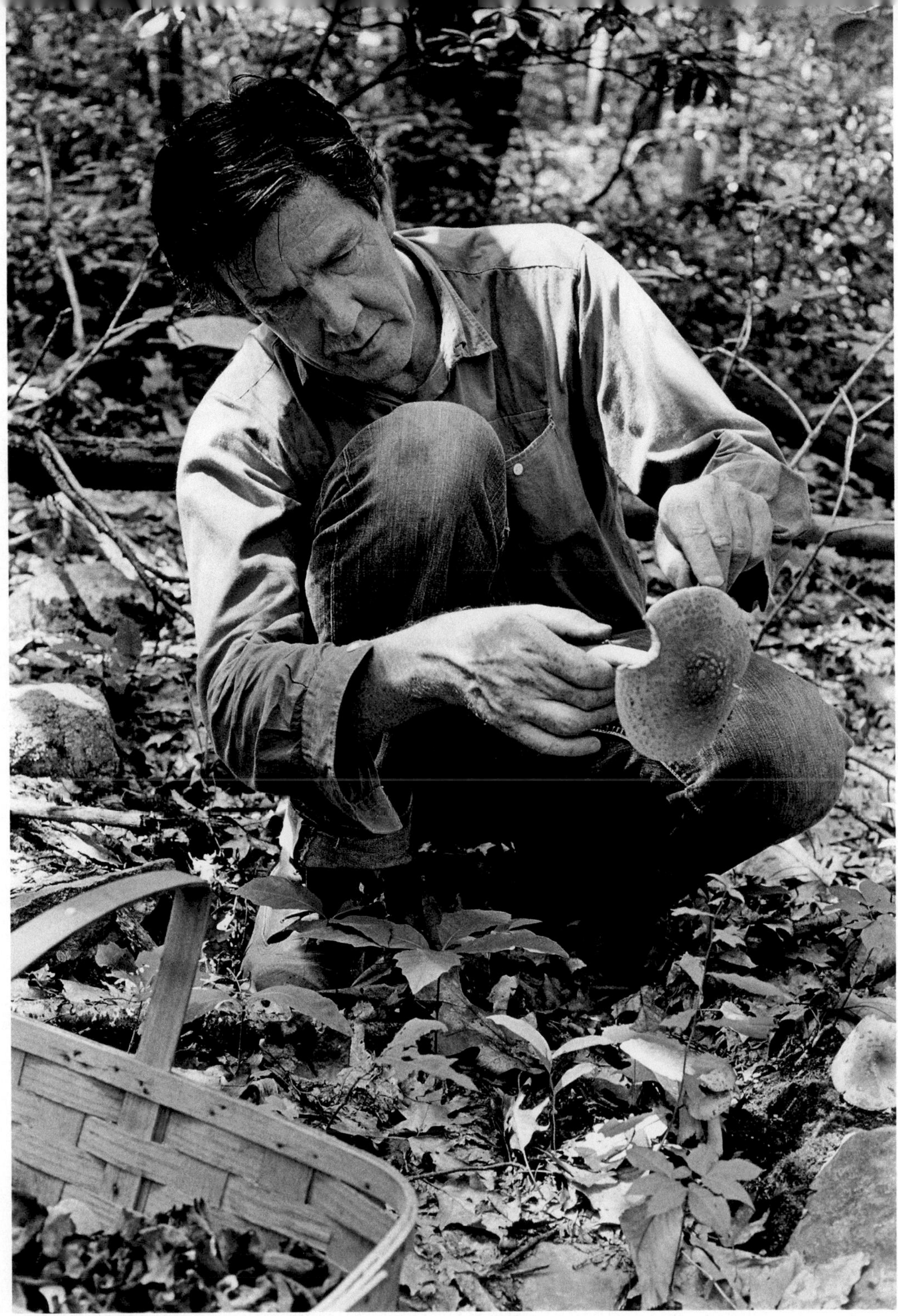

"Think carefully, Mr. Cage," Mike Bongiorno, the Italian game show host urged, while asking the $5-million-lire-question on the grand finale of *Lascia o raddoppia* (Leave it or double it). "You must tell us the twenty-four names of the white-spored *Agaricus* contained in Atkinson's *Studies of American Fungi*." Much to the surprise of both the audience and the host, the American composer responded confidently that he could "enumerate the list alphabetically." "You can what?" asked the host, flabbergasted, upon which John Cage rattled off all of the names of Atkinson's agarics, in correct alphabetical order. With the prize money of $10,000, he bought a piano and a Volkswagen bus for his partner, Merce Cunningham's, new dance company. "I'd like to thank the mushrooms and all the people of Italy!"

Quoted from *Lascia o raddoppia*, Milan, February 5, 1959

William Gedney, *John Cage*, 1967

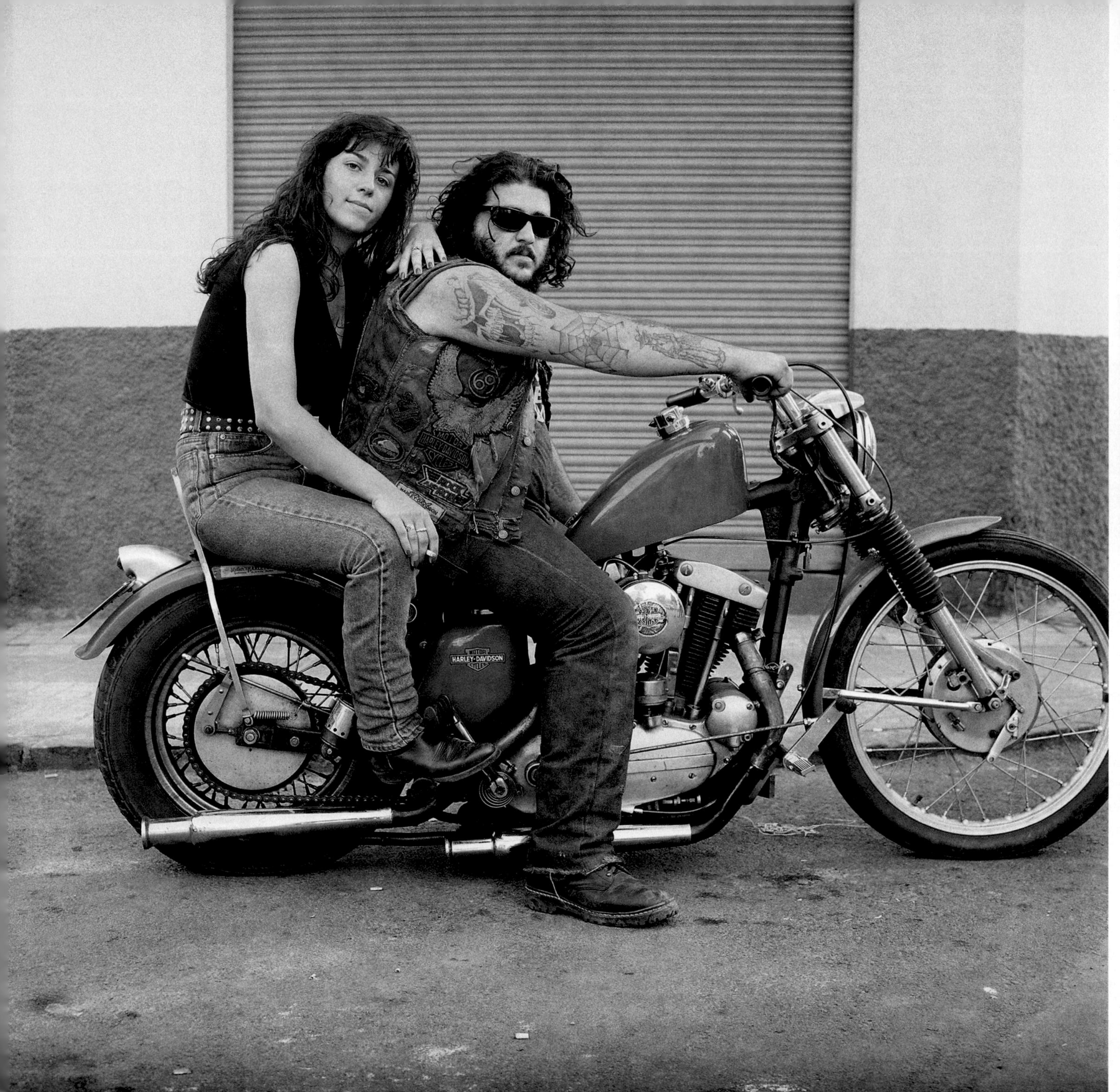

"I ramped things up. I stole from my mother's purse. One thousand francs: in pesetas, twelve thousand. With that and a gold Dupont lighter that belonged to my father, I bought a Derbi Antorcha Tricampeona (the three-time champion). The first thing I did was to beef up the engine by adding a 16 cc Dell'orto carburetor, and I dressed her like a little slut with a kit Puig gas tank, and a single-seat tail painted in English green. That little baby could really move, buzzing like an angry wasp. Sunday mornings gave me immeasurable ecstasy and moments of glory in my particular: campus and beyond. I had a predilection for the upper curve of the auditorium and the Villa de la Dehesa..."

From Alberto García-Alix, *Moto*, 2015

Alberto García-Alix, *El Gordo y Kity*, 1991

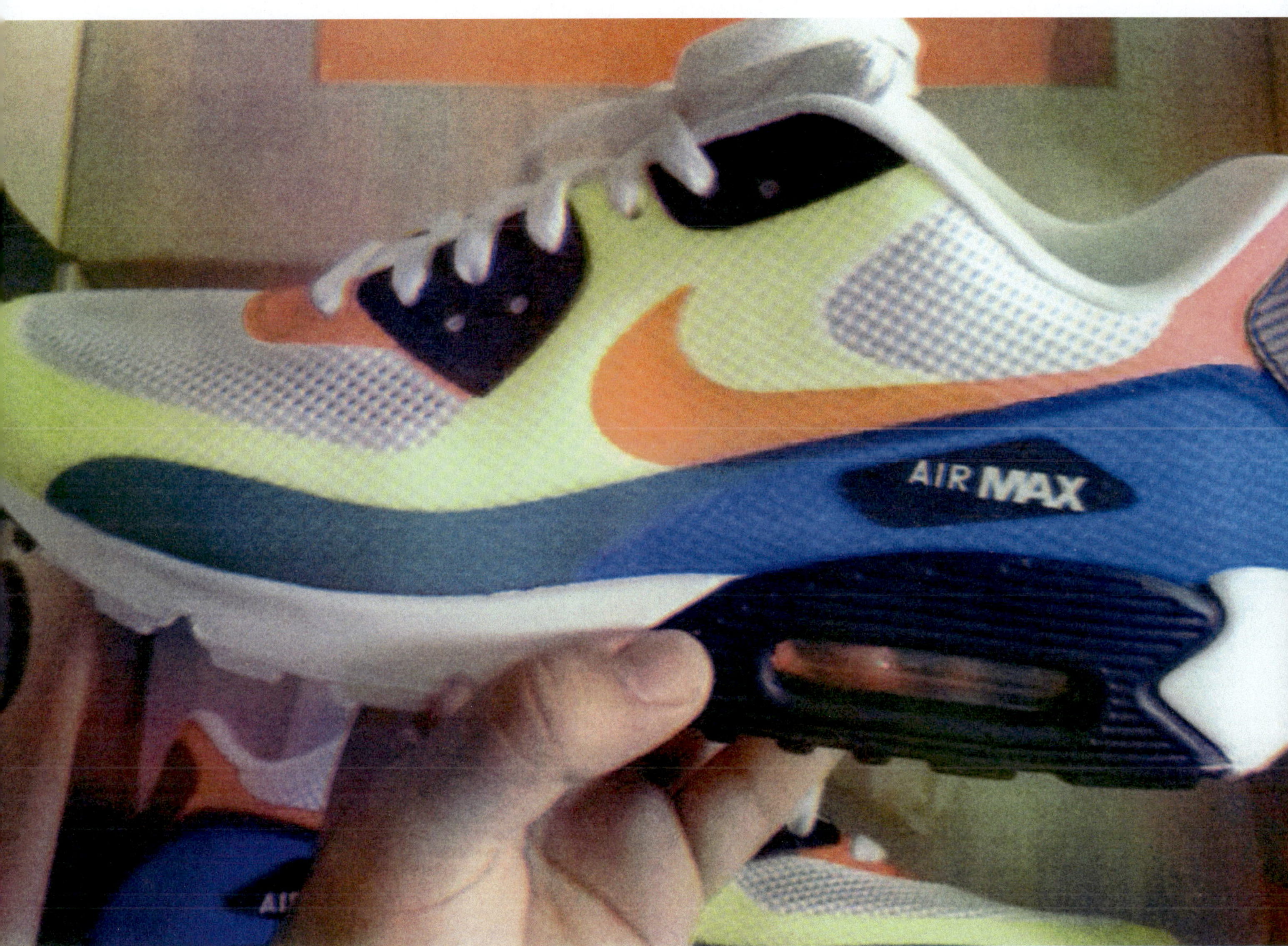

"Nike Air Max 90 Hyperfuse Olympic. What the Max. Here's the latest pair I bought. Just came out this year. Nike based the colors on the Olympic logo. It's the first time I could imagine never actually wearing a pair. They're truly fabulous. They were the last size in stock, so the sales assistant gave me a fifteen euro discount. I'll stop collecting sneakers because I just don't feel like buying them anymore. I'm not a sneaker addict. I don't like that attitude, or the fact that some people live just for their sneakers. One day, no doubt, I'll buy some again, but that's enough for now."

From Hana Miletić, *The Molem Collective*, 2013

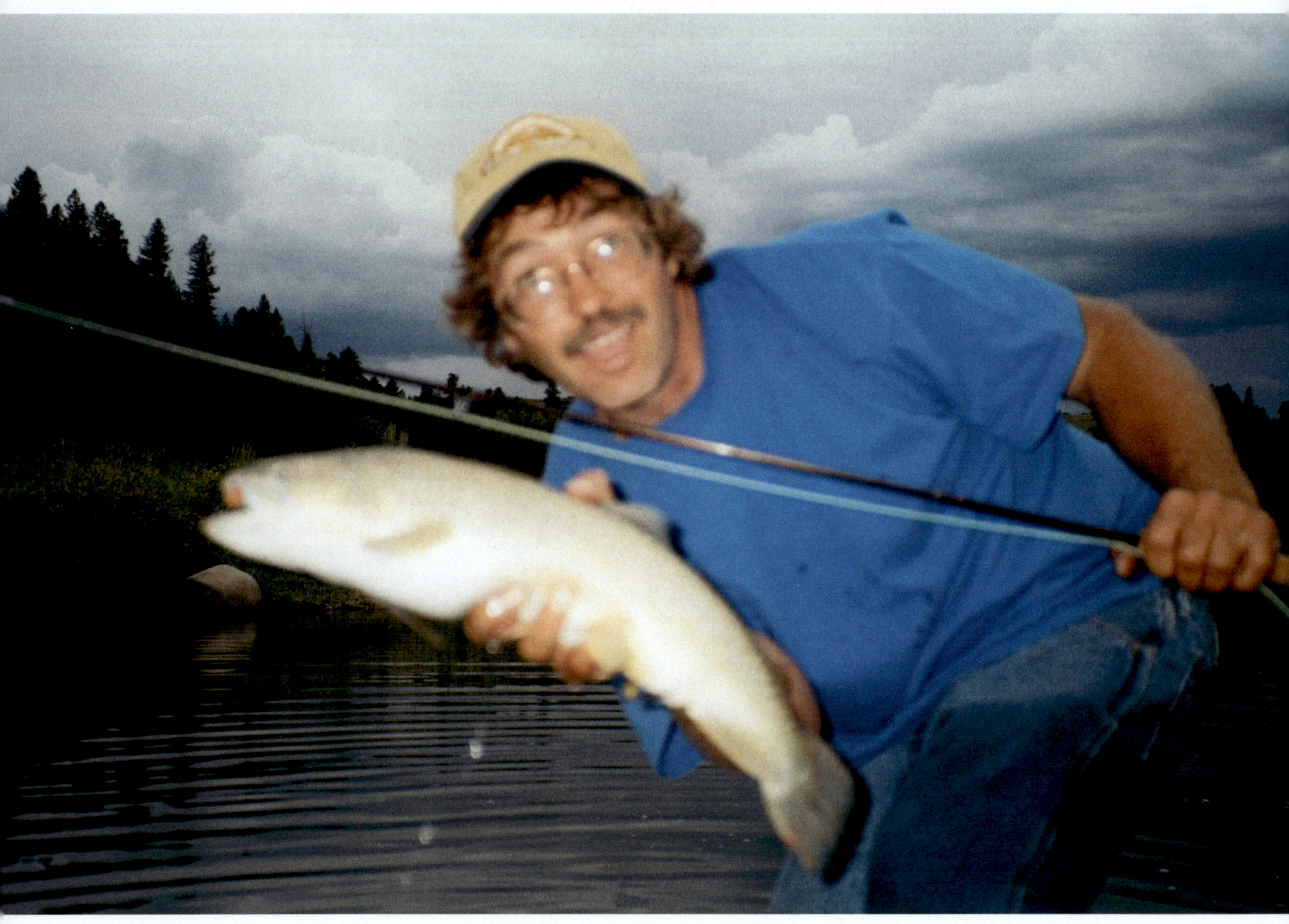

"I've had it.
I've gone fishing now for seven
years
and I haven't caught a single trout.
I've lost every trout I ever hooked.
They either jump off
or twist off
or squirm off
or break my leader
or flop off
or fuck off.
I have never even gotten my
hands on a trout.
For all its frustration,
I believe it was an interesting
experiment
in total loss
but next year somebody else
will have to go trout fishing.
Somebody else will have to go
out there."

From Richard Brautigan, *Trout Fishing in America*, 1967

Benedikt Bock, from *ALEXANDER HALL*, 2017

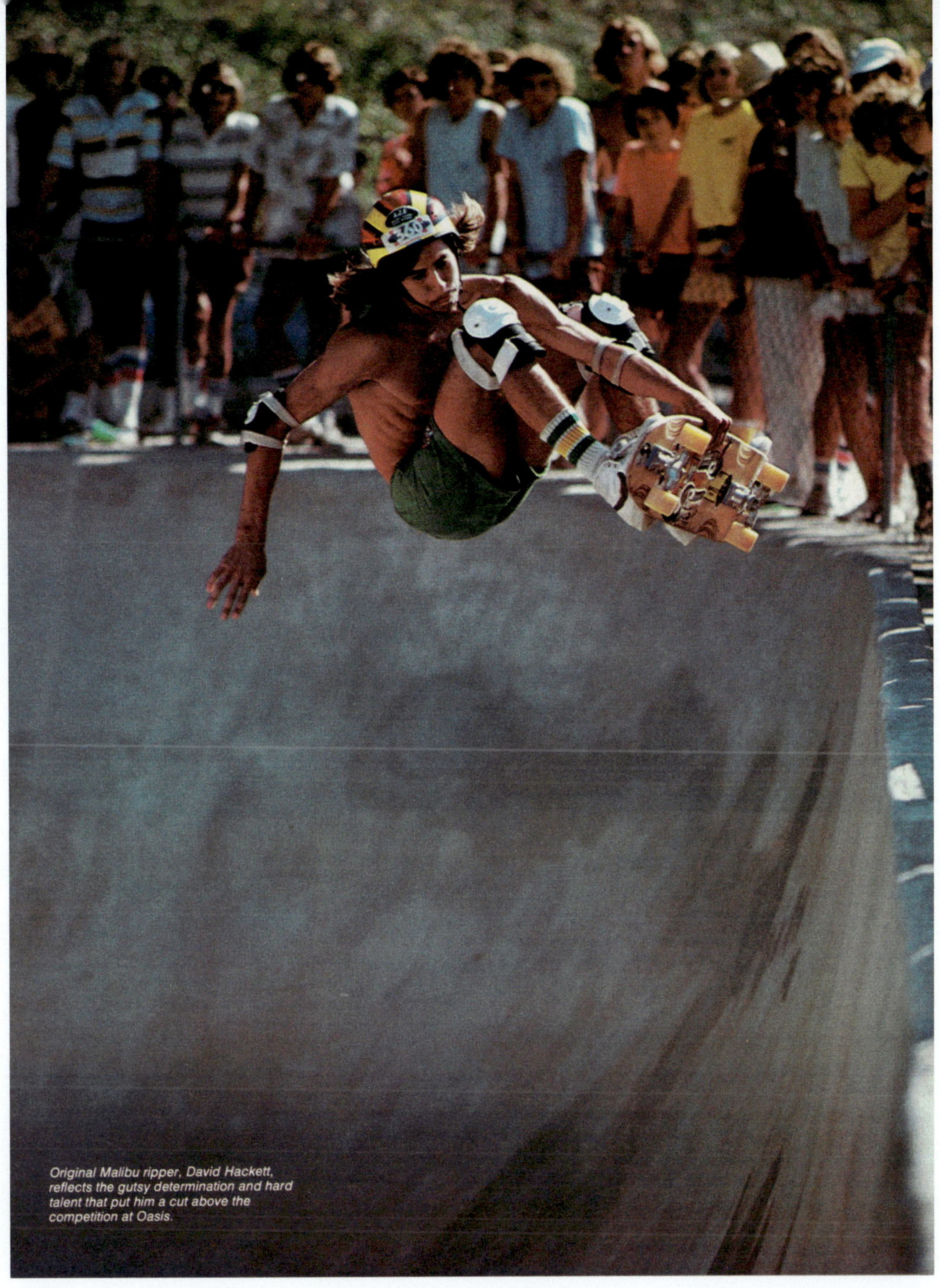
Original Malibu ripper, David Hackett, reflects the gutsy determination and hard talent that put him a cut above the competition at Oasis.

"Due to a major drought, the use of water is limited in California. In Los Angeles, one is no longer allowed to water one's garden and pools become empty: a godsend for the new wave of pool skaters. Techniques for locating pools multiply: with Jay Adams standing on the roof of his pickup truck, Stacy Peralta drives around the streets of Beverly Hills. In certain real estate agencies, the ex-Z-Boys find adresses of uninhabited mansions. A controversial anecdote recounts how Jay Adams and Shogo Kubo would go so far as to pay a pilot to fly over certain neighborhoods. When the pools are not completely empty, a pump linked to a generator allows for speedy drainage. The sessions are often quite rapid (sometimes not going beyond ten minutes), with skaters taking turns to keep an eye out for the police, disappearing at the first peal of a siren."

From Raphaël Zarka, *On a Day with No Waves*, 2011

Craig Fineman, from *Skateboarder Magazine*, 1979–1980

Bruce Baumgart, winner of the Five-Man Free-For-All at the First Intergalactic Spacewar Olympics, brandishing control buttons in triumph

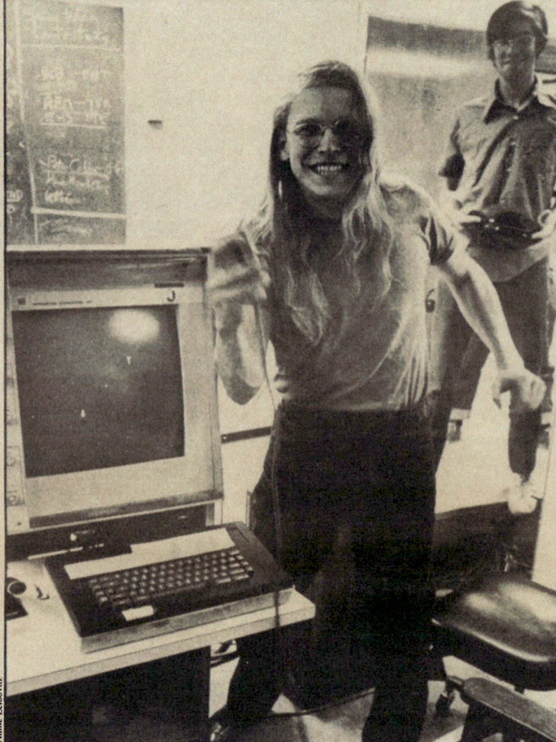

metric display hacks, computer music programs, the color video image maker . . . Four intense hours, much frenzy and skilled concerted action, a 15-ring circus in ten different directions, the most bzz-bzz-busy scene I've been around since Merry Prankster Acid Tests . . . and really it's just a normal night at the AI Project, at any suitably hairy computer research project. Something basic . . .

These are heads, most of them. Half or more of computer science is heads. But that's not it. The rest of the counterculture is laid low and back these days, showing none of this kind of zeal. What, then?

The Hackers

I'm guessing that Alan Kay at Xerox Research Center (more on them shortly) has a line on it, defining the standard Computer Bum:

"About as straight as you'd expect hotrodders to look. It's that kind of fanaticism. A true hacker is not a group person. He's a person who loves to stay up all night, he and the machine in a love-hate relationship . . . They're kids who tended to be brilliant but not very interested in conventional goals. And computing is just a fabulous place for that, because it's a place where you don't have to be a Ph.D. or anything else. It's a place where you can still be an artisan. People are willing to pay you if you're any good at all, and you have plenty of time for screwing around."

The hackers are the technicians of this science—"It's a term of derision and also the ultimate compliment." They are the ones who translate human demands into code that the machines can understand and act on. They are legion. Fanatics with a potent new toy. A mobile new-found elite, with its own apparat, language and character, its own legends and humor. Those magnificent men with their flying machines, scouting a leading edge of technology which has an odd softness to it; outlaw country, where rules are not decree or routine so much as the starker demands of what's possible.

A young science travels where the young take it. The wiser computer research directors have learned that *not* trusting their young programmers with major responsibility can lead immediately to no research. AI is one of perhaps several dozen computer research centers that are flourishing with their young, some of them with no more formal education than they got at the local Free School. I'm talking to Les Earnest, the gent who went for beer. He's tall, swarthy, has a black and white striped beard, looks like a Sufi athlete. He's telling me about what else people build here besides refinements of Spacewar. There's a speech recognition project. There's the hand-eye project, in which the computer is learning to see and visually correct its robot functions. There's work on symbolic computation and grammatical inference. Work with autistic children, "trying to get them to relate to computers first, and then later to people. This seems to be successful in part because many of these children think of themselves as machines. You can encourage them to interact in a game with the machine."

Another window on the interests of AI and of the hackers is a posted printout of the file of AI's system programs, some 250 elaborate routines available. Scanning: *Hand Eye Monitor . . . Go Game . . . DPY Hack Broom Balancing . . . Comparison Portion of Soup . . . Retrieves Selected AP News Stories . . . Display Hack . . . Mad Doctor . . . New TV Editor . . . Fortune Cookie Program . . . Another Display Hack . . . Kalah Game . . . Oh Where, Oh Where Has My Little Job Gone . . . Paranoid Model . . . Pruning Program . . . The Wonderful News Program . . . Old Spacewar . . . New Spacewar . . . Send Everyone a Message . . . Old Version of Daemon . . . Tell Everyone the System Is Going Down . . . Music Compiler Sort Of . . . New Music Compiler . . .*

A distinction exists between low-rent and high-rent computer research, between preoccupations of support group (hackers) and of research group. The distinction blurs often. Les Earnest: "Sometimes it's hard to tell the difference between recreation and work, happily. We try to judge people not on how much time they waste but on what they accomplish over fairly long periods of time, like a half year to a year." He adds that Spacewar players "are more from the support groups than the research groups. The research groups tend to get their kicks out of research."

Spacewar is low-rent.

Spacewar

Low-rent . . . but pervasive. Alan Kay: "The game of Spacewar blossoms spontaneously wherever there is a graphics display connected to a computer."

The first opportunity was at the Massachusetts Institute of Technology (MIT) Electrical Engineering Department back in 1961-1962. The earliest mini-computer, Digital Equipment Corporation's PDP-1, was installed in the kludge room with a cathode ray tube display hooked on. ("Kludge"—any lash-up, often involving chewing gum, paper clips, scotch tape; it works if no one trips over a wire; unadaptable; a working mess.) There it was that Steve Russell and his fellow hackers Alan Kotok, Peter Samson and Dan Edwards introduced Spacewar to the world.

I phoned Russell at the sprawling old fabric mill in Maynard, Massachusetts, where Digital Equipment Corporation manufactures the most popular research and education computers on the market. Russell currently is a researcher for them working on man-machine interface problems—adapting computer nature to fit human nature. Back in 1962 he was a hacker, 23 or so, a math major two years out of Dartmouth working in the brand new field of computer science for John McCarthy at MIT.

His account of the invention of Spacewar is not only intriguing history, it's the most sophisticated analysis of good game design I've ever run across—elegant work. But that's in retrospect; back then it was just kids staying up all night.

"We had this brand new PDP-1," Steve Russell recalls. "It was the first mini-computer, ridiculously inexpensive for its time. And it was just sitting there. It had a console typewriter that worked right, which was rare, and a paper tape reader and a cathode ray tube display. [There had been CRT displays before, but primarily in the Air Defense System.] Somebody had built some little pattern-generating programs which made interesting patterns like a kaleidoscope. Not a very good demonstration. Here was this display that could do all sorts of good things! So we started talking about it, figuring what would be interesting displays. We decided that probably you could make a two-dimensional maneuvering sort of thing, and decided that naturally the obvious thing to do was spaceships."

Naturally?

"I had just finished reading 'Doc' Smith's *Lensman* series. He was some sort of scientist but he wrote this really dashing brand of science fiction. The details were very good and it had an excellent pace. His heroes had a strong tendency to get pursued by the villain across the galaxy and have to invent their way out of their problem while they were being pursued. That sort of action was the thing that suggested Spacewar. He had some very glowing descriptions of spaceship encounters and space fleet maneuvers."

"Doc" Smith:

"The *Boise* leaped upon the Nevian, every weapon aflame. But, as Costigan had expected, Nerado's vessel was completely ready for any emergency. And, unlike her sister-ship, she was manned by scientists well-versed in the fundamental theory of the weapons with which they fought. Beams, rods and lances of energy flamed and flared; planes and pencils cut, slashed and stabbed; defensive screens glowed redly or flashed suddenly into intensely brilliant, coruscating incandescence. Crimson opacity struggled sullenly against violet curtains of annihilation. Material projectiles and torpedoes were launched under full-beam control; only to be exploded harmlessly in mid-space, to be blasted into nothingness or to disappear innocuously against impenetrable polycyclic screens."

—*Triplanetary* (1948)

Steve Russell: "By picking a world which people weren't familiar with, we could alter a number of parameters of the world in the interests of making a good game and of making it possible to get it onto a computer. We made a great deal of compromises from some of our original grand plans in order to make it work well.

"One of the important things in Spacewar is the pace. It's relatively fast-paced, and that makes it an interesting game. It seems to be a reasonable compromise between action—pushing buttons—and thought. Thought does help you, and there are some tactical considerations, but just plain fast reflexes also help.

"It was quite interesting to fiddle with the parameters, which of course I

—*Continued on Next Page*

"Ready or not, computers are coming to the people," claimed Stewart Brand, reporting on the first video game tournament, the "Intergalactic Spacewar Olympics," in Palo Alto, California, for *Rolling Stone* magazine. The event, which took place at Stanford University's Artificial Intelligence Laboratory on October 19, 1972, was photographed by Annie Leibovitz and gathered two dozens of researchers and programmers, "long-haired graduate students [who] clustered around a PDP-10 time-sharing computer, entered a few commands, conjured up tiny triangular spaceships on the computer's monitor, and proceeded to blast each other out of the sky." The Spacewarriors, "'out of their bodies' in the game," seemed much like the "high-tech version of the turned-on dancers of the Trips Festival," and the computer itself like a new kind of LSD.

Quoted from Fred Turner, *From Counterculture to Cyberculture*, 2008

Stewart Brand, from "Spacewar," in *Rolling Stone Magazine*, 1972. Photo: Annie Leibovitz

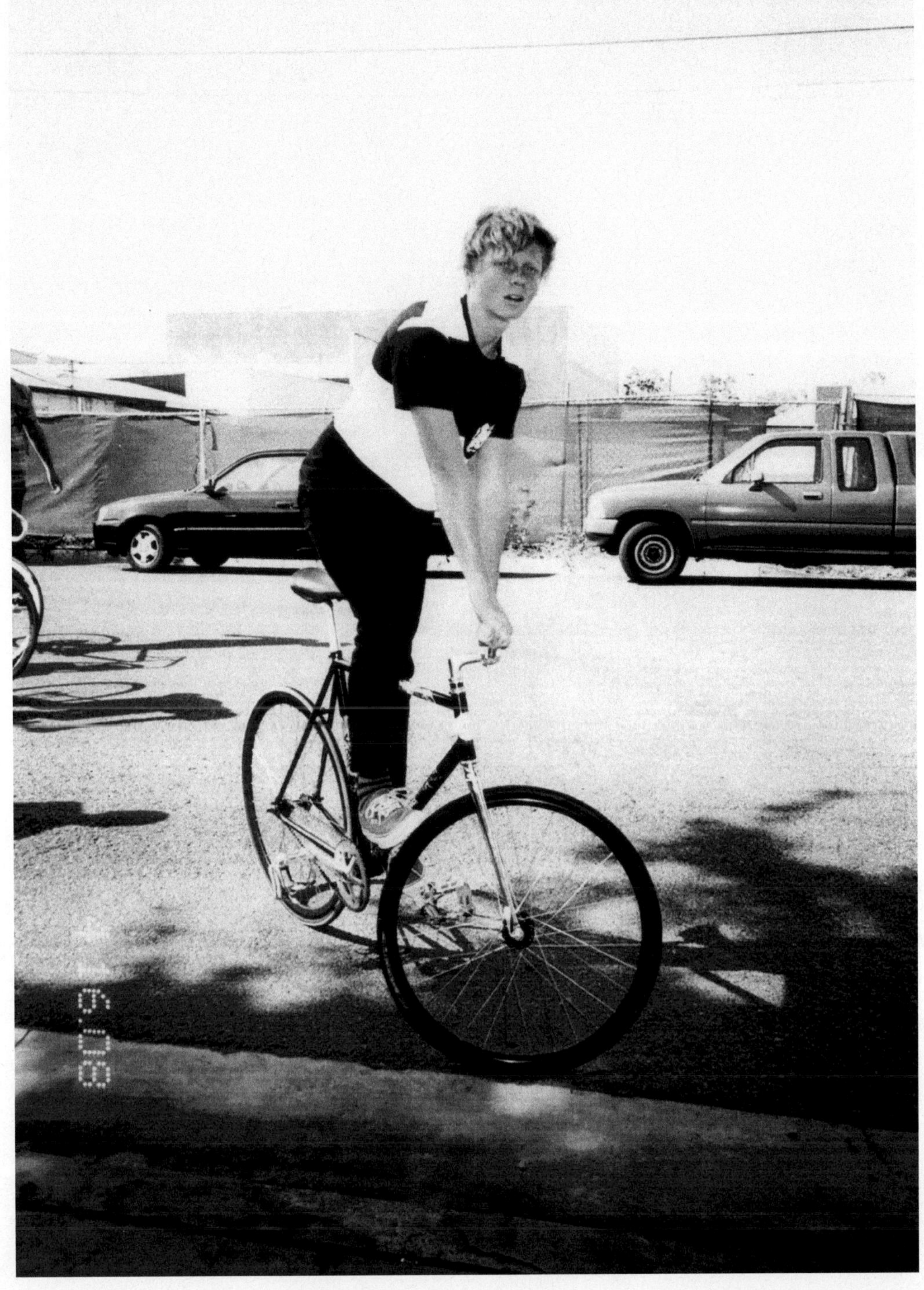

"Suburbia

where the suburbs met utopia
where the suburbs met utopia

Lost in the high street, where the
dogs run
roaming suburban boys
Mother's got her hairdo to be
done
She says they're too old for toys
Stood by the bus stop with a felt
pen
in this suburban hell
and in the distance a police car
to break the suburban spell
Let's take a ride
and run with the dogs tonight in
suburbia
You can't hide
Run with the dogs tonight
in suburbia

Break the window by the town hall
Listen! A siren screams
there in the distance like a roll call
of all the suburban dreams
Let's take a ride
and run with the dogs tonight
in suburbia
You can't hide
run with the dogs tonight
in suburbia

I only wanted something else to
do but hang around"

From Pet Shop Boys, *Suburbia*, 1986

Ari Marcopoulos, from *Directory*, 2011

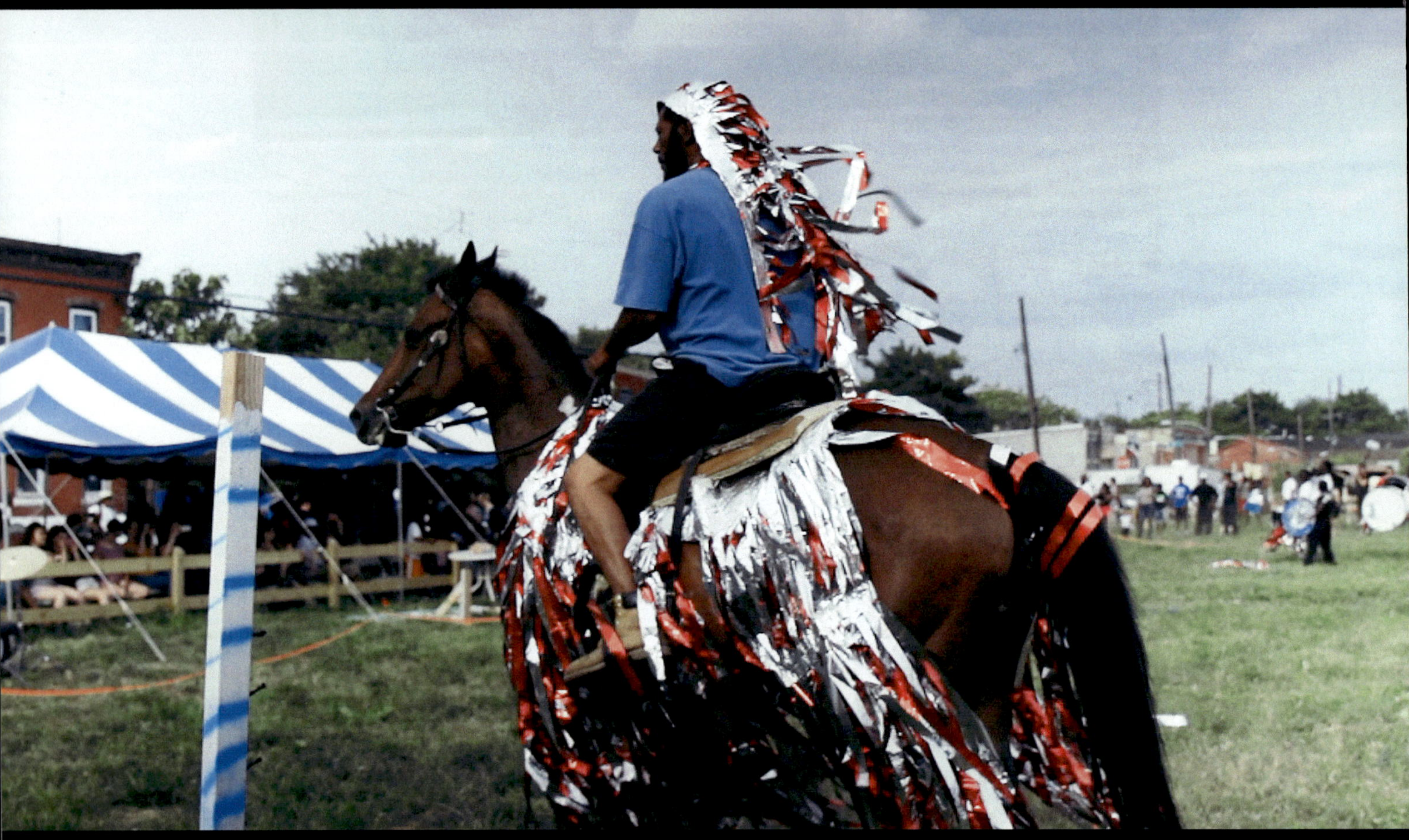

"I had long since developed into a first class cow boy and besides being chief brand reader in Arizona and the pan handle country. My expertness in riding, roping and in the general routine of the cow boy's life, including my wide knowledge of the surrounding country, gained in many long trips with herds of cattle and horses, made my services in great demand and my wages increased accordingly. To see me now you would not recognize the bronze hardened dare devil cow boy, the slave boy who a few years ago hunted rabbits in his shirt tail on the old plantation in Tennessee, or the tenderfoot who shrank shaking all over at the sight of a band of painted Indians. I had long since felt the hot sting of the leaden bullet as it plowed its way through some portion of my anatomy. Likewise I had lost all sense of fear, and while I was not the wild blood thirsty savage and all around bad man many writers have pictured me in their romances, yet I was wild, reckless and free."

From Nat Love, *Life and Adventures of Nat Love, Better Known in the Cattle Country as "Deadwood Dick,"* 1907

Mohamed Bourouissa, from *Horse Day*, 2015

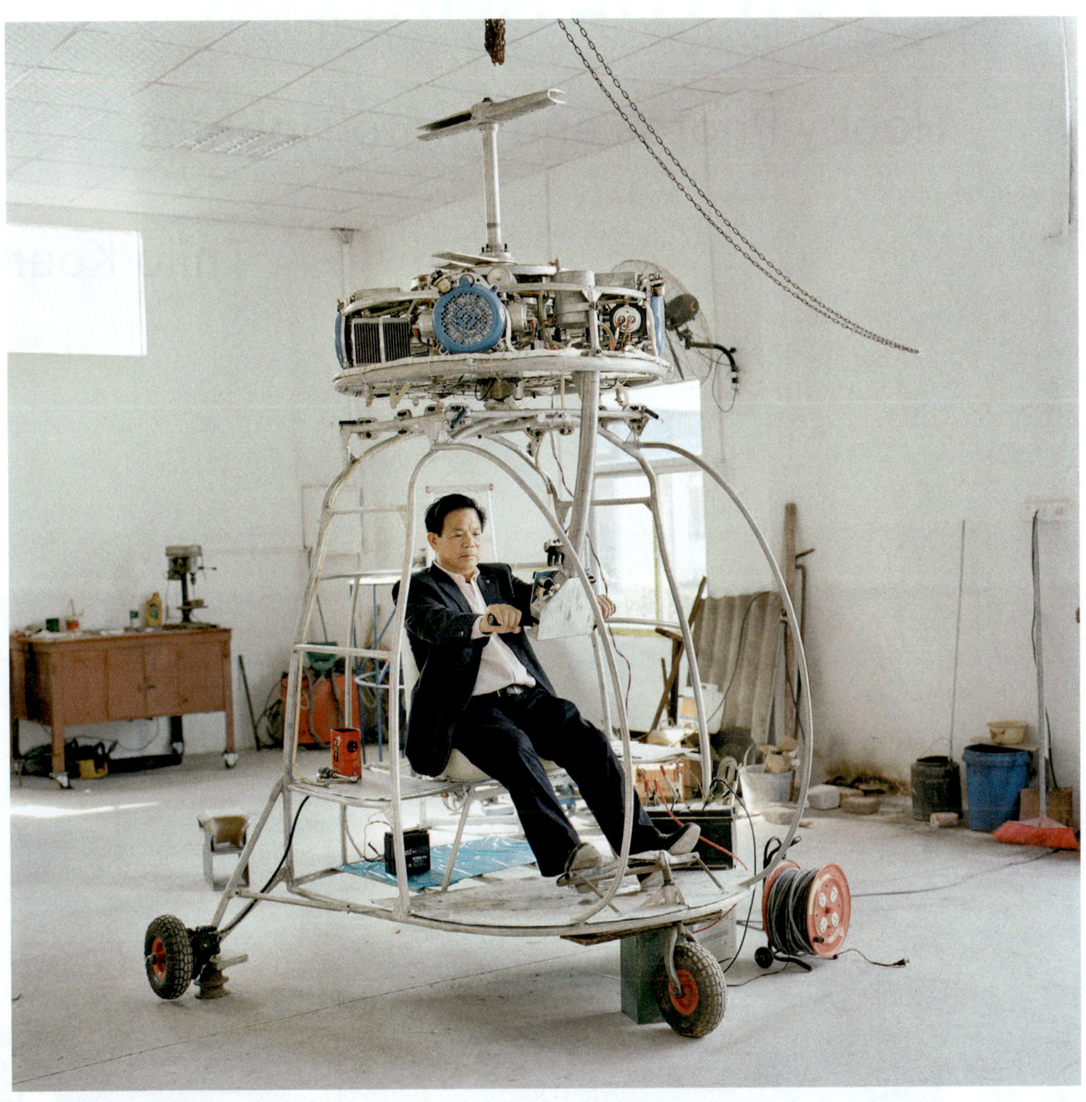

Xiaoxiao Xu, from *Aeronautics*, 2000

NOTHING IS TOO DIFFICULT FOR THE AMATEUR

Hobby Photos and Photo Hobbies

Thilo Koenig

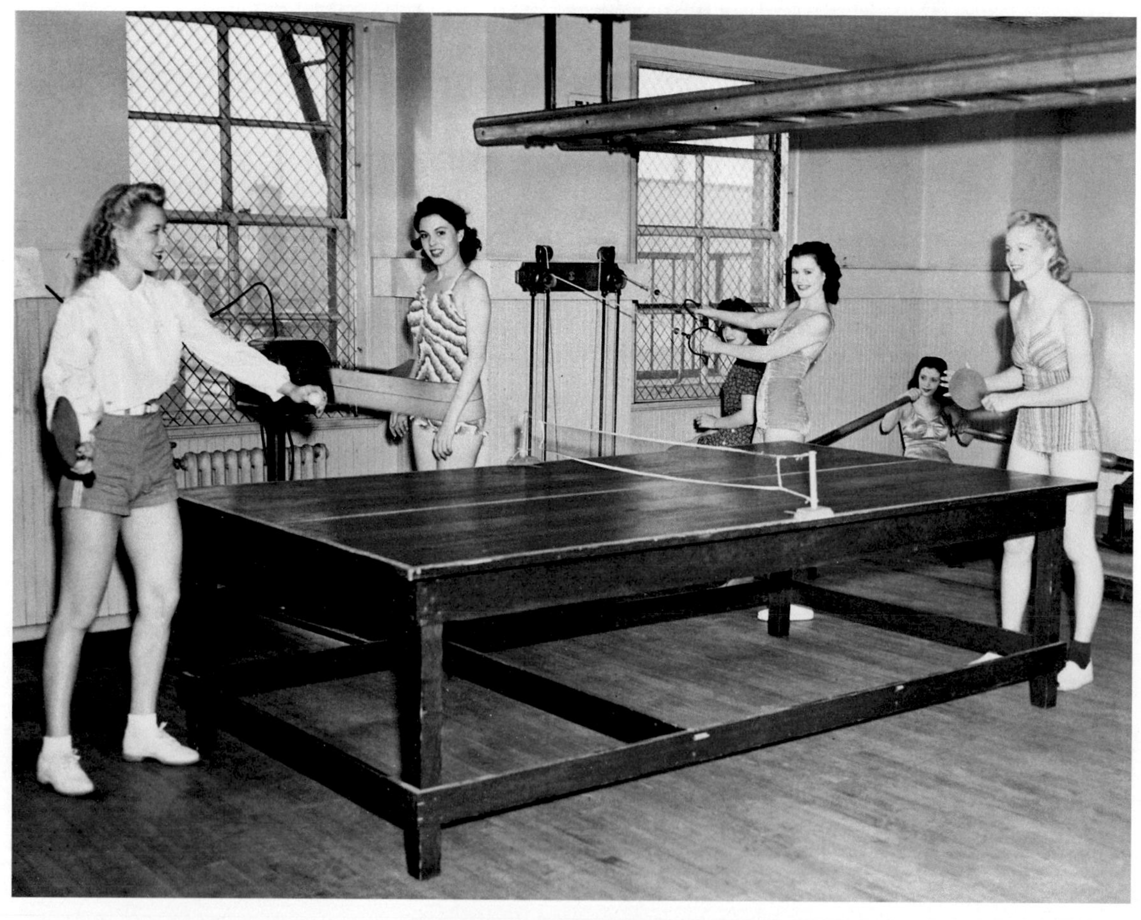

Alec Soth, from *Ping-Pong*, 2013

"For as soon as the distribution of labour comes into being, each man has a particular, exclusive sphere of activity, which is forced upon him and from which he cannot escape. He is a hunter, a fisherman, a herdsman, or a critical critic, and must remain so if he does not want to lose his means of livelihood; while in communist society, where nobody has one exclusive sphere of activity but each can become accomplished in any branch he wishes, society regulates the general production and thus makes it possible for me to do one thing today and another tomorrow, to hunt in the morning, fish in the afternoon, rear cattle in the evening, criticise after dinner, just as I have a mind, without ever becoming hunter, fisherman, herdsman or critic."

Karl Marx/Friedrich Engels
The German Ideology, 1846

"Without the amateurs, there will be nothing happening in the next few years."

Martin Heller/Walter Keller
"Herzblut fliesst überall," 1987

In 1966, the young American artist Bruce Nauman shot four short films in collaboration with William Allan "without considering art." Conceived as instructional 'how to' guides, they presented each step involved in an activity from beginning to end: from preparing the equipment to catching a fish in the first, *Fishing for Asian Carp,* followed by *Abstracting the Shoe,* a parody on abstract art, then *Legal Size*, in which a standard sized envelope is enlarged manually, and *Span,* about the construction of a wooden rig for spanning a tarp across a river. Not only do the films poke fun at hobby and DIY manuals, but they also directly sabotage traditional concepts of art—in much the same way that Marcel Duchamp did with his readymades and his chess game. In Happenings, Pop Art and Conceptual Art of the 1960s and 70s, DIY manuals and everyday hobby activities became integral parts of an 'anti-art' movement that increasingly made use of photography and film. In 1969, for instance, Robert Smithson simply submitted an instruction card detailing how to take the necessary photos, using a then popular Instamatic amateur camera, and how to display them, for his *400 Seattle Horizons.* Douglas Huebler similarly provided carefully typed instructions on how to take conceptual photo series and how to present them.

The 1960s American counterculture of hippies and dropouts was all about exploring the DIY tradition as an alternative lifestyle option, creating self-crafted geodesic domes in the spirit of Buckminster Fuller, producing batik textiles and pottery in a new take on the Arts and Crafts movement, shunning consumption and specialist divisions of labor in favor of putting former hobby techniques at the heart of their self-determined daily lives, while, at the same time, visual artists were countering the concepts of high art in every genre with more 'authentic' processes, or showing works that were based on existing hobbies, leisure themes, and hobbyist materials. Gordon Matta-Clark, for instance, opened the restaurant FOOD in 1971 with other New York artists, while Mike Mandel took portraits of famous photographers in sporting poses for his 1974 *Baseball-Photographer Trading Cards,* creating an ironic spoof on the collectible baseball cards that were once so popular. In 1978, Donald Judd used planks to put together simple geometric wooden chairs which he later produced as a series. The upshot of all this was that, according to Ralph Rugoff, "Conceptual art shifted the role of the artist from trained expert to a kind of nomadic, cross-disciplinary free agent engaged with research, process, context, and documentation."

Amateur pursuits and hobbies are phenomena linked to a modern form of leisure, which did not emerge in its present form until after the Reformation. Before that, everyday life was structured by nature and religion. Activities unrelated to daily necessity were the sole preserve of the aristocracy. With the Protestant ethic (Max Weber), working and earning became moral values, underpinned by an internalized sense of duty and thus imbued with the purpose of life itself. People became responsible for their own use of time, their heightened awareness of which was shaped by the emergence of the bourgeoisie and the Industrial Revolution, as job performance was now quantifiable in measurable terms. Whereas working time and personal time still more or less overlapped in the early days of industrialization, the later nineteenth century saw increasing limitations being set on working hours, and the introduction of the six-day week. Contractually regulated working hours and free personal time thus became complementary elements. Where there had previously been a distinction between those who worked and those who did not, the distinction between work and leisure was now embodied within each individual.

This newly acquired free time did not, however, only mean idleness. On the contrary: the moral lessons came soon enough, urging people to use their time responsibly and usefully. According to Steven M. Gelber, the concept of the hobby, which had once been equated with household activities or even questionable private obsessions, did not take on specifically positive connotations as a meaningful and potentially useful pastime, balancing out professional work, until the 1880s. As free time increased, particularly after the First World War and especially during the unemployment crisis of the 1930s and far into the post-war period, hobbies and DIY took on a new significance as necessary self-help techniques. From here on, a broad-based infrastructure of magazines, manuals, and clubs began to flourish, complemented from 1945 onward by specialist hobby supply outlets and prefabricated modules. The hobby room, or man cave, became synonymous with the pursuit of such institutionalized leisure activities. The 1950s are widely regarded as the last heyday of classic hobby culture.

Yet for all the personal responsibility—as a relaxing and satisfying counterpoint, at best, to paid employment—hobbies are nonetheless inextricably linked with the world of work. The hobby described by Robert A. Stebbins as "serious leisure" (in contrast to occasional "casual leisure") follows the same logic as work itself; even a hobbyist can achieve specialist skills and recognition in a chosen field, and, through that, perhaps carve out a career. Unlike paid employment, a hobby can be pursued with less division of labor, with neither pressure to perform nor outside interference. In that respect it might be said to have a certain 'pre-industrial' quality. Seen in the light of the Marxist utopia of a free and self-determined choice of activities, Theodor W. Adorno regarded such active leisure pursuits as largely heteronomous under the prevailing conditions of a still unfree capitalist world: free time that is nothing but a shadow of continued working time merely extends the individual's lack of freedom, and the "do it yourself" approach to tasks that could be undertaken more professionally by others is just an illusion in which such "pseudo-activities" are, themselves, also industrialized and commercialized!

Photography rapidly became one of the most popular hobbies, on a par with collecting, handicrafts, outdoor activities, and sports. From early on, media history was influenced not only by the first professional photographers, graphic artists, and painters who switched to this new technology but by non-professionals as well. Amateur photography, however, did not really get off the ground until the 1880s, when technical innovations made it possible to take photographs more easily and more quickly. Lighter, hand-held cameras, pre-produced so-called dry-plate negatives with higher light sensitivity, faster lenses, instant shutters, photometers, and roll films, all made it possible for even the technically unversed to dabble in photography with no prior knowledge or mastery of the chemical processes involved. Kodak's consumer-friendly system based on the slogan "You press the button, we do the rest" (from 1888) was merely the most overt example of the medium's radically altered accessibility, making it available to ever wider swathes of the population, even though photography did not become a mass phenomenon until the twentieth century. As soon as the camera became simpler to use, new forms of imagery emerged: snapshots that captured unusual poses for the first time, in turn firing the interest of painters, visual 'flaws' such as blurring or fragmentation, and amusing shots of randomly documented situations. John Szarkowski considered such examples of amateur photography to have had a far bigger impact on the development of modern media usage than any aesthetic discourse.

In Happenings, Pop Art and Conceptual Art of the 1960s and 70s, DIY manuals and everyday hobby activities became integral parts of an 'anti-art' movement that increasingly made use of photography and film.

Yet at almost the same time as hobbies took on their current significance and amateur photography became increasingly widespread, there was a distinct split into different camps. From the late 1880s onward, the artistically aspiring 'amateur photographers' or 'pictorialists' who championed the recognition of photography as a fine-art genre in its own right sought to distance themselves from the so-called snappers, or lay photographers, who wanted to record everyday and family life for their own private use, generally without any compositional ambitions. As predominantly non-professional photographers themselves, they entered into international correspondence with publications and exhibitions betweeen the 1890s and 1910 in a bid to promote the visual distinctiveness of amateur photographers as opposed to trained professional photographers (forming a third group). In photography, as in the painting of the time, dilettantism was a term that had positive connotations for people such as the then director of the Hamburg Kunsthalle, Alfred Lichtwark, who hoped for a non-academic revival in the arts. The pictorialists, however, consciously sought to create their authored compositions for public display in the art world, unlike the snappers who often had their photos developed and printed for their albums or the drawer, for memory's sake or as surprising

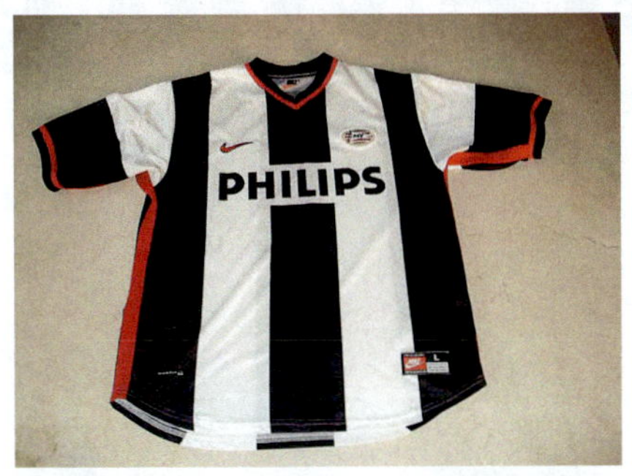

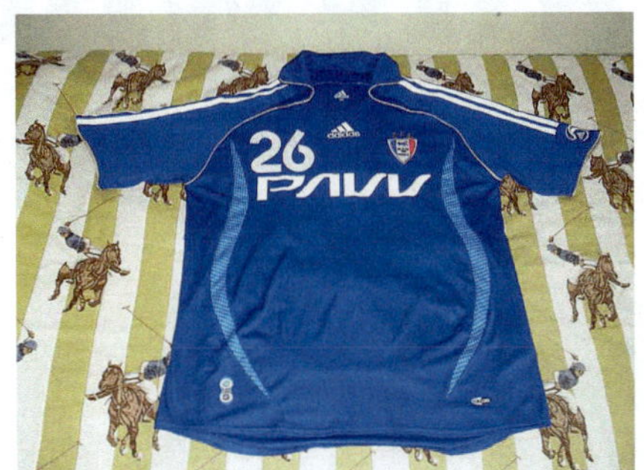

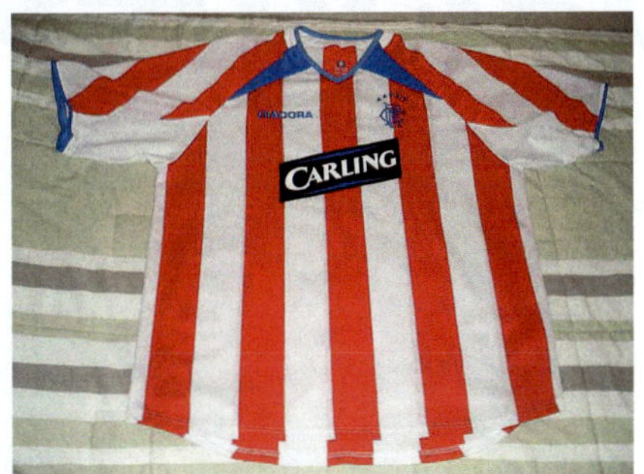

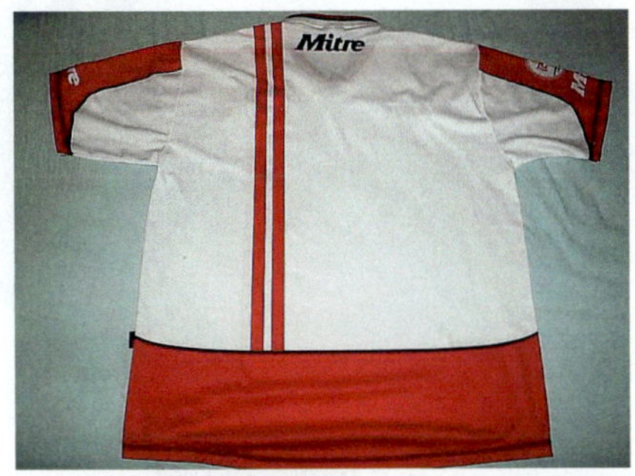

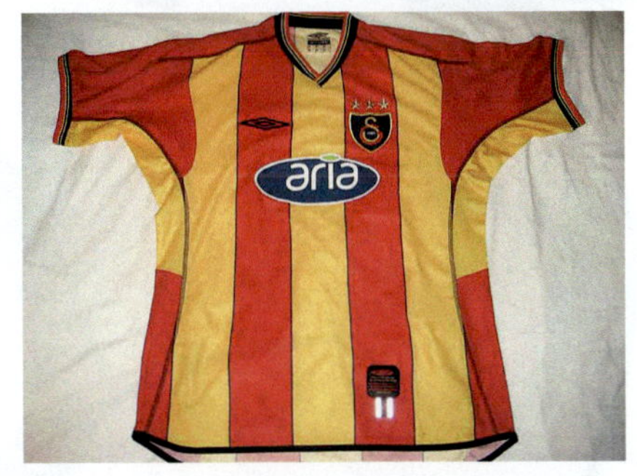

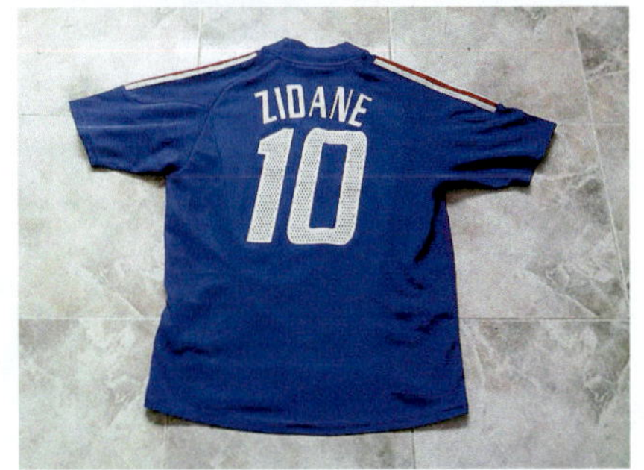

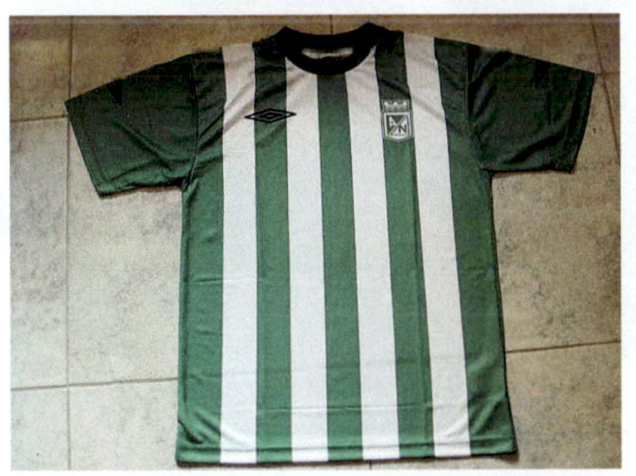

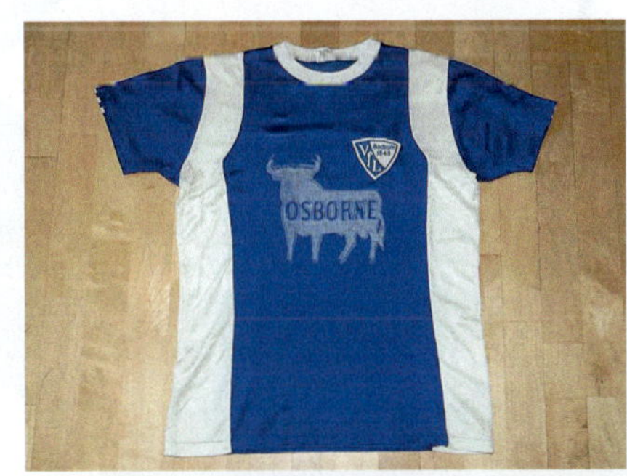

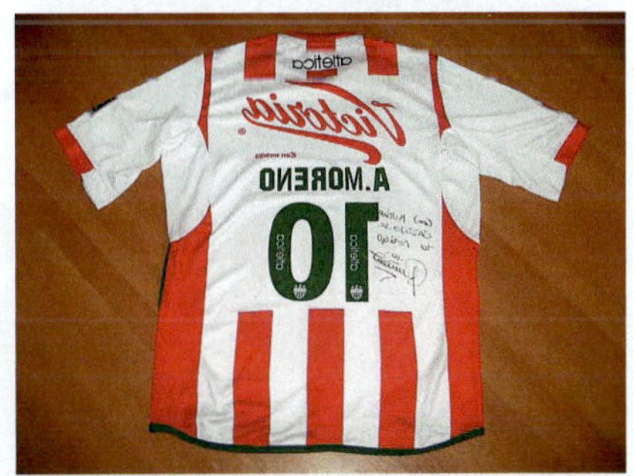

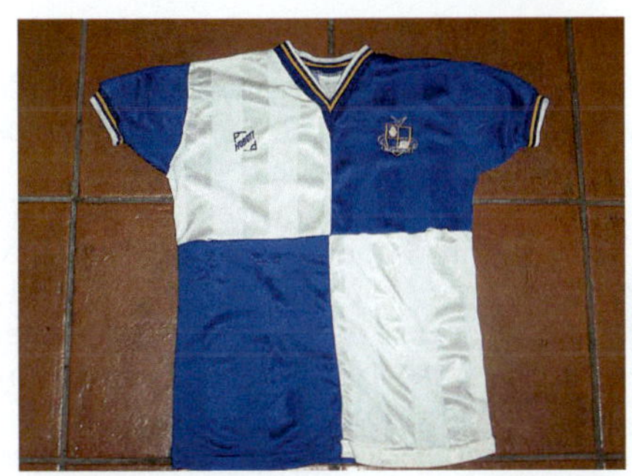

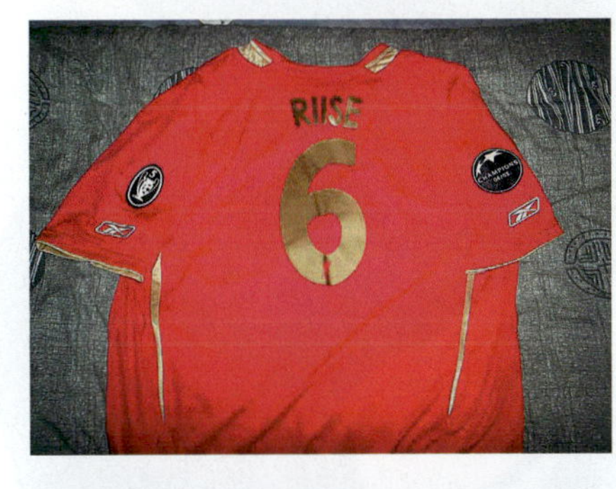

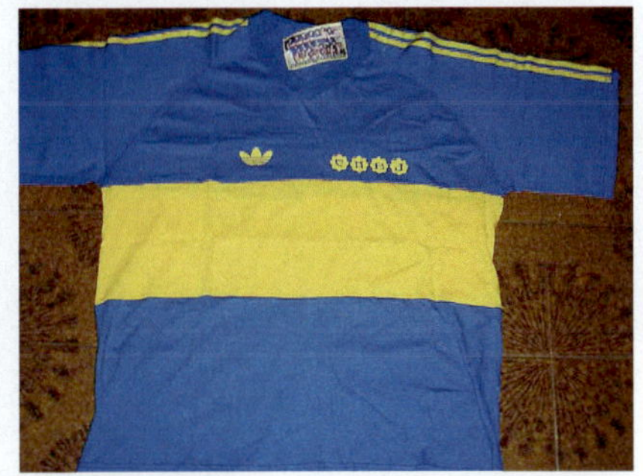

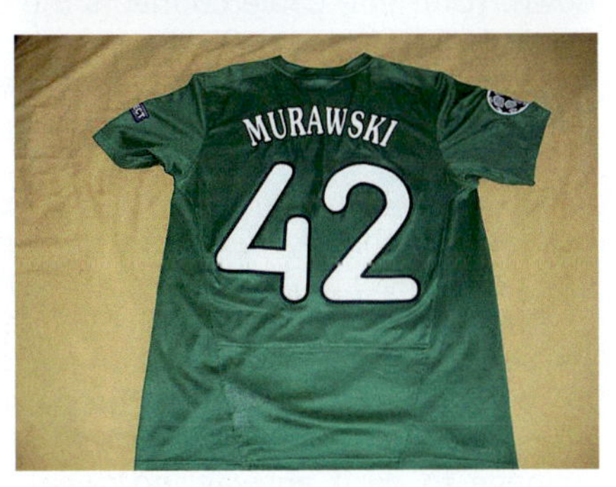

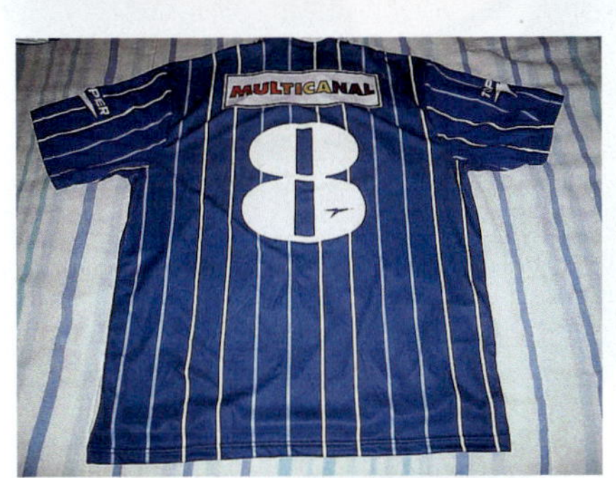

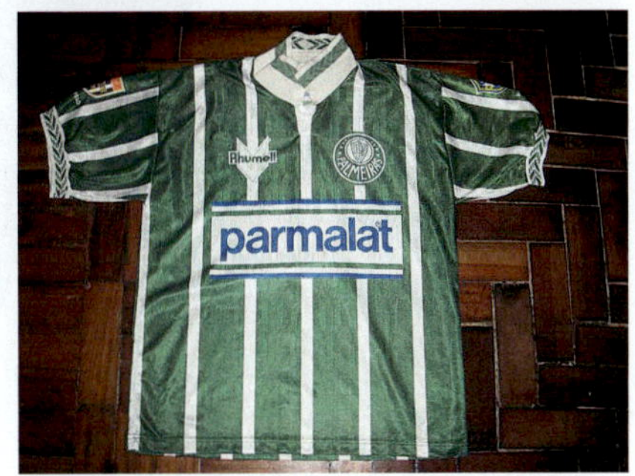

Joachim Schmid, *Other People's Photographs – Shirts*, 2008–2011

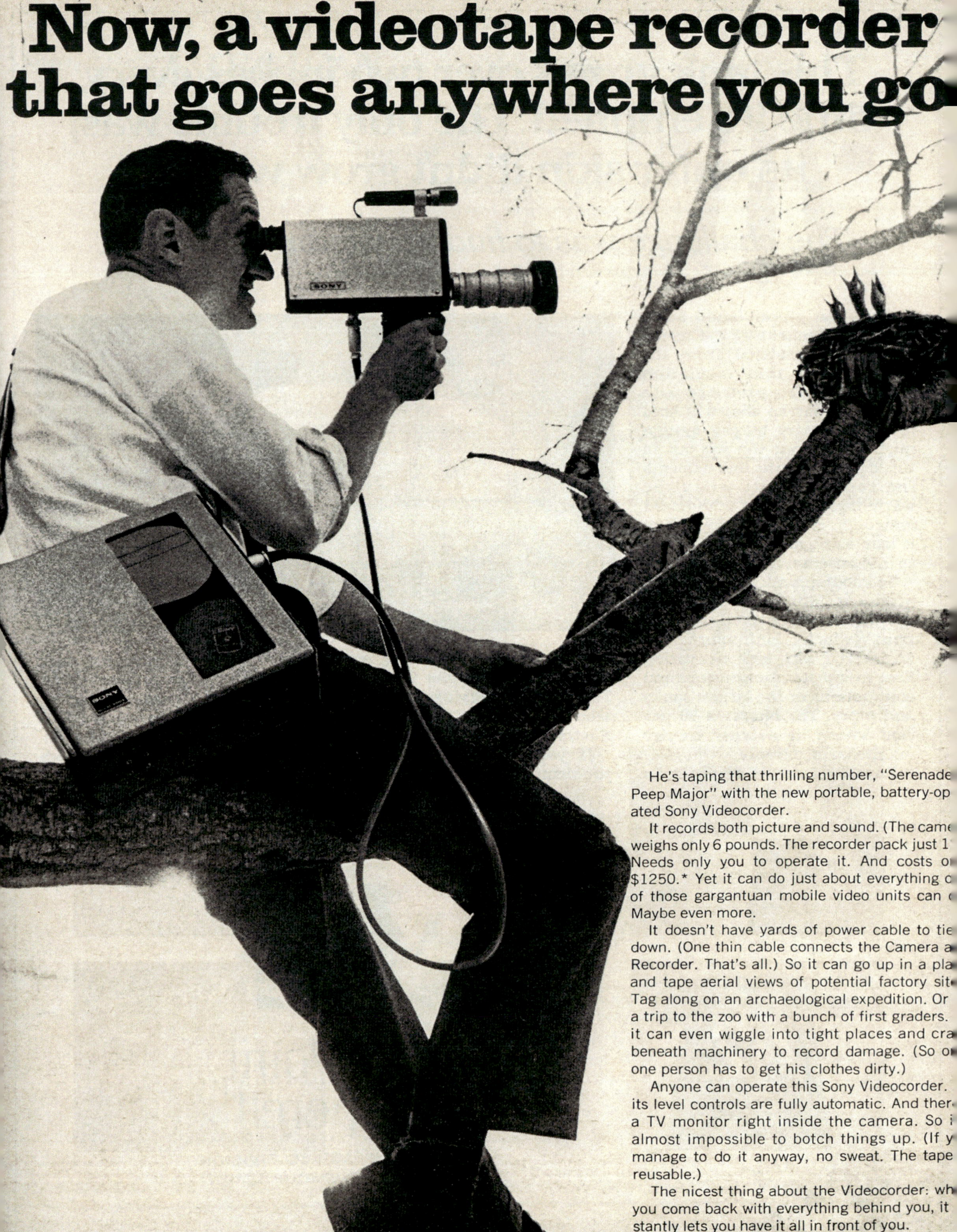
Now, a videotape recorder that goes anywhere you go
SONY
SONY
He's taping that thrilling number, "Serenade Peep Major" with the new portable, battery-op ated Sony Videocorder.
It records both picture and sound. (The came weighs only 6 pounds. The recorder pack just 1 Needs only you to operate it. And costs o $1250.* Yet it can do just about everything of those gargantuan mobile video units can Maybe even more.
It doesn't have yards of power cable to tie down. (One thin cable connects the Camera a Recorder. That's all.) So it can go up in a pla and tape aerial views of potential factory sit Tag along on an archaeological expedition. Or a trip to the zoo with a bunch of first graders. it can even wiggle into tight places and cra beneath machinery to record damage. (So o one person has to get his clothes dirty.)
Anyone can operate this Sony Videocorder. its level controls are fully automatic. And ther a TV monitor right inside the camera. So i almost impossible to botch things up. (If y manage to do it anyway, no sweat. The tape reusable.)
The nicest thing about the Videocorder: wh you come back with everything behind you, it stantly lets you have it all in front of you.
SONY® PORTABLE VIDEOCORDE
*Manufacturer's suggested retail price—including battery charger and zoom lens.

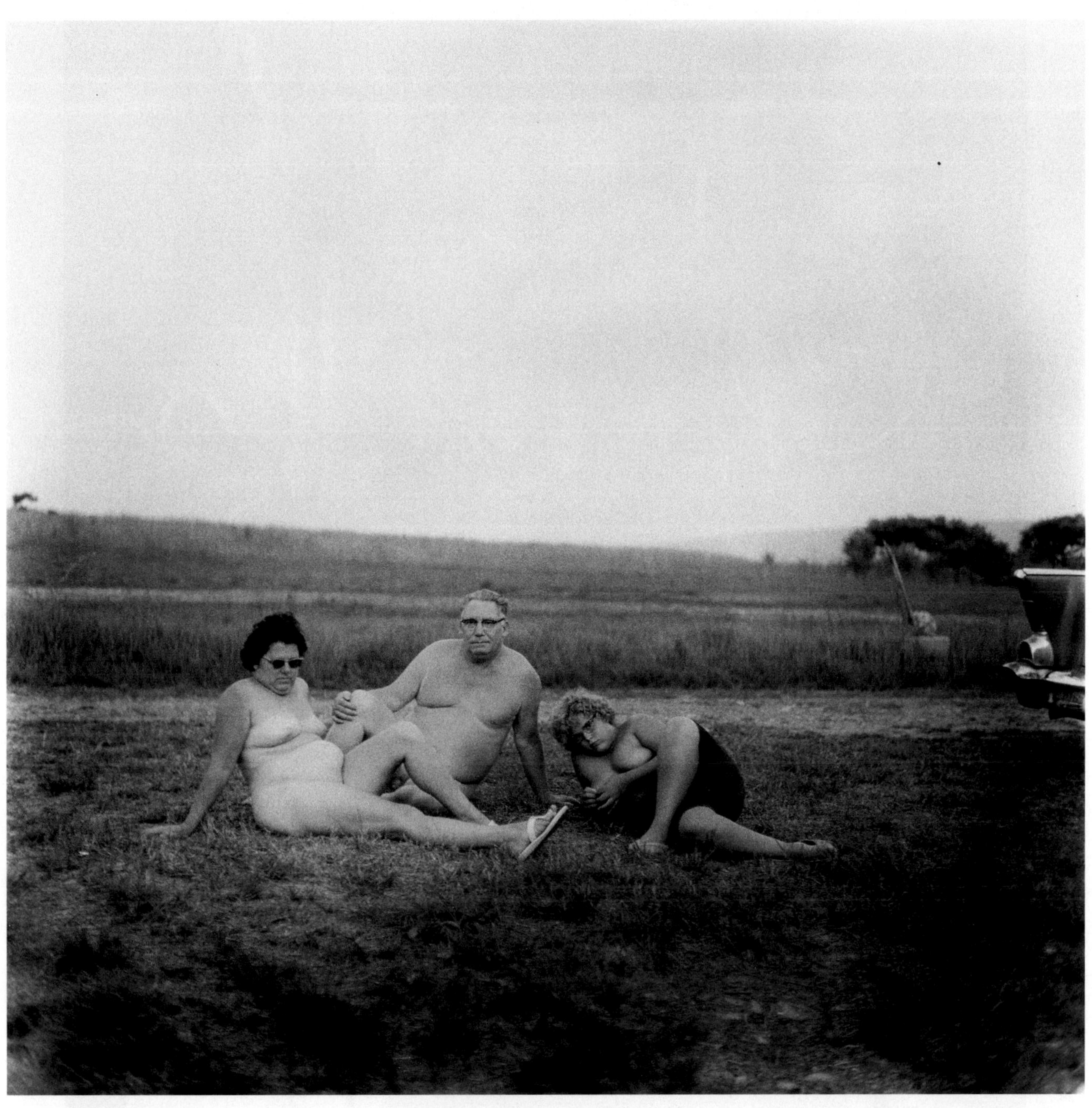

Diane Arbus, *A Family One Evening in a Nudist Camp, Pennsylvania*, 1965

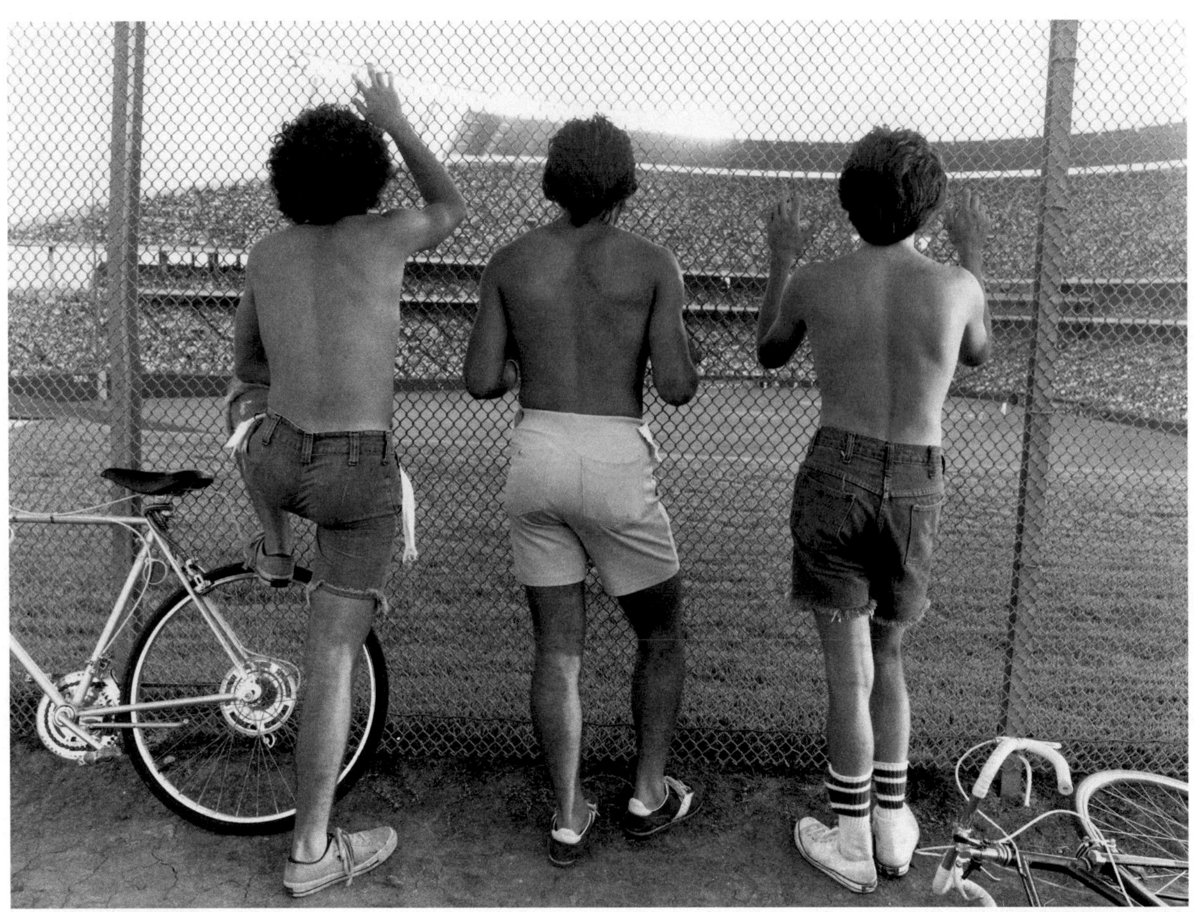

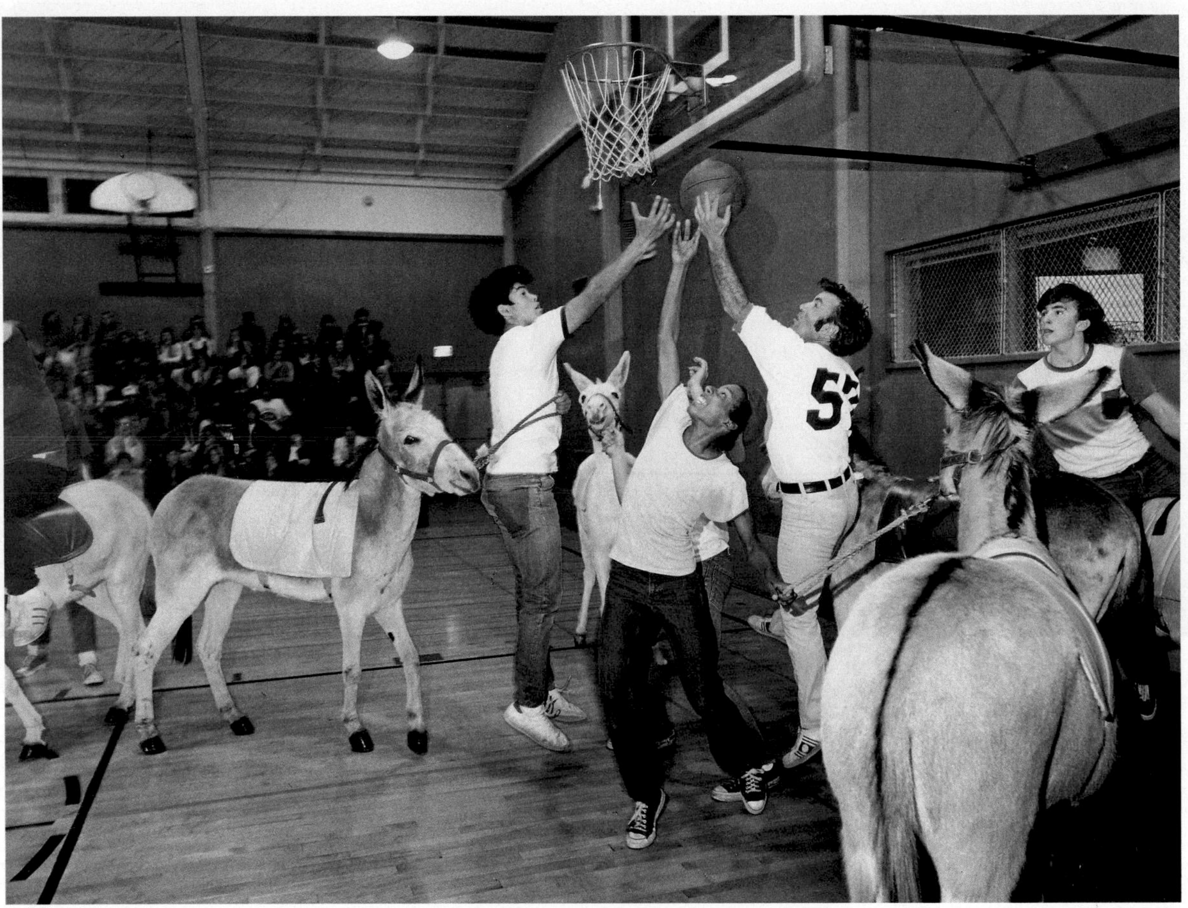

Bill Owens, from *Leisure*, 1976

After the worker-photographers of the Weimar Republic and the proletarian photo-reporters of the Soviet Union, who aimed to provide a direct view of social reality, it was once again the art rebels of the 1970s who saw the casual snapshot as a new 'folk art' with which they could undermine the stereotypes of the photographic aesthetic.

world views. Both approaches might be described as a hobby in the sense of "serious leisure" (though some pictorialists did not practice photography only in their free time, but actually pursued it as an elitist main occupation).

In some ways, the compositional aspirations of amateur art-photography have been continued in the hobby photo scene that still follows the advice and guidance of specialist magazines and tutorials when it comes to improving composition or digitally optimizing images and finding out which techniques are available; photos are submitted to competitions and awards collected. The snappers, on the other hand, whose ubiquitous images flood the Internet these days, have often served as guarantors of an authentic media practice 'from below.' After the worker-photographers of the Weimar Republic and the proletarian photo-reporters of the Soviet Union, who aimed to provide a direct view of social reality, it was once again the art rebels of the 1970s who saw the casual snapshot as a new 'folk art' with which they could undermine the stereotypes of the photographic aesthetic. But as early as the 1960s, Pierre Bourdieu described photography as being "half-way between 'vulgar' practices" and "noble cultural practices." And he expressly warned against regarding snapshots—taken, among other things, as a memory *ersatz* or to jolt the memory, like "a magical substitute for that ... which time has destroyed," or as a form of "self-realization"—merely as an individual improvisational act with neither tradition nor aspiration, pointing out that little was as strongly subject to rules and conventions as amateur photography and its products.

Working with snapshots from very different sources—private archives, flea markets, found images—has nevertheless become an important strategy of conceptual and trace-securing art practices. Hans-Peter Feldmann, Elmar Mauch, Fiona Tan, Erik Kessels, and Alec Soth have all collated substantial collections and have edited such images entirely according to their own personal criteria. In the late 1980s, Joachim Schmid and Adib Fricke began collecting found photos and preparing them for the context of art. In 1990, under the motto "no new photographs until the old ones have been used up," Schmid founded the "Erste allgemeine Altfotosammlung" (first general collection of used photographs) to which people donated many amateur snapshots.

In 1976, under the slogan "power to the amateurs," the magazine *Volksfoto* run by Dieter Hacker and Andreas Seltzer sought to process the "invisible mountain" of stored-away photos and to encourage snappers to take pictures not only of selected, beautiful aspects in their lives. Instead, by way of "operational photography," they were urged to undertake in-depth documentary research and even use the camera "as a weapon": "Although everything we see makes our wish seem utopian," Dieter Hacker wrote, "we want a world that is determined by the amateurs—which is to say, everyone. That is why we have to become aware of our own needs and abilities, and learn from the professionals what is useful to us, in order to defeat them."

Oliver Sieber, from *Übungsräume*, 2000

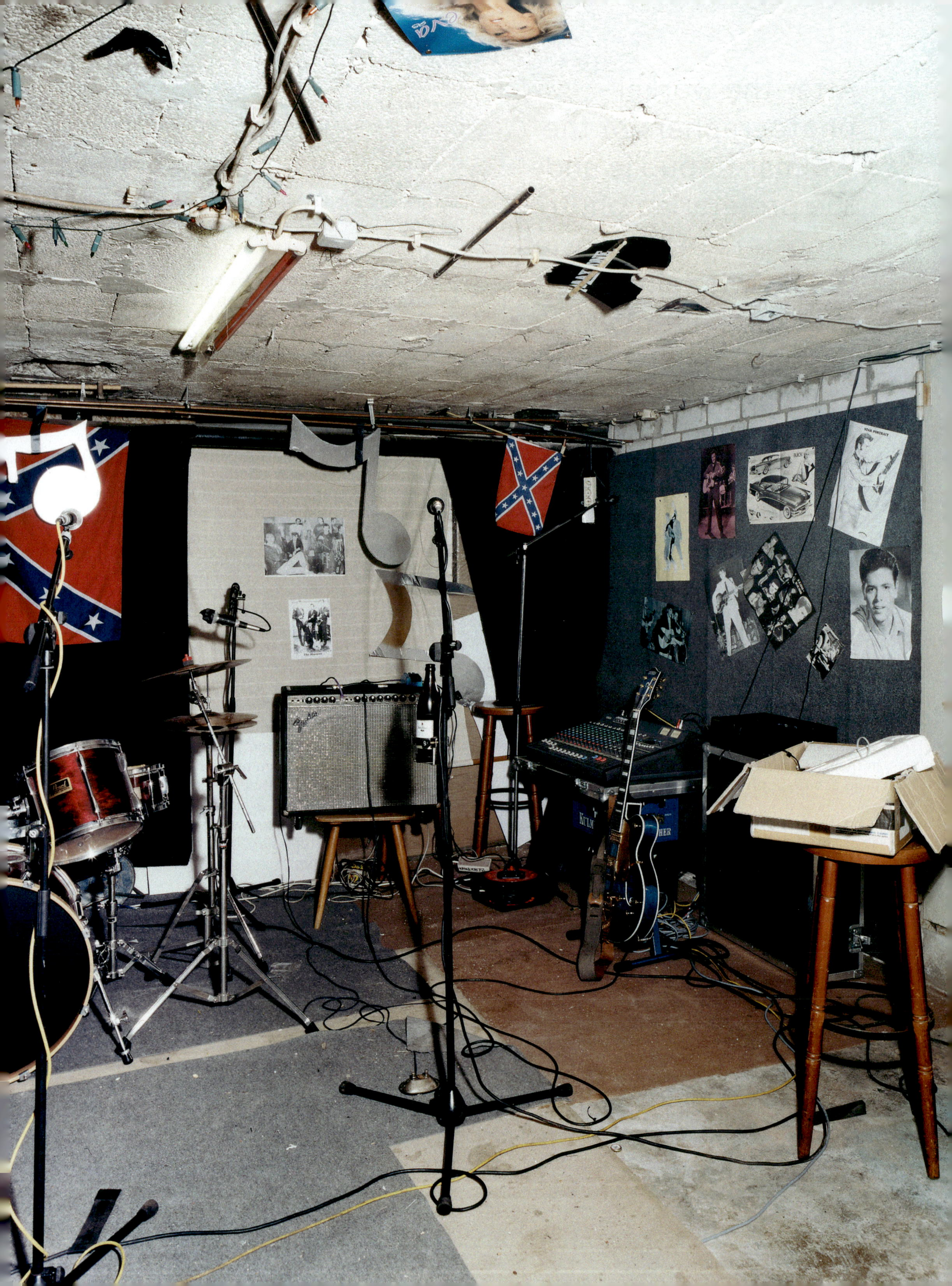

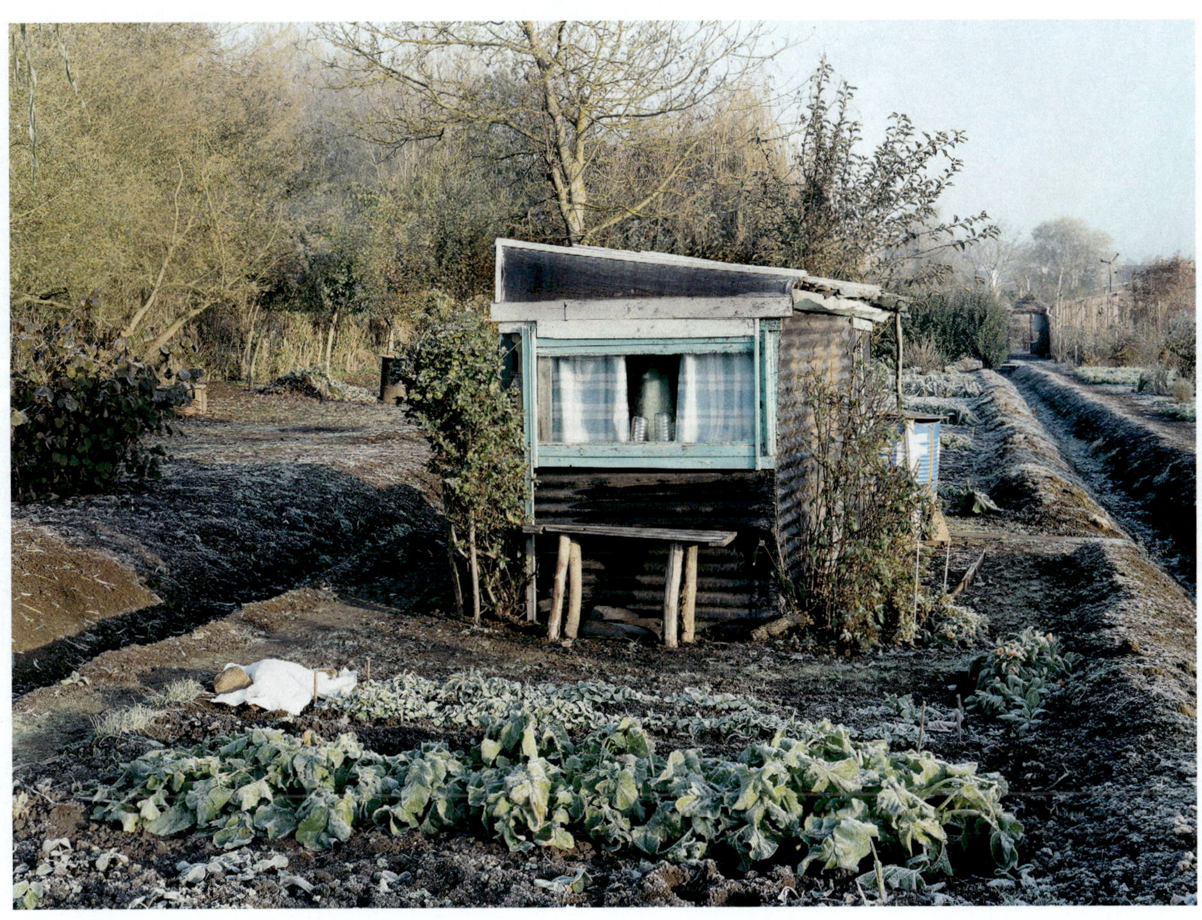

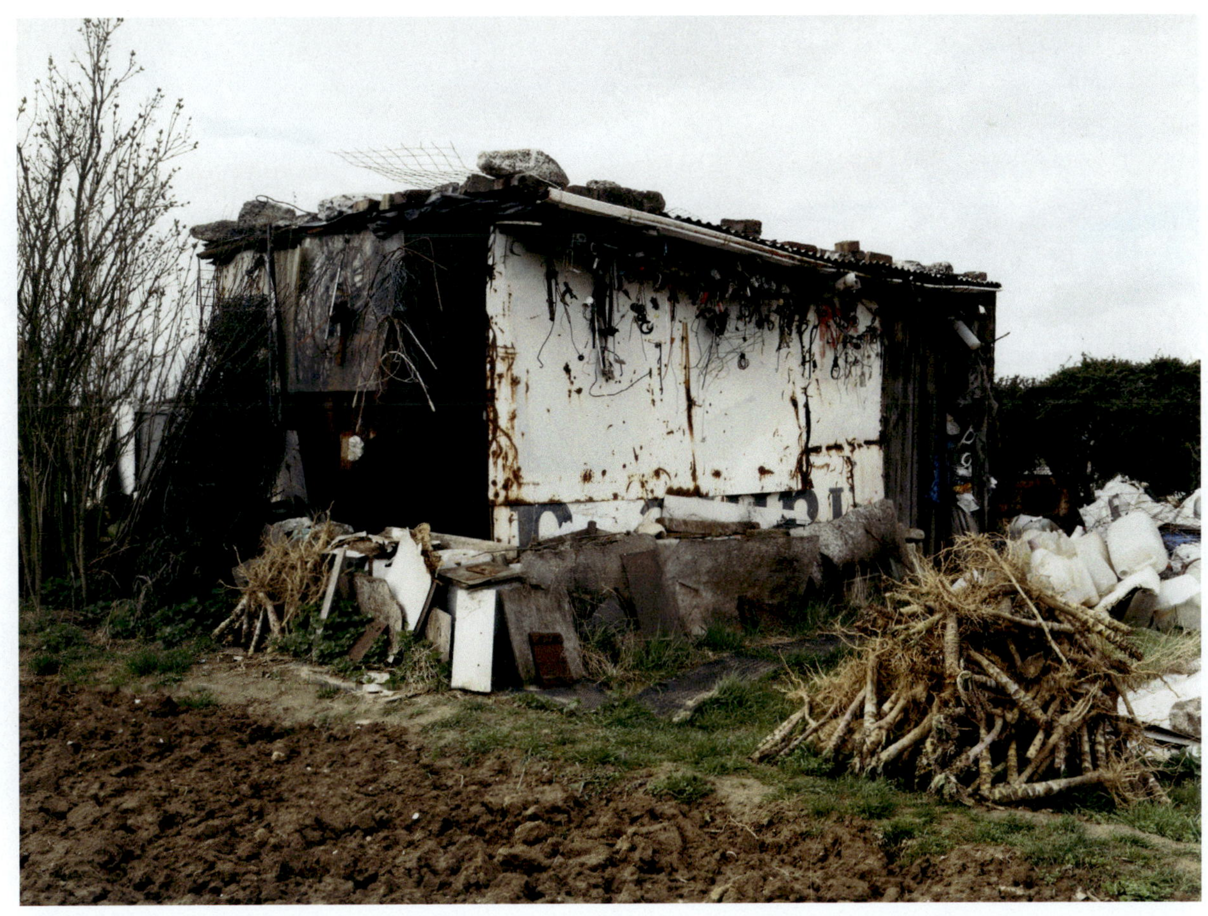

Simone Nieweg, *Feldgarten mit Hütte, Noyon, Oise*, 2005

Schuppen mit Drahtwerk, Louvres, Val d'Oise, 2006

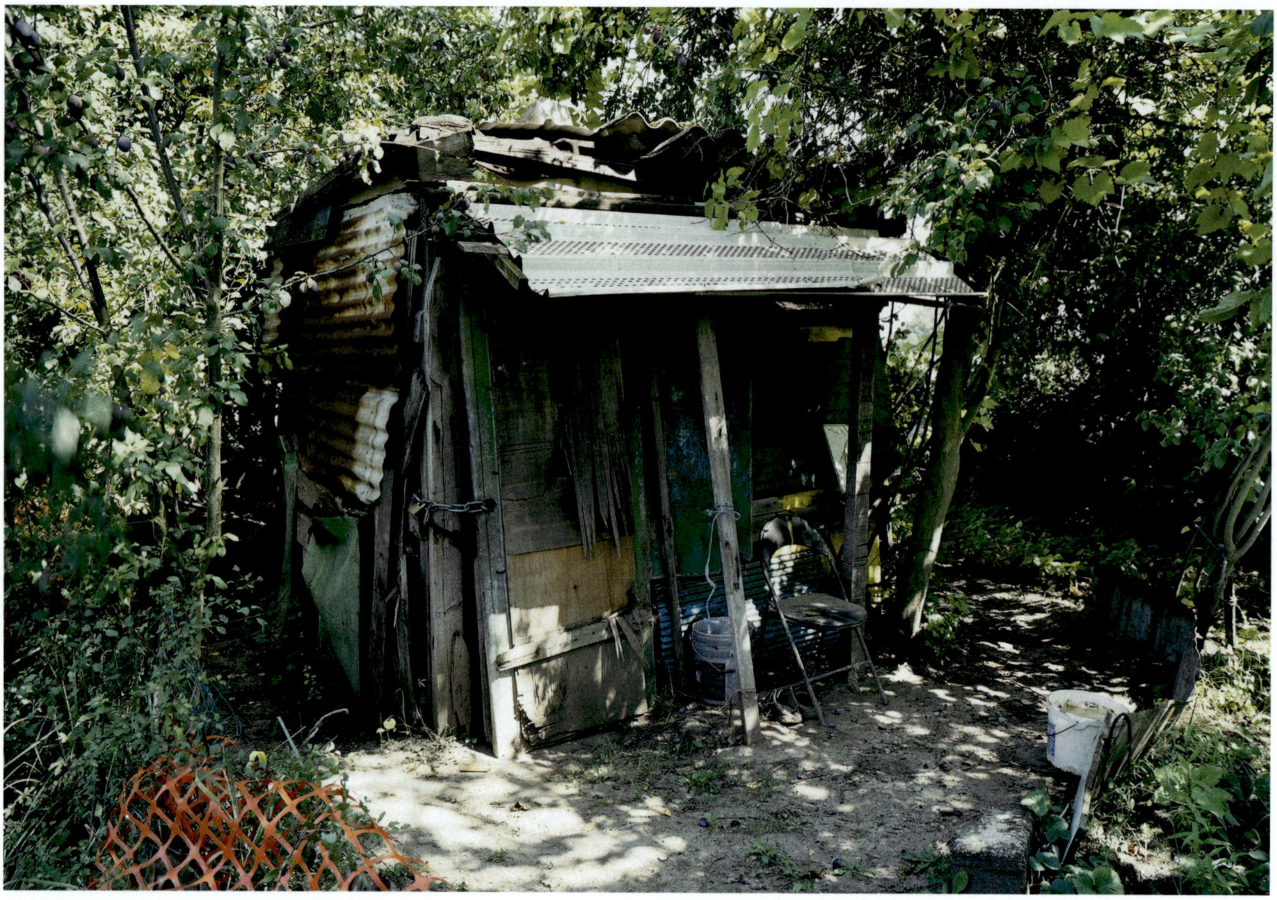

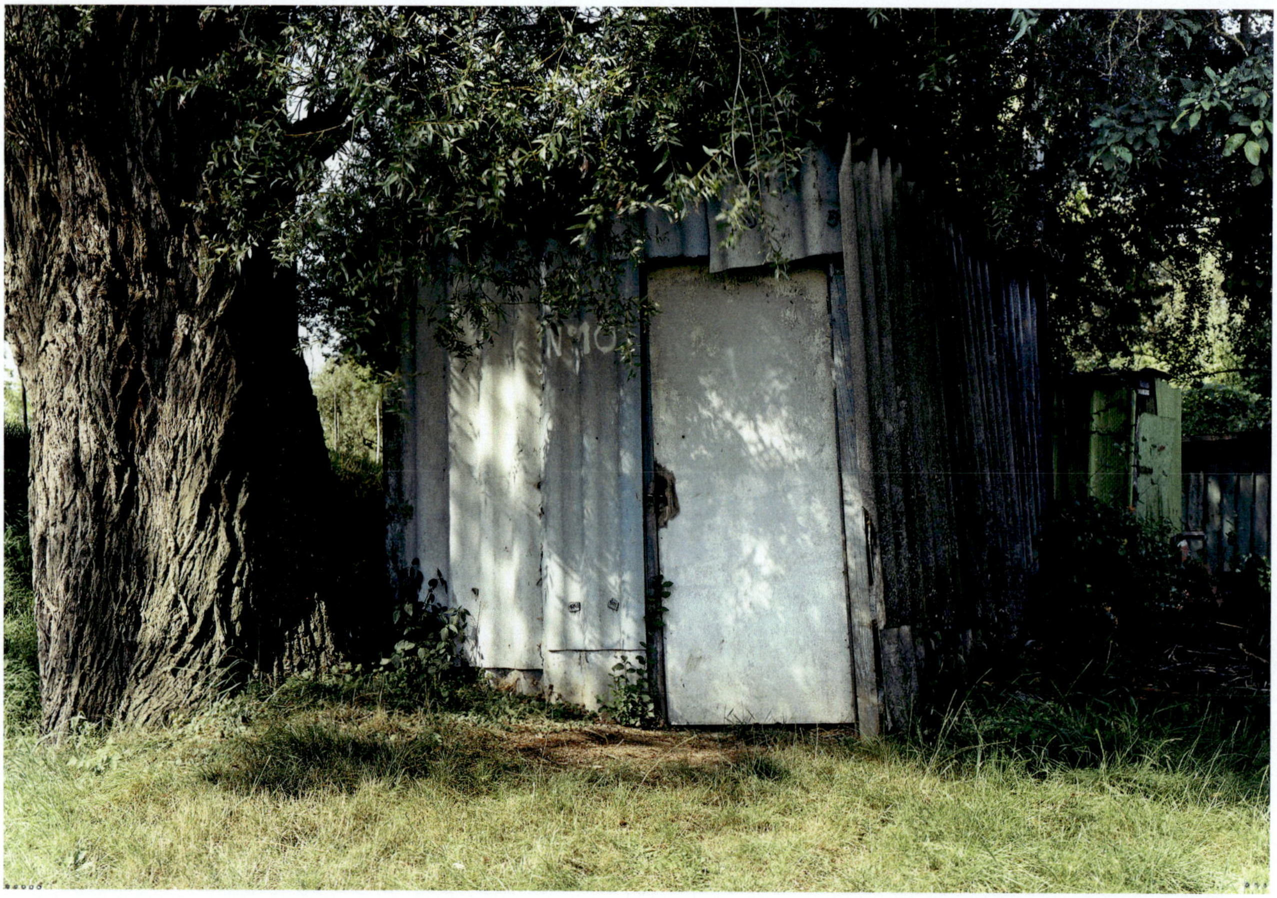

Simone Nieweg, *Hütte unter Pflaumenbäumen, Ay-sur-Moselle*, 2009

Hütte Nr. 10, Ay-sur-Moselle, 2009

SAWN-UP FROG

A Recipe to Honor Gordon Matta-Clark and His FOOD Restaurant

Samuel Herzog

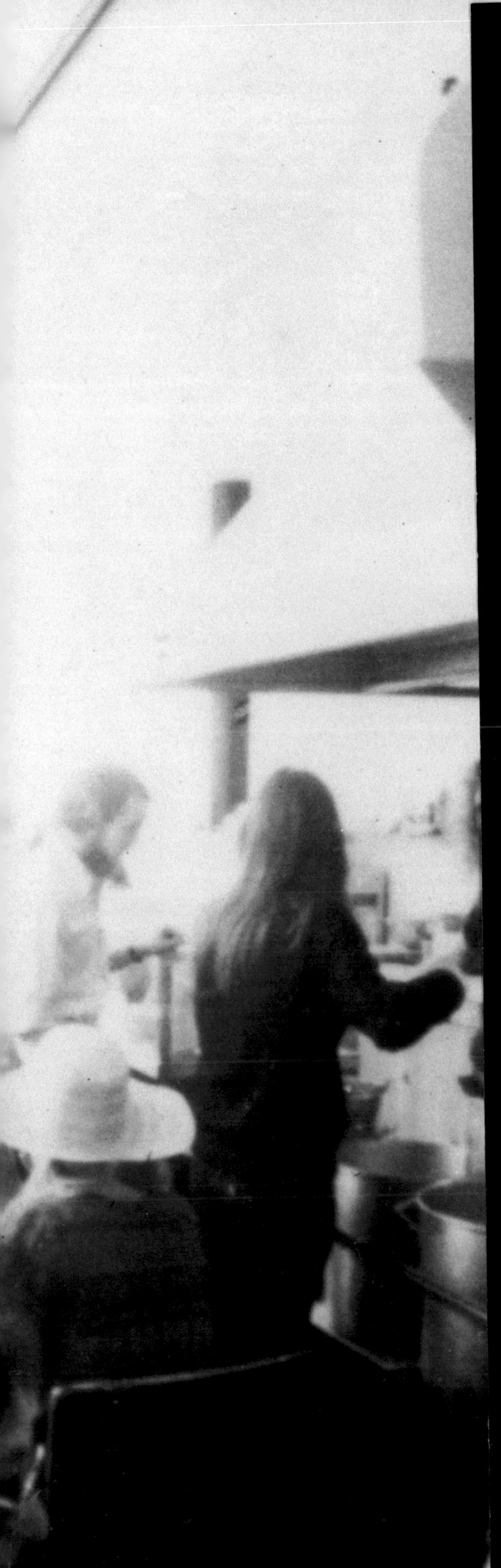

Gordon Matta-Clark, from *FOOD*, 1972

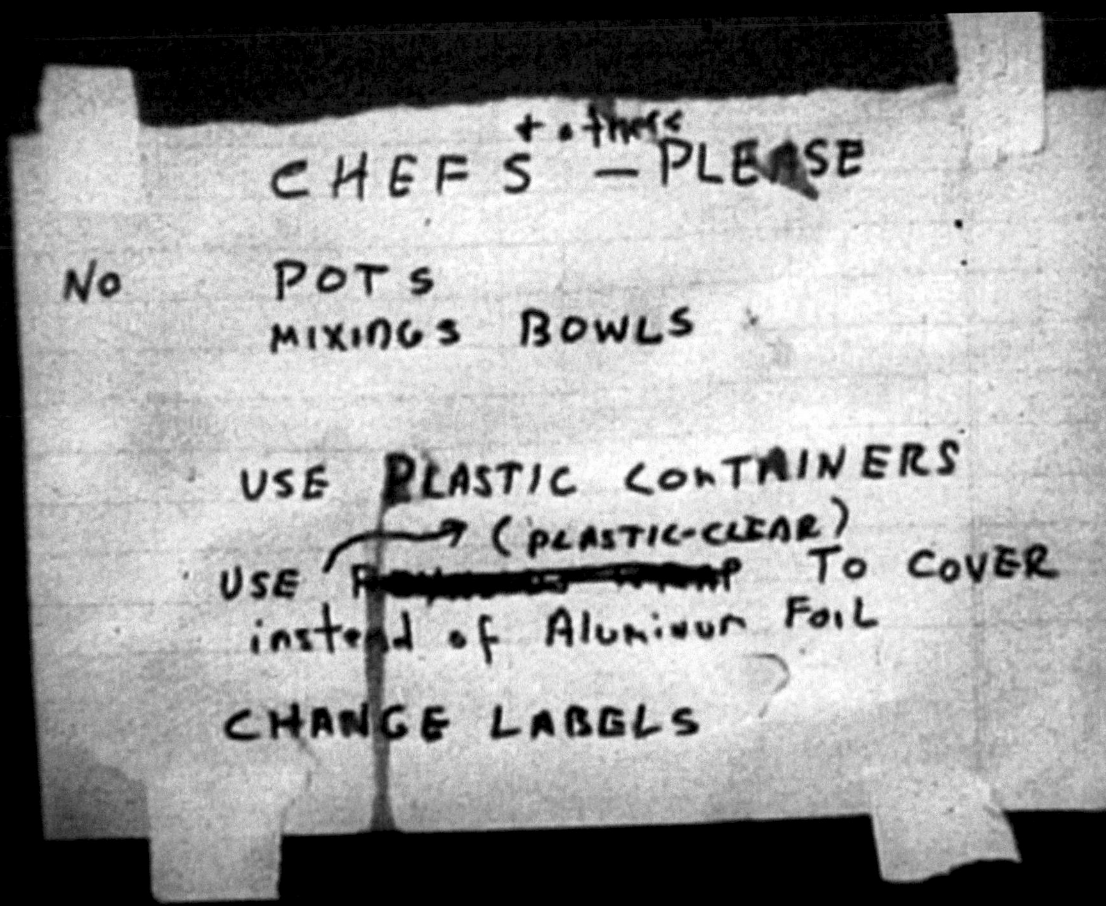

Cosmos Andrew Sarchiapone, *FOOD*, ca. 1971–1973 (Goodden/Matta-Clark/Girouard/Harris/Lew)

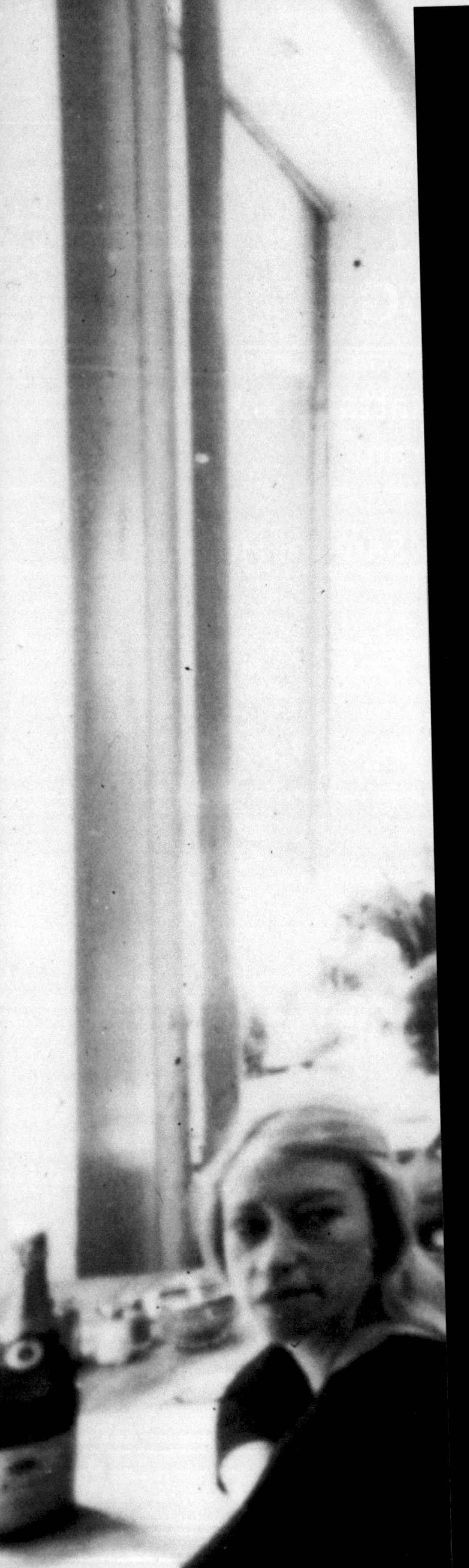

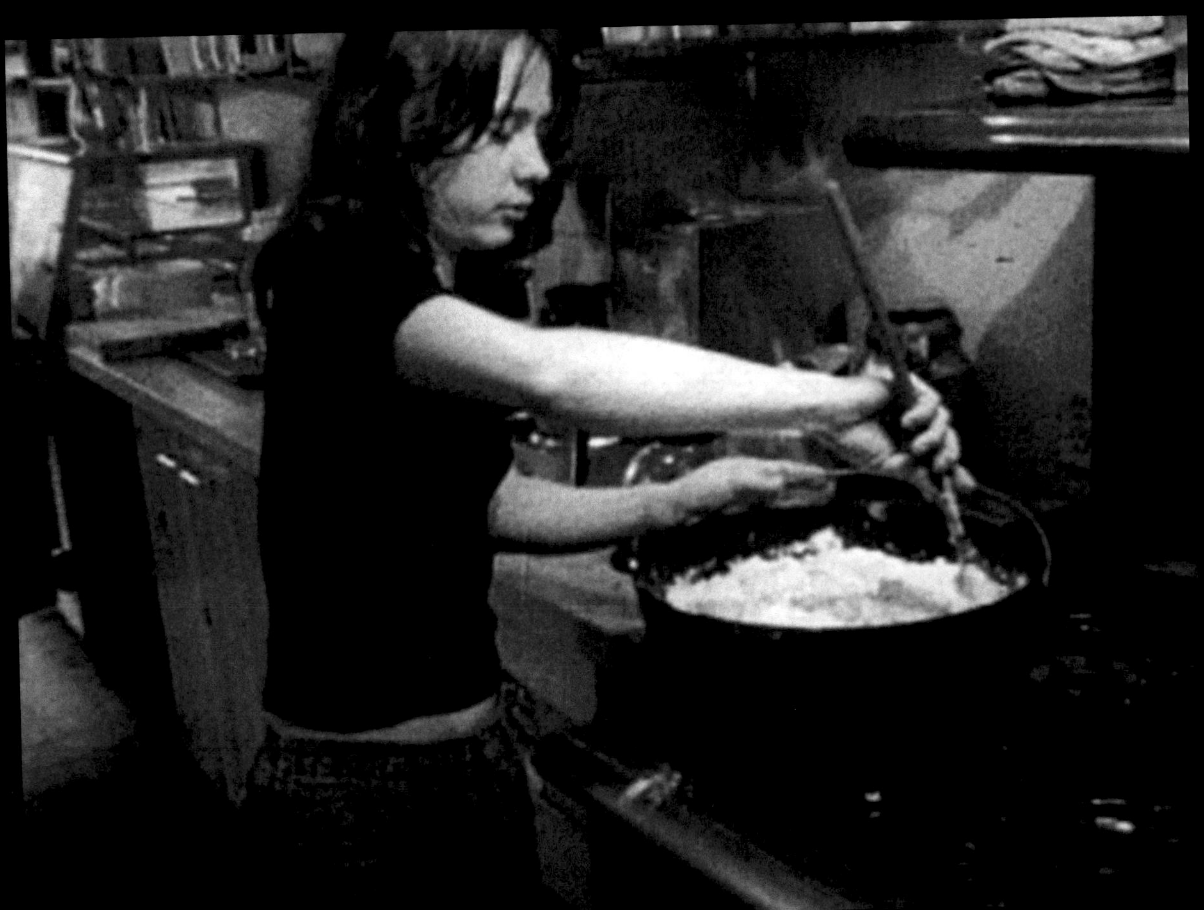

Hobby chefs, such as myself, are known to take on some quite ambitious challenges. My project of writing a cookbook with recipes to honor famous artists of our times has also proved to be a vain undertaking. Following on from the gilded goose's egg for James Lee Byars and the locust soufflé for Hamish Fulton, I then came to Gordon Matta-Clark.

Matta-Clark was a fan of Jonathan Swift, who made a rather bold suggestion in 1729 as to how one could stave off the famine in Ireland: namely by eating little children. Inspired by this cannibalistic idea, Matta-Clark's preparations for *Matta's Proposal* (1971) included asking fellow artist Lee Jaffe to become an edible artwork and, in doing so, kick-start an "incredible edible art movement." Needless to say, *Baby à la Matta-Clark* sounded like it could be just perfect for my cookbook. So I asked around my circle of friends and acquaintances to see whether anyone would like to donate one of their offspring for a few culinary experiments. The response was less than enthusiastic.

After that, I spent quite some time mulling over what else might be available to devour—just as Matta-Clark had devoured the wealth and the very lifetime of photographer and dancer Caroline

Gordon Matta-Clark, from *FOOD*, 1972

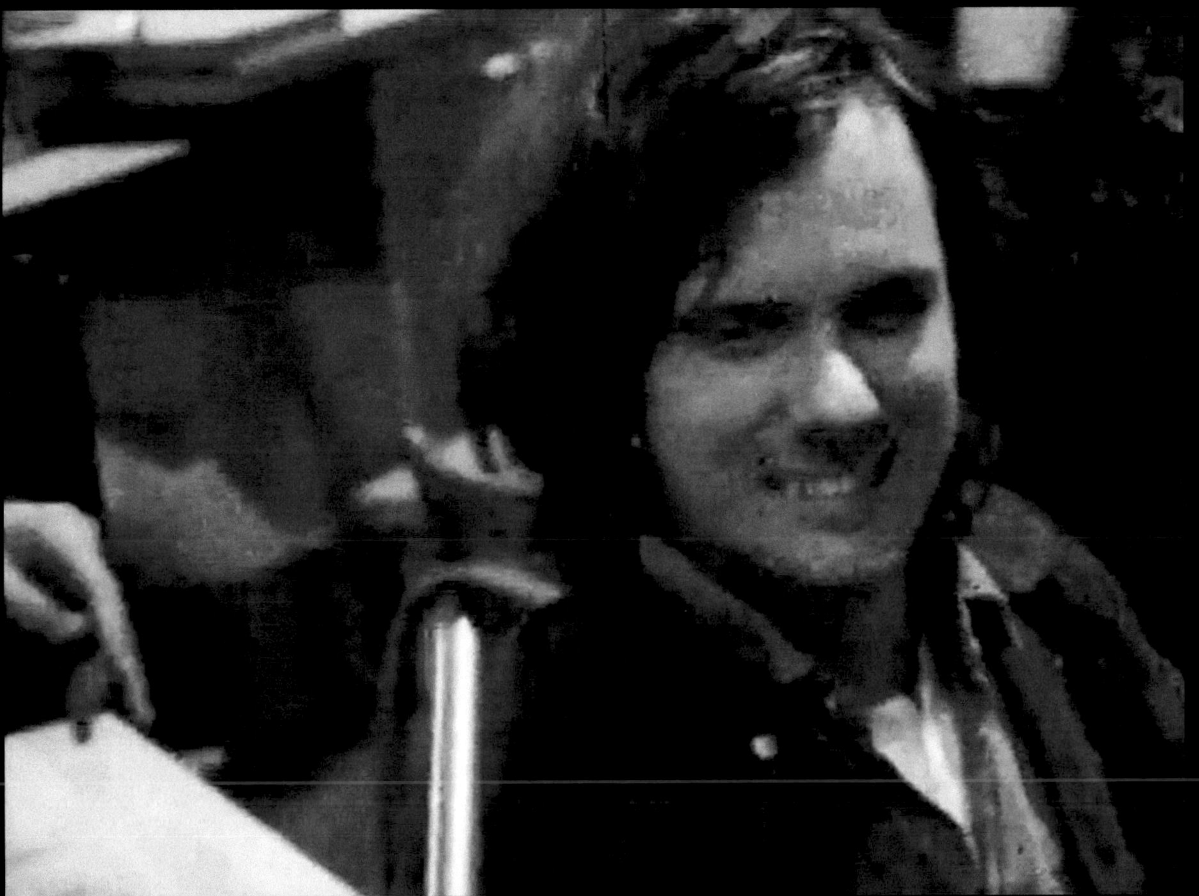

Goodden, by using her money to launch his FOOD restaurant at 127 Prince Street, New York, in 1971, slap-bang in the middle of SoHo, which was, at the time, still something of a cultural and economic wasteland. For Goodden, FOOD was also a business venture, whereas for Matta-Clark it was primarily an opportunity to live out his fascination for food as an artistic and transformatory process. A project he quite literally got fed up with, however, after two years.

One Sunday dinner at FOOD, which Matta-Clark particularly relished, springs to mind. He used hard-boiled eggs, removed the yolk and replaced it by live shrimps. Some of the guests shrieked at the sight of the shrimps crawling from the inside of the egg. Others left the premises without a word. Still others bravely swallowed the whole thing. "Wonderful reactions—Gordon enjoyed all of it," recalls Goodden. Boiled egg with tortured shrimp—another great recipe for my cookbook! Unfortunately, live shrimps are just about as easy to find in Switzerland as barbecue-ready infants.

A dish from *Sculptors Dinner* by Mark di Suvero would whet my appetite. He had food served through the windows of the restaurant from a crane; screwdrivers and hammers served as cutlery. It remains unclear whether this dinner ever actually took place,

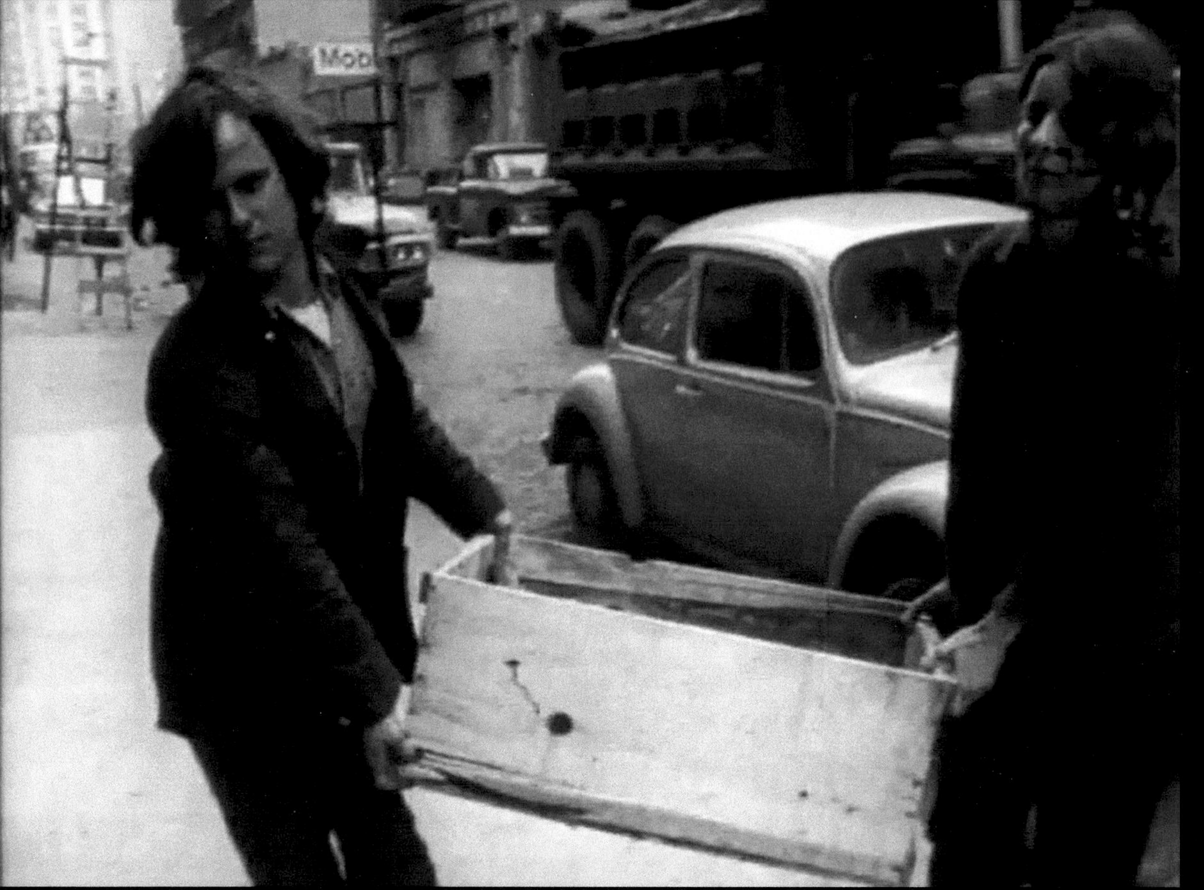

or whether it is simply one of those "apocryphal stories" (Alanna Heiss) that FOOD invariably seemed to generate. The walnut-stuffed flamingo from Lemusa is another dish I'd love to replicate, but the directors of the local zoo have not responded yet.

Ultimately, a lot of pretty down-to-earth dishes were also served at FOOD. For instance, on the opening night, September 25, 1971, there was garlic soup, gumbo, and chicken stew. The restaurant was also one of the first to serve raw fish, making it a kind of vanguard of sushi. Yet none of this stacks up for me when it comes to creating a monument in the form of a recipe for an alchemist like Matta-Clark. There was another highlight, though—the *Bone Meal*, which was akin to a culinary Sunday sermon by the artist. He introduced his *Matta-Bones* with a dish of home-made aspic, followed by an oxtail soup, and then a huge platter of bones including marrow-bone, chicken carcasses, and haunches of beef, stuffed with wild rice and mushrooms—all *splittings* and *cuttings* of animal skeletons. After the meal, guests could even take home a necklace of cow bones. And then there was one other *Matta-Bones* dish with which the French tend to shock the rest of the world: *Frog Legs Provençal*. Eureka! At last I have found my recipe: *Sawn-up Frog à la Gordon*—well, if that isn't *le dernier cri*!

PETS, HOBBIES, AND THE INTERNET

A Conversation with the Artist Collective NEOZOON

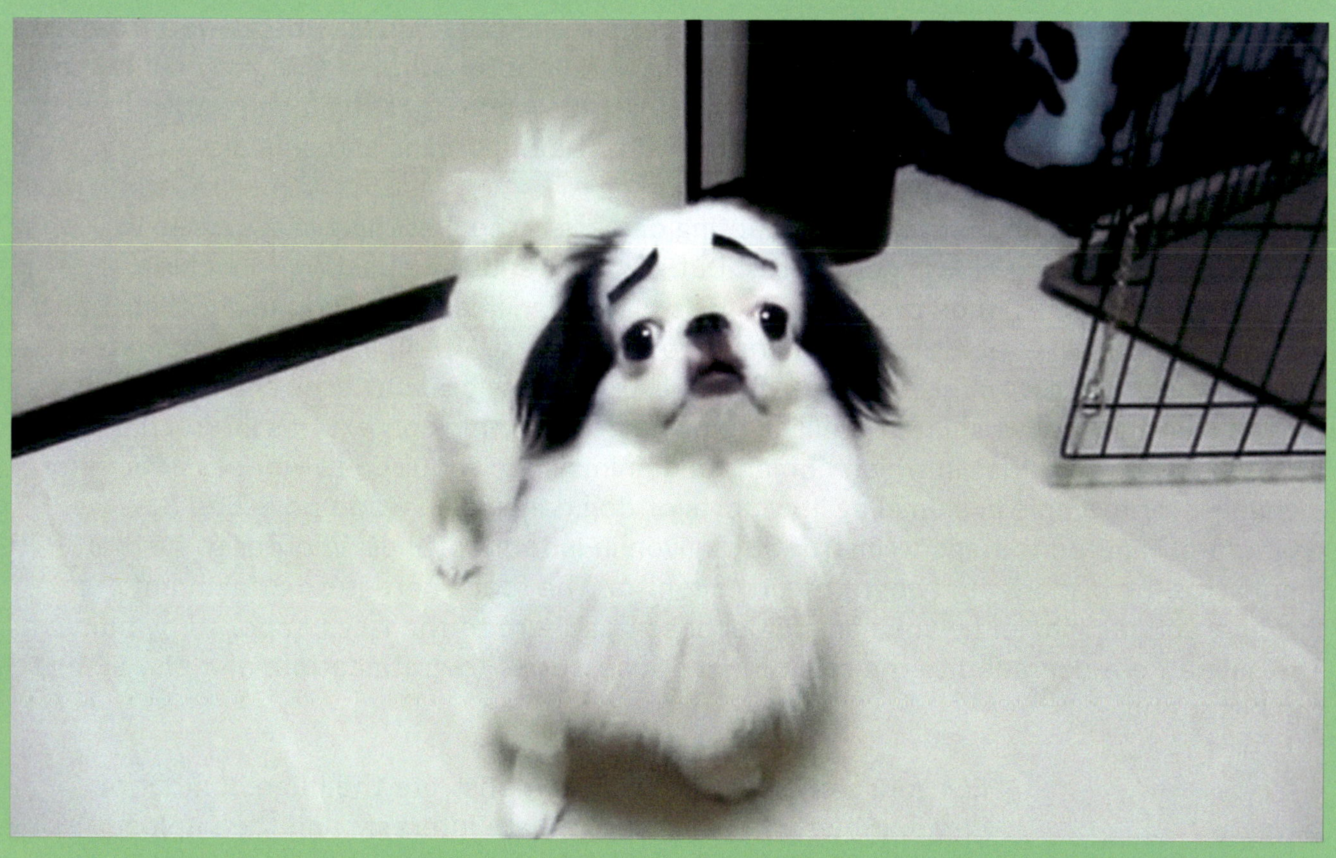

Erec Gellautz: Your work primarily focuses on the relationship between humans and animals. How did you decide on this direction, which is also reflected in your name—NEOZOON—a term for species of animals which have been introduced into new habitats by humans?

NEOZOON: We were both individually interested in the relationship between humans and nature before we founded NEOZOON. In 2009, when we explicitly oriented ourselves towards exploring the human-animal relationship, we began with a large-scale street art project. The idea came when we found a huge quantity of discarded fur coats from second-hand clothing collection companies. From them we cut out hundreds of life-size animal silhouettes and stuck them on buildings in several major cities. A simple act of recycling which, without having to have much background knowledge, communicated a visual message quickly while playfully opening new intellectual horizons. The ensuing questions regarding the exploitation of animals, which occupied both the public and us, have led to an ever more intensive examination of this subject and ultimately reinforced our thematic focus.

EG: In *Good Boy—Bad Boy* (2011), you compiled footage you found on the Internet for the first time. The work undeniably celebrates the humorous aspects of the special link between pets and net culture, but irritation and a sense of awkwardness also arise through the repetition of almost identical sequences of praise and reproach, training and playing. The depicted routines of interactions between people and pets can also be viewed from the perspective of leisure and hobby cultures that are now found both on- and offline. What relevance does this perspective have on shaping the coexistence between humans and animals?

NZ: When you think about hobbies, collecting objects is the first thing that comes to mind—not the keeping of living creatures. But if you extend the question to include recreational activities, then of course animals play a significant role; you might think of leisure-time hunters, rabbit breeders and pigeon fanciers. Although it isn't immediately perceptible in people who keep pets, in establishing behavioral patterns and little tricks, for the owners it's always about fulfilling human needs. In this context, it's interesting to observe leisure activities in which humans and animals are required to work as a team for a change, for example in animal agility sports or dog dancing. In *Good Boy—Bad Boy*, we deliberately limited footage to instructions given in indoor settings, in order to further emphasize the disparity between the protagonists. The focus here is on attainment, training, and punishment—when an animal doesn't adhere to the rules imposed by humans. The animals are degraded to the role of mere accessories to gratification, and play along to the bitter end.

EG: Your works impressively demonstrate the huge number of communities who film their private interests and then upload their videos. What kind of scenes do these include that you access via

From *Good Boy—Bad Boy*, 2011

YouTube which one wouldn't otherwise normally come across? And what role does sharing online have for these groups? How has found video footage changed and how have your artistic strategies evolved over the years?

NZ: Our practice has changed in that we now know exactly which keywords to use to find certain groups and subjects. Of course, special-interest videos don't just 'float to the surface' very often, like those with 100,000 clicks. Almost everyone who posts videos online is looking for followers or like-minded people, and sometimes interests are only awakened by others on the Internet. We are curious about many different groups, but mostly those which in some way—either consciously or unconsciously—have something to do with other species. Whether it's people who train their pets, people who adhere to a particular diet, or those who like to watch other people trampling on food, we are primarily interested in the phenomenon itself—for us it's never about the individual but the masses. Viewed in this way, our works are essentially sociological studies of the human species.

EG: Even if people today, in the so-called anthropocene era, have become the most important geological, biological, and atmospherical factor, the individual often perceives a loss in the efficacy of his or her actions. Hobbies can be seen as a release

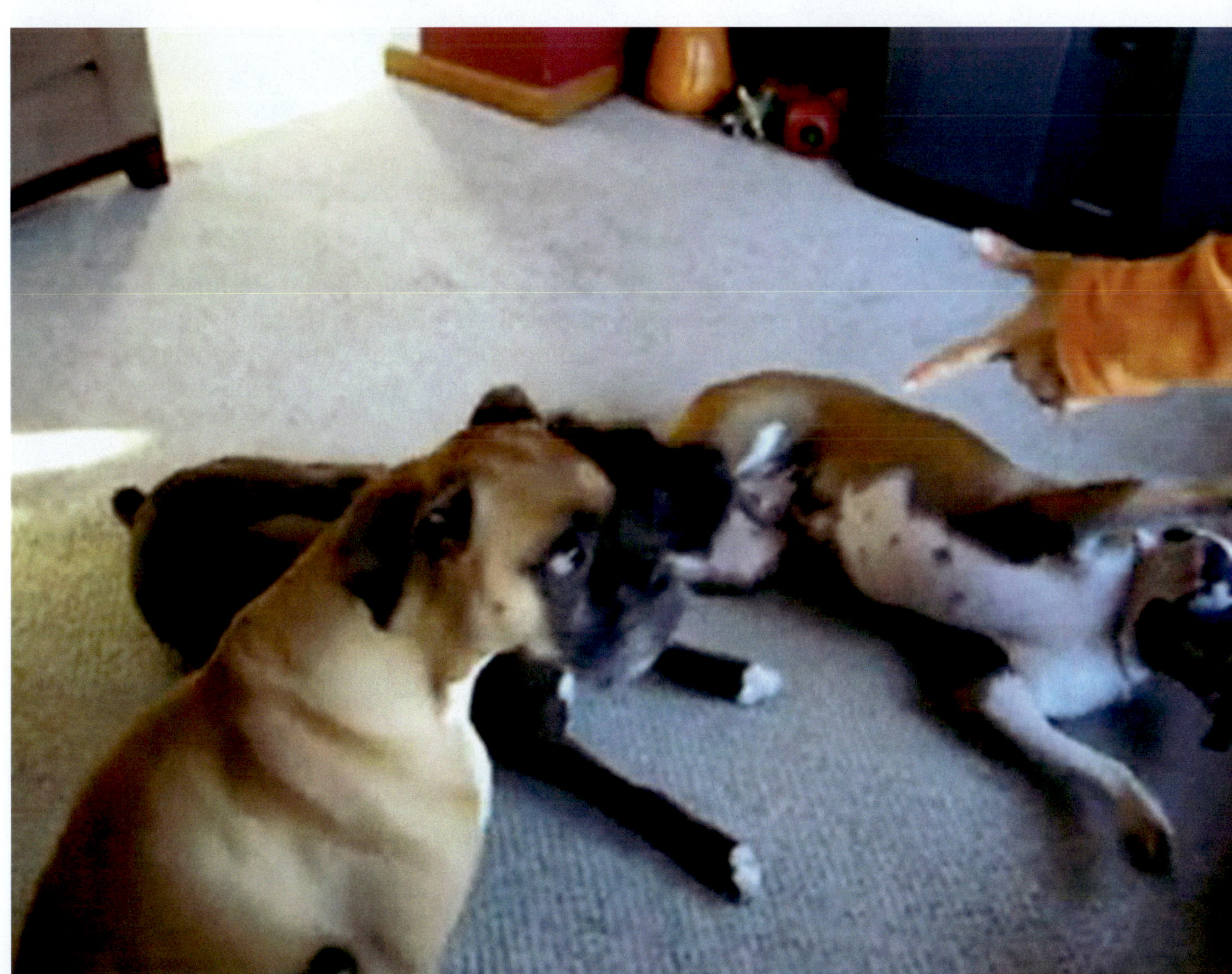

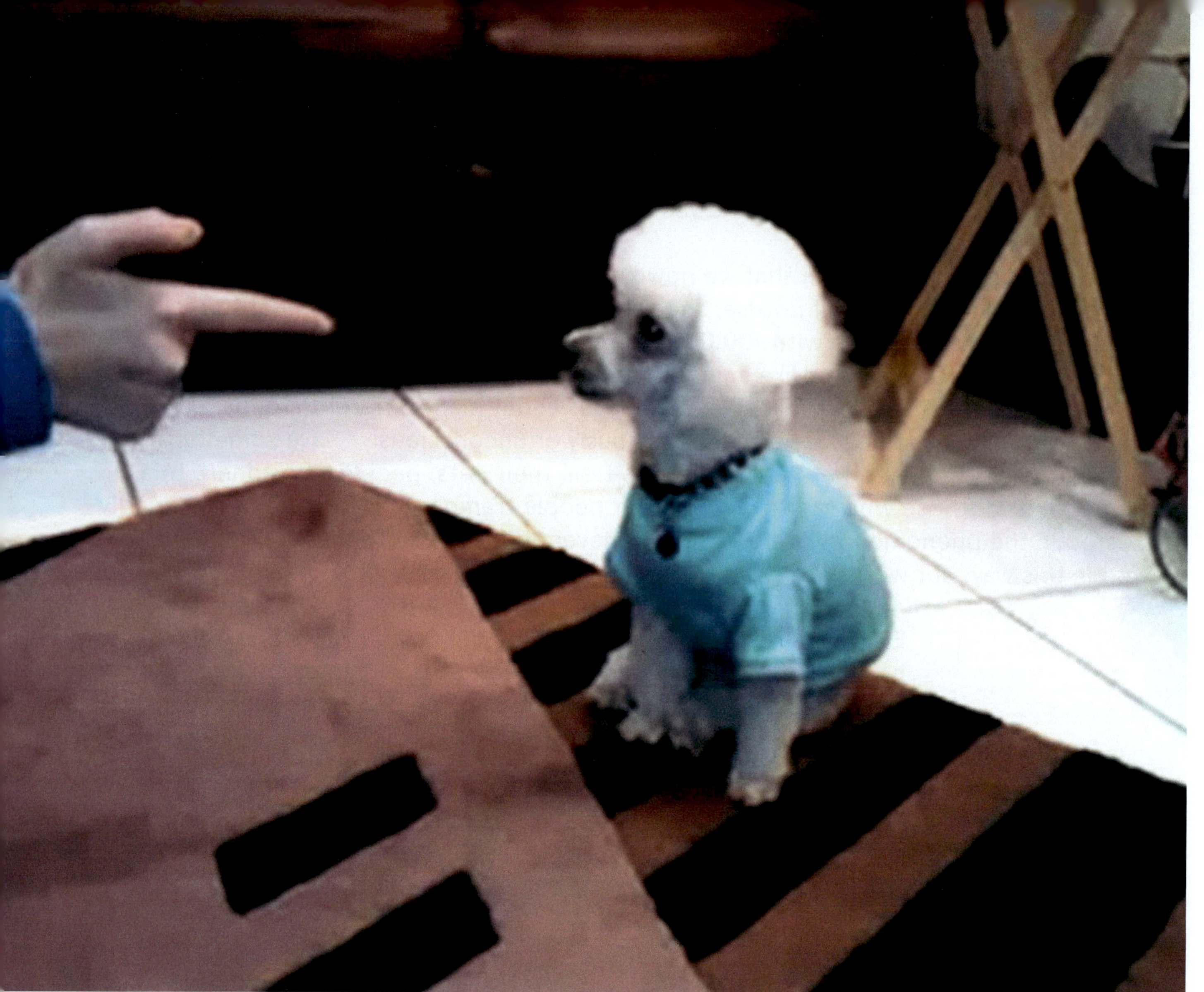

mechanism for this, as they often fulfill the desire for meticulous control even though it is limited in scope. This also applies to the keeping of pets, as it comes with an absolute determining power over a living creature. Are pets ultimately equatable to 'emotional livestock'? And could the hobby concept potentially lead to new findings with regard to a sociological perspective on owners?

NZ: Because by way of exception we don't eat these animals, we use them for something else, like our emotions. The way we interact with animals has always been characterized by a significant fear of the 'other'—it is about the desire to master nature. Domesticated animals play a very special role in this. We have succeeded in adapting them to suit our needs, and in doing so have managed to master them. Seen in this way, there really is a parallel with the hobby concept; for the owners of animals in our film it is solely about demonstrating the execution of this power of control.

EG: Can you see a pattern if and how social awareness regarding our relationship with pets and the problems of industrial farming

From *Good Boy—Bad Boy*, 2011

and meat consumption has developed? dOCUMENTA 13 (2012) provided impetus for perceiving things from an animalistic perspective, and since then many exhibitions have questioned the anthropocentric viewpoint. Is there also an increased awareness with regard to animal rights in everyday life?

NZ: Definitely. Society's awareness of animal rights has risen considerably in recent years, which has of course to do with the widespread realization that our dietary habits are detrimental to the earth's climate. But also in the field of the humanities, there is an increased interest in questioning the relationship between animal suffering and human benefit, or how it feels to belong to another species. Against this background it is interesting to question whether animals are always seen as mere providers of something, or if they could also be viewed as actors with individual rights. Who is actually doing what with whom, and is it possible for us to renounce the anthropocentric perspective? This paradigm shift in the humanities has definitely made an important contribution to the change in perception in recent years. But despite this development, humankind's relationship to animals is still full of contradictions—and that is where our work comes in.

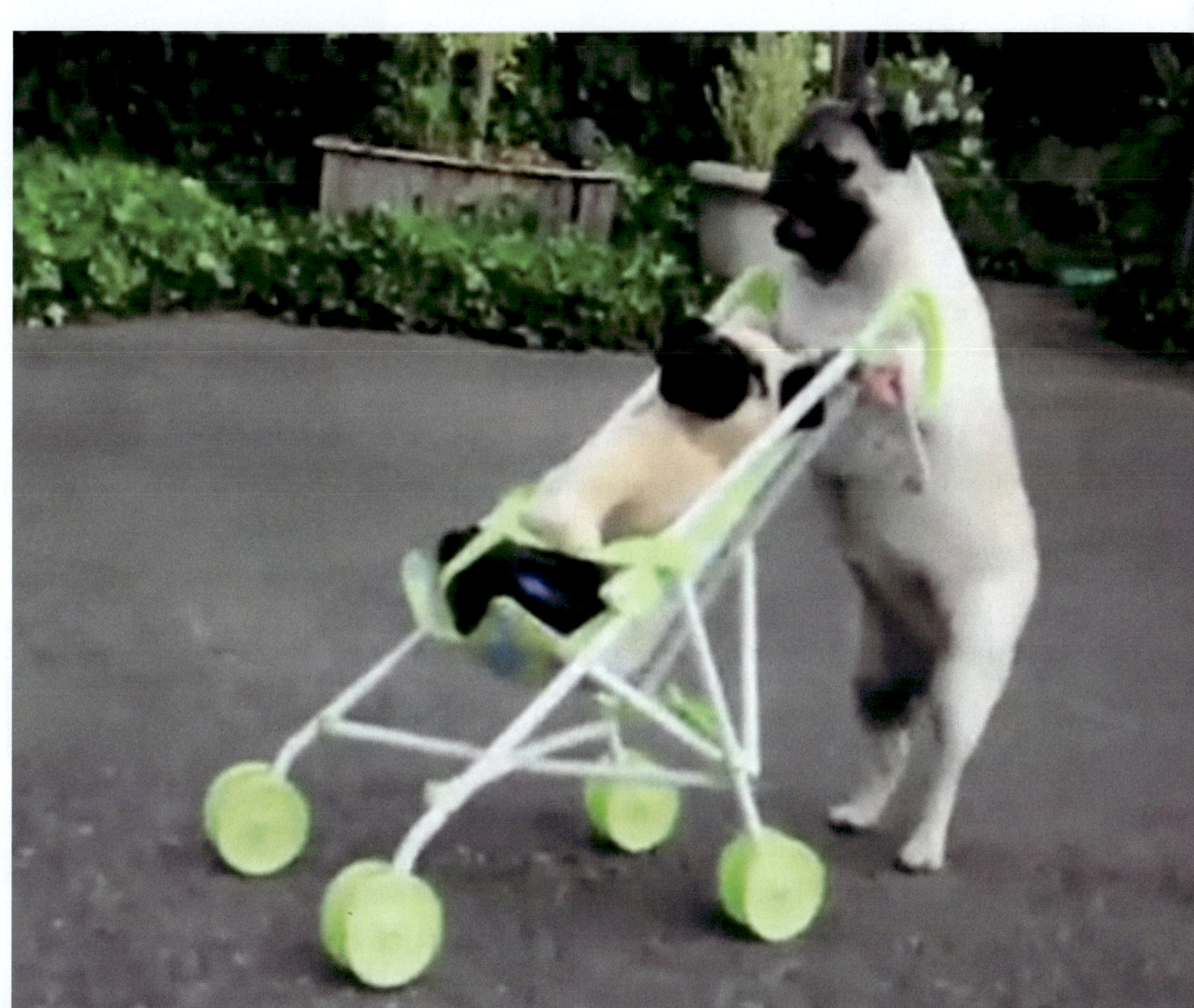

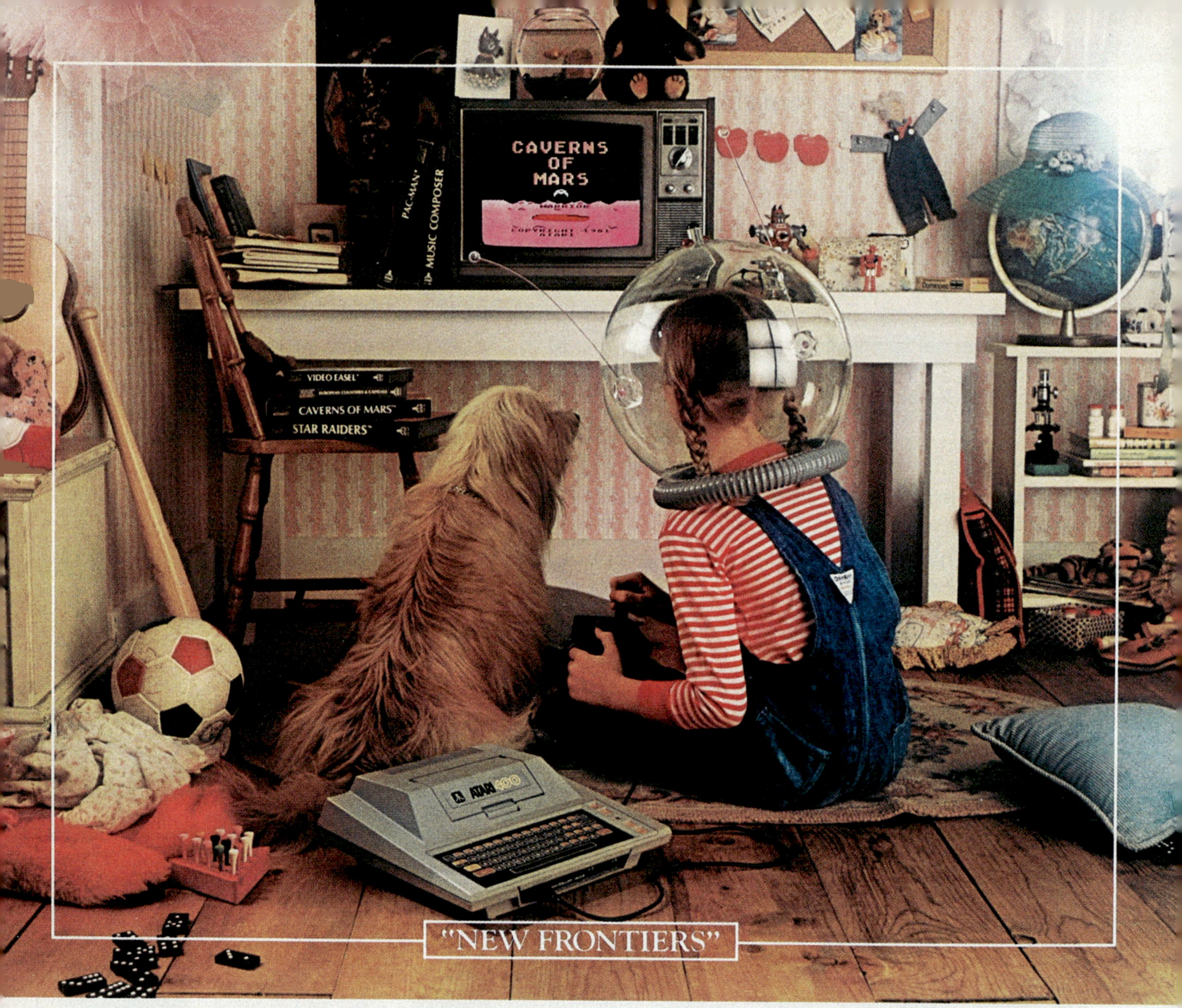

"NEW FRONTIERS"

LEARN TO BRAVE NEW WORLDS.

Your kids already know how to use a computer if they've ever sped through hyperspace with Star Raiders™ or challenged magnetic force fields with the new Caverns of Mars.™

And when you use an ATARI® Home Computer you'll also discover how easily new worlds can open up for you.

ATARI has programs that help solve problems of everyday life, like Mortgage and Loan Analysis.*

Or educational programs like My First Alphabet,™ which is an easy-to-use and beautifully graphic way to teach letters and numbers to children.

In fact, the ATARI Home Computer is your whole family's vehicle to a more imaginative, exciting and manageable world. And the best part is that getting there can be so much fun.

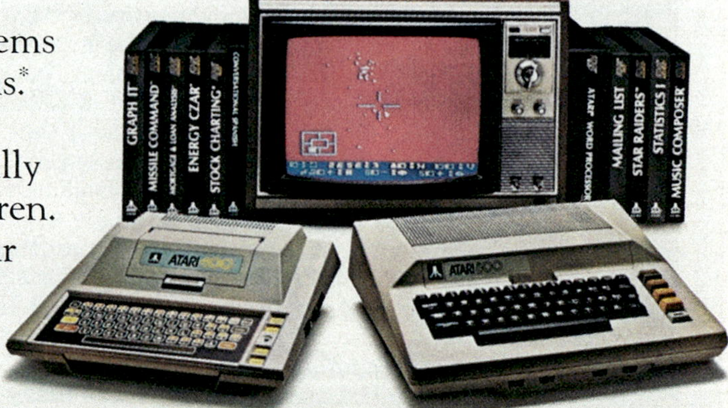

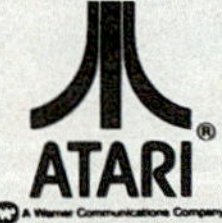

For more information, write: Atari, Inc., Dept. G3P , P.O. Box 16525, Denver, CO 80216. *A Control Data CYBERWARE™ product manufactured under license from Control Data Corporation © 1980. Estimated availability of Caverns of Mars and My First Alphabet, mid-1982.

ATARI® HOME COMPUTERS

We've brought the computer age home.™

FREE TIME FOR SALE

The Hobbyist in Advertising

Olivia Baeriswyl

A young girl sits on the floor, surrounded by the instruments, sports equipment, games, and books that fill her room. Wearing an alien-like space helmet and with the family's shaggy dog for company, she immerses herself in the video game *Caverns of Mars*.

It is a scene that could have played out in many households in the early 1980s. In actual fact, it has been taken from an advertisement by Atari (p. 42), the biggest developer and producer of video games at the time, printed in the June 1982 issue of *Discover* magazine. The strategically placed Atari products—the computer, the video games, the console—and the accompanying text soon make it clear that it is a staged scene within the context of an advert. But the 'snapshot' feel, the chaotic surroundings and the act of playing lend the scene a vibrant realism, one that we participate in for a moment while flicking through the pages.

Since the end of the 1960s, advertising photography has exhibited this increasingly activity-based character, in which the experience—either in bright colors or black and white—is of primary importance; often with an accompanying text that expands upon the fragmentary narrative. In this way, recreational activities are not just alluded to by the depiction of a product, rather products are conversely incorporated as objects in the storylines of these stage-managed worlds. The solitude of the camping trip (p. 78), the Harley-Davidson tour into the desert twilight (p. 100)—such advertisements connect the products with certain moods and create parallel worlds that are supposed to offer a break from the stress of everyday work life: for example the motorbike as a "freedom machine" and escape vehicle for every *Playboy* reader browsing the magazine in 1974. The concept of freedom portrayed is multi-faceted: moments of individualism, retreat, and tranquility are shown in equal measures as those of activities and entertainment together with family or friends. Frequently, the photographs show formal similarities to amateur photography in their use of stylistic techniques like blurredness or the snapshot aesthetic, thus seeming like authentic records from the world of leisure culture. But it is not only the images themselves that take their aesthetic cues from movement. Mobility as a sales argument is a common motif in many advertisements of the time—Sony makes explicitly use of it with its Walkman, a companion in almost all leisure activities (p. 4); or its TV sets (p. 2), which turn into portable outdoor entertainment systems. New, increasingly mobile media products carry the dynamic afforded to them by the text and imagery of advertising, and at the same time influence the spread of the product to a wider public.

Everyday life, work, and leisure are regularly juxtaposed with each other as themes in advertising, without necessarily excluding one other. Atari, for instance, advertises the entertainment offered by its video game consoles at the same time as telling us how its home computer can provide assistance in coping with the "problems of everyday life." Apple takes a similar approach in its 1977 advertisement for the Apple II home computer (p. 53), which can be used as an education tool, an administrative aid, and an entertainment device for the whole family. In its 1967 advertisement for their portable video recorder, Sony made an even more specific appeal to a specialist audience of archaeologists, company owners, and teaching personnel, who they believed could benefit from the device (p. 24). But here too, as with Atari and Apple, there is a focus on the product's easy-to-use nature—thus also appealing to the amateur.

Technological equipment for everyone? These advertisements attempt to address as wide an audience as possible. In terms of target groups, laypeople and experts are treated alike when functionality and ease of accessibility are highlighted, yet the Apple and Harley-Davidson products are marketed with complicated technical jargon. The magazines in which these advertisements appear also feature playful amateurishness next to professional expertise. For example, *Scientific American*, in which Sony advertises its video recorder, addresses a scientifically interested readership, but also incorporates laypeople into the discourse with its column "The Amateur Scientist," which encourages people to carry out experiments in their own homes. *Byte* magazine, too, in which the Apple advertisement appears, uses a highly technical language throughout—both in its advertisements and its editorial contributions. But those who understand this language, however, are offered space for experimentation, for DIY, and are provided with the necessary guidelines and instruments to undertake it.

Precisely these instruments are needed to perform many hobbies, like the fishing rod, the console, or the motorbike. Embedded between advertisements for spirits and aspirin—additional means for coping with the problems of everyday life—these advertised products illustrate the permanent human condition of imprisonment described by Theodor W. Adorno. Rather than being liberated by our apparently free time and the recreational industry, they only serve to emphasize it. Marketing and advertising, however, not only condition consumers that they should have a hobby, they also influence which one it should be and what it should look like. The stage-managed advertisements create and reinforce the image of each respective hobby and the accompanying framework in which it should take place.The protagonists in the Apple advertisement demonstrates which household is able to afford the computer, who operates it, and who watches them doing this; the Sony TV advertisement shows how an archetypal father-son trip should look, and the skater advertisement feeds in to the stereotype of the male skater (p. 103). Role allocation in terms of gender, ethnicity, and social class within the world of leisure is consolidated in advertising photography. The orchestrated scenes influence how we picture 'the hobby,' and act as an identification interface which controls how we see ourselves within it. Their placement in specialist magazines, with their specific readerships, in turn contributes to the formation of hobbyist groups. These examples from the world of advertising clearly illustrate that photography as a medium—one capable of both verifying old realities and generating new ones—plays a significant role in the shaping and performing of hobbies.

Role allocation in terms of gender, ethnicity, and social class within the world of leisure is consolidated in advertising photography. The orchestrated scenes influence how we picture 'the hobby,' and act as an identification interface which controls how we see ourselves within it.

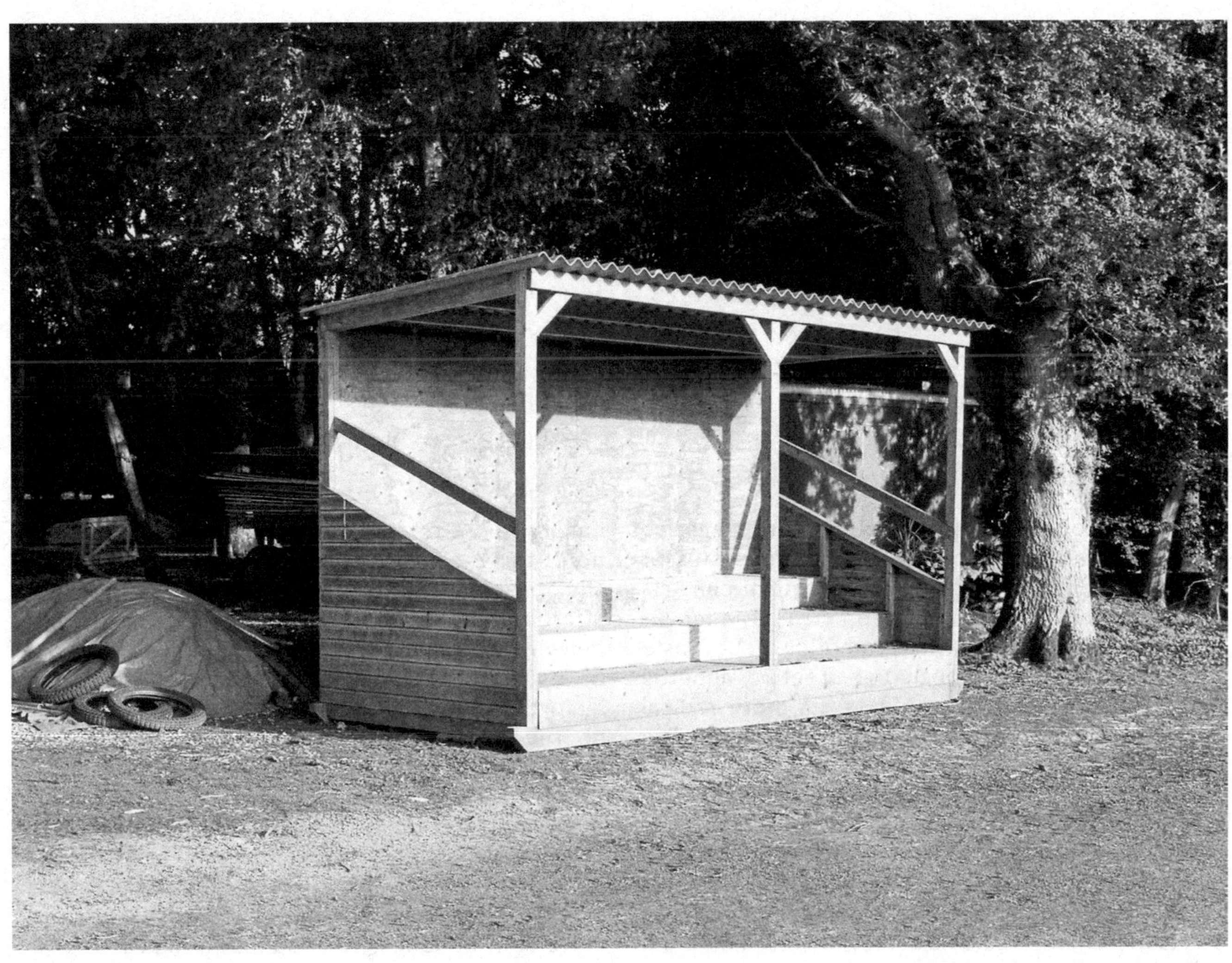

David De Beyter, *Tribune*, 2015

MAKING IT

Pick up a Spot Welder and Join the Revolution

Evgeny Morozov

In January of 1903, the small Boston magazine *Handicraft* ran an essay by the Harvard professor Denman W. Ross, who argued that the American Arts and Crafts movement was in deep crisis. The movement was concerned with promoting good taste and self-fulfillment through the creation and the appreciation of beautiful objects; its more radical wing also sought to advance worker autonomy. The problem was that no one in America seemed to need its products. The solution, according to Ross, was to provide technical education to the critics and the consumers of art alike. This would stimulate demand for high-quality objects and encourage more workers to take up craftsmanship. The cause of the Arts and Crafts movement would be achieved, he maintained, only "when the philosopher goes to work and the working man becomes a philosopher."

In a long rebuttal, Mary Dennett, who later became an important advocate for women's rights, pointed out that the roots of the problem were economic and moral. Reforming the school curriculum wouldn't do much to change the structural conditions that made craftsmanship impossible. The Arts and Crafts movement was spending far too much time on "rag-rugs, baskets, and ... exhibitions of work chiefly by amateurs," rather than asking the most basic questions about inequality. "The employed craftsman can almost never use in his own home things similar to those he works on every day," she observed, because those things were simply unaffordable. Economics, not aesthetics, explained the movement's failures. "The modern man, who should be a craftsman, but who, in most cases, is compelled by force of circumstances to be a mill operative, has no freedom," she wrote earlier. "He must make what his machine is geared to make."

Dennett's tireless social activism bore fruit in other realms, but she lost this fight to aesthetes like Ross. As the historian Jackson Lears describes it in *No Place of Grace* (1981), the Arts and Crafts movement no longer represented a radical alternative to the alienated labor of the factories. Instead, it provided yet another therapeutic escape from it, turning into a "revivifying hobby for the affluent." Lears concluded, "The craft impulse has become dispersed in millions of do-it-yourself projects and basement workshops, where men and women have sought the wholeness, the autonomy, and the joy they cannot find on the job or in domestic drudgery."

Although the Arts and Crafts movement was dead by the First World War, the sentiment behind it lingered. It resurfaced in the counterculture of the nineteen-sixties, with its celebration of simplicity,

From *The Updated Last Whole Earth Catalog. Access to Tools*, 1974

[M]ushroom Hunter's Field Guide
[Sa]vory Wild Mushroom

[Fi]nding a strange, slimy, luminous colored growth on dark [ro]tting wood is surprise and pleasure; to extend that exper[ien]ce into identifying it and possibly *EATING* it is even [be]tter. For the beginner one batch of mushrooms can [oc]cupy a whole day, from finding them, through waiting [fo]r a good spore deposit and making a decision, to cook[in]g them. An efficient guidebook is essential to avoid [fru]strations.

The McKenny book is compact, but not especially well organized for use. It contains clear and concise descriptions of 83 varieties of fungi, some of them peculiar to the Puget Sound region, the rest common throughout the U.S., and 33 black-and-white and 48 color photographs. There is also an article on mushroom poisons and the many fine recipes make one want to rush to the woods and immediately gather baskets of Chanterelles, Morels and Ceps. Not so easy!

Smith's book, which I prefer, is more technical in language and scope, although, as a field guide, it avoids identification methods involving microscopes and chemicals. It is much more complete, covering 188 varieties with a black-and-white photo of each plus 84 color photos, and it is organized in keys which are super to use if you like being methodical. It is not necessarily true, however, that it is quicker to follow the system in thumbing through either book, as in wandering in the woods, luck and perseverance further.

[Suggested and reviewed by Sandra Tcherepnin]

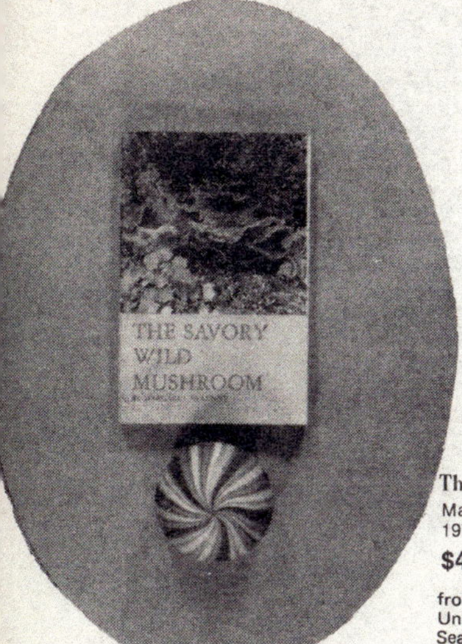

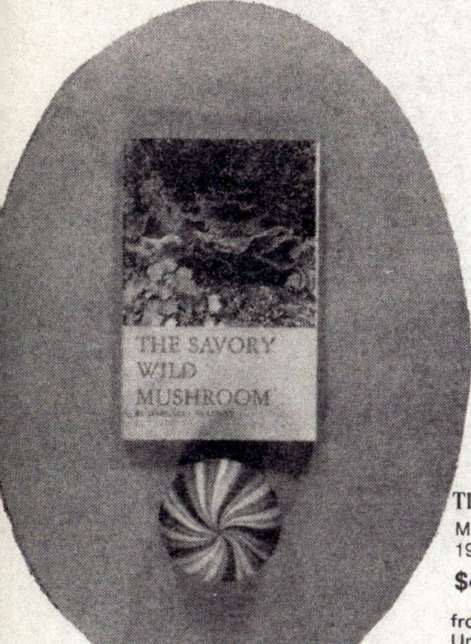

The Mushroom Hunter's Field Guide
Alexander H. Smith
1958; 1967; 264 pp.

$9.95 postpaid

from:
University of Michigan Press
615 East University
Ann Arbor, Michigan 48106
or
WHOLE EARTH CATALOG

The Savory Wild Mushroom
Margaret McKenny
1971 rev. ed. 296 pp.

$4.95 postpaid

from:
University of Washington Press
Seattle, Washington 98195
or
WHOLE EARTH CATALOG

On a tramp through the fields and forests, carry with you a small jar of butter, creamed with salt and pepper. On finding any edible mushroom (except morels or elfinsaddles), collect a few dry sticks and fire them. Split a green stick (alder or willow) at one end. Put the mushroom in the cleft, hold it over the fire until tender, season with the butter. Eat from the stick.

from "The Savory Wild Mushroom"

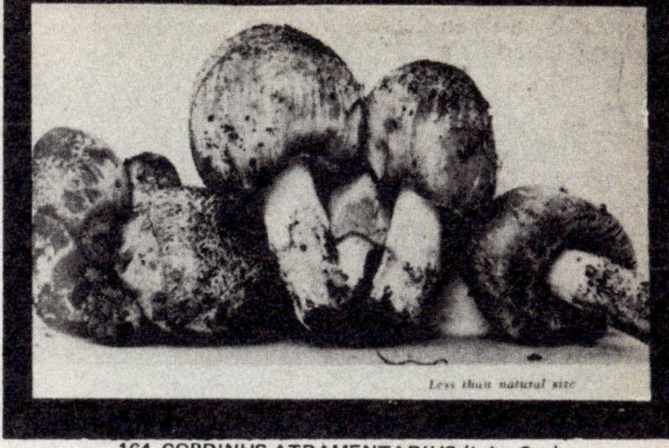

164. COPRINUS ATRAMENTARIUS (Inky Cap)

Edibility. Edible, but some people experience a peculiar type of intoxication from eating this species and afterward drinking an alcoholic beverage. I have now discovered three people in Michigan with this type of sensitivity.

from "The Mushroom Hunter's Field Guide"

A Key to the American Psilocybin Mushroom

magic mushroom information, not found in normal mushroom guides.

—jd

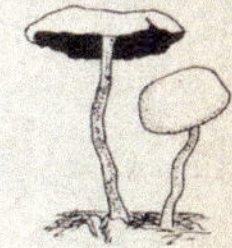

Psilocybe quebecensis

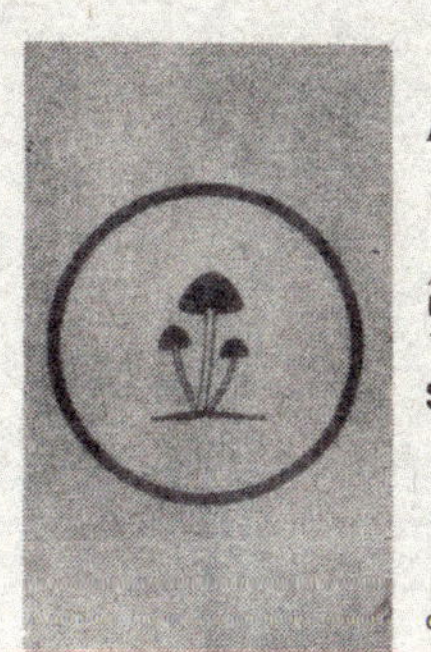

A Key to the Psilocybin Mushroom
Leonard Enos
1972; 80 pp., color plates

$5.00 postpaid

from:
The Youniverse Project
8135 Lincoln Street
Lemon Grove, California 92045

or WHOLE EARTH CATALOG

All but one of the species have revealed an interesting and striking chemical characteristic that is very constant in fresh specimens. When the Fruit are scratched, bruised by handling, or injured in any way they stain blue, or, if the surface color is yellowish, green or greenish blue. This harmless phenomenon is apparently caused by the oxidation of an enzyme in conjunction with the psilocybin and is a main point of identification. Certain chemical reagents are known to accelerate this bluing. The best, of these indicators, p-methylaminophenol sulphate or metol, gives a constant and strongly positive reaction on the flesh of the stem, becoming very deep violet within 1-30 minutes. This chemical, which is in crystal form, is inexpensive and can be prepared from any chemical house or photographic shop that handles darkroom supplies. Metol will dissolve in about 20 times its weight of distilled water, and the solution must be used immediately since it is unstable. A canteen of distilled water and a small plastic bottle are all the tools needed to make up the solution in the field. Be sure to shake the solution vigorously to shorten the dissolving time.

[E]dible and Poisonous Mushrooms of Canada

[T]he world is full of them. They grow in lawns and woodlots, by [ro]ads and rivers, in parks and pastures, but most abundantly in the [mo]ney woods in the fall. Most people do not see them. They are [th]ere, but invisible; outside the range of conscious awareness. Once [yo]u become aware of them, they seem to spring up in droves.

[F]or the beginning pot-hunter, The Savory Wild Mushroom [(]Margaret McKenny, U. of Wash. Press) or the Mushroom Hunter's [H]andbook (Alexander Smith, U. of Mich. Press) are excellent non-[te]chnical guides. Pretty soon you can spot an Amanita, Agaricus, [R]ussula or Corprinus or such off-beat types as Chantrelles and [B]oletes. But there comes a day when, after an afternoon's ramble [th]ru a park or forest you come home with about thirty different [sp]ecies, most of which are not in the book. Now what?

[T]here are a number of older and more technical manuals which can [u]sually be found in libraries. The Mushroom Handbook by Louis [K]reiger has been reprinted by Dover in paperback and so is [r]eadily available, but is rather difficult to use.

[O]n a recent trip to Canada I found what I think is the best new book [o]n the subject, Edible and Poisonous Mushrooms of Canada. It is [a]uthoritative, but still readable, though you might have to keep one [f]inger in the glossary at first. There are new and simplified keys for [t]racking down over 400 different species, and best of all, most of [t]hem are illustrated with color photos taken in the field. With this [b]ook, and a lot of patience, you should become a local expert.

[Reviewed by Walt Downing.
Suggested by Barbara Kirshenblatt-Gimblett]

[E]dible and Poisonous Mushrooms of Canada
[J.] Walton Groves
[1]962; 298 pp.

[$]11.70 postpaid

[fr]om: Queen's Printer
Information Canada
Publishing Division
Ottawa, Ontario
Canada

or WHOLE EARTH CATALOG

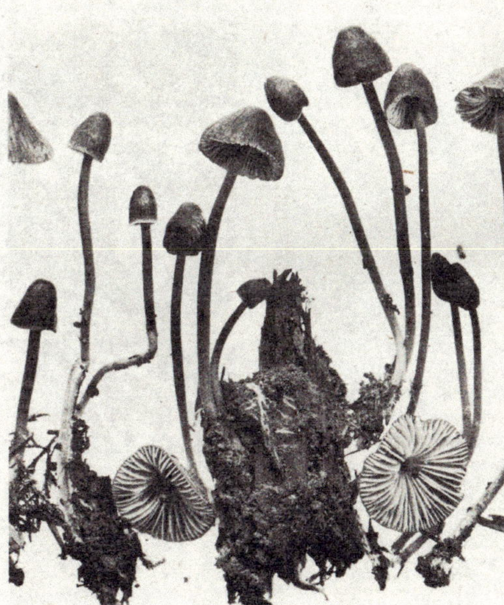

Figure 266. *Mycena alcalina.*

Mycological Societies

Your coverage of mushroom identification books is fine, but I have graduated from Smith and McKenny (both of which I have) to *A Guide to Mushrooms and Toadstools* by Morten Lange and F. Bayard Hora, Dutton. It is very complete and has color painting instead of photographs, which I like, and every species is shown in color. I belong to the San Francisco Mycological Society and I recommend that anybody who is interested in mushroom identification join the nearest mycological group for help with locating and identifying. Write to the North American Mycological Association, 4245 Redinger Road, Portsmouth, Ohio 45662, for the address of the nearest group.

Sent by

Mary Schooner
San Francisco, CA

[F]ruits of Hawaii

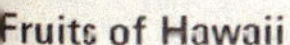

[A]fter due research I can report that it's true, you can live [o]ff the land in Hawaii for very little. Fruit grows everywhere, [a]nd this book is an excellent guide to which of it is edible [a]nd where to find it and how to cook it. If you liked the [e]arly 60's, you'll love Hawaii.

—SB

[F]ruits of Hawaii
[C]arey D. Miller, Katherine Bazore, Mary Bartow
[1]965; 229 pp.

$6.00 postpaid

[f]rom:
University of Hawaii Press
[5]35 Ward Ave.
Honolulu, Hawaii 96814

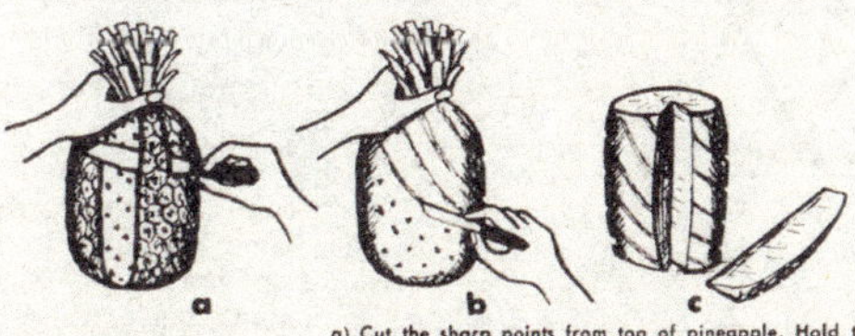

a) Cut the sharp points from top of pineapple. Hold top firmly in left hand and, with a large, heavy knife, start peeling strips from top downward until entire rind is removed. (The top may be removed before cutting off rind.)

b) Remove the eyes by cutting diagonal grooves around pineapple.

c) Cut off top and slice fruit lengthwise into wedges. Each serving then has some of the sweetest and most desirable portion of the fruit. The core may be removed from each slice.

d) If larger pieces are desired, cut entirely through the peeled fruit lengthwise and serve the slice whole.

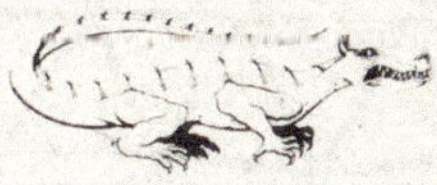

PRAYER

The Way is uncharted. The map cannot be spoken. Names are in words, but nature lives only in nature. The source of creation is nameless, but the matrix of all is named. The secret eludes eyes clouded by longing. Prejudiced eyes must stop cold at the surface. The secret is self-contained.

May we be mindful of these truths. May we become pure enough to pass through the gate to the root of the universe.

PACIFIC DOME
continued

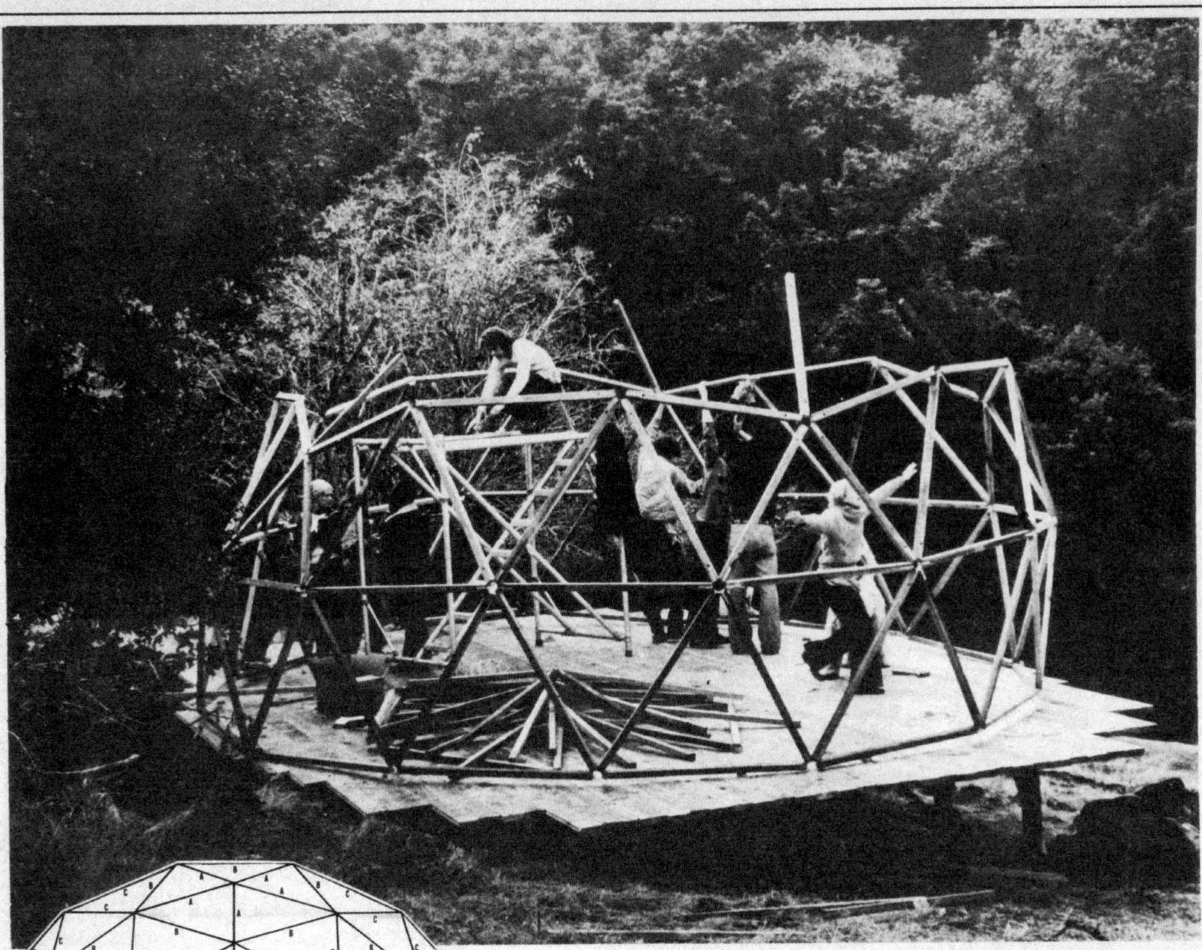

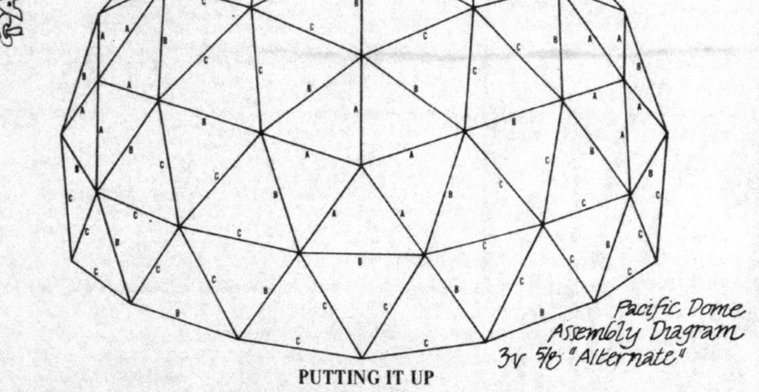

Pacific Dome Assembly Diagram 3v 5/8 "Alternate"

PUTTING IT UP

Invite friends, try to pick a nice day, have some homemade bread for when it's completed. You'll want to spend some time sitting inside after it's up.

A scaffold makes things much easier. you can rent one, with wheels.

Set model in center. Start at bottom course. It is best to have one person who just designates what goes where. Work around, and up. *Temporarily tie it down if there's a wind*. It will start holding itself up during the second course.

Strap as you go. One man on strapper, another working the crimper.

Next, attach to floor. Take an average from center of floor. Place each strut an equal distance from center. We strapped ours down like this:

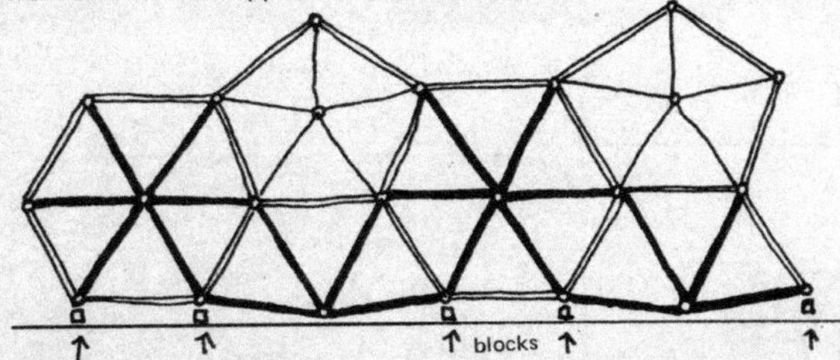

Drill holes in floor and strap each hub to floor. Strap it securely, so dome won't blow off. If you don't strap, work out a means of bolting down.

If you use plastic hubs there should be blocks inside base course hubs so weight of dome is not resting on pieces of plastic.

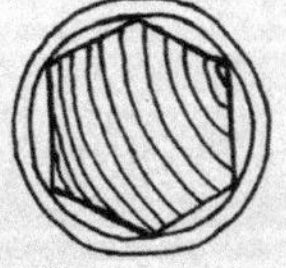

Cut floor off to fit dome.

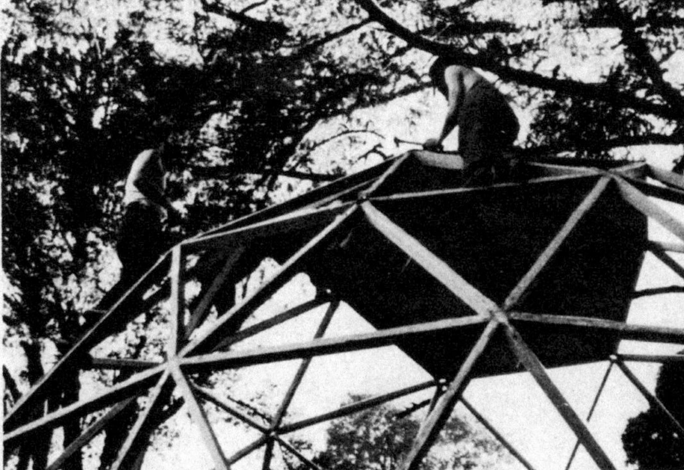

SKINNING DOME

You should wait a while, sleeping under framework, seeing where the morning sun rises and planning carefully where to admit light. This will vary according to season. When this is decided you can start with the plywood skinning. Make sure struts are equally spaced around hubs. You can do this as you go, lining up struts with marks on hubs. Be careful, as errors will accumulate.

If you caulk, staple strips of polyethylene to struts with rustproof staples. Best to start from top, as it leaves room underneath to stand on struts.

Nail triangles on with hot dip galvanized nails. Electro-galvanized nails will rust. One nail about every 4" or 6". Or rent a pneumatic staple gun that shoots rustproof staples and *be careful* of people below.

Have a helper handing triangles up to you.

The struts must be accurately positioned around hubs.

Nailing should be done very carefully. Don't leave any hammer marks on surface, as they will complicate the sealing of joints. Go slowly here. Everyone wants to nail on triangles. Two or three nailers is about right, but check each one out to make sure he is hammering well, and placing triangles carefully. We had a careless nailer on one dome and later had to custom fit some triangles.
At bottom course, where large triangles overlap, first nail on one, then a few nails to hold the overlapping one, and saw down the middle.

Calculating for interior membrane: see note on this in Big Sur dome. You will use a different radius times the chord factor for calculating interior paneling.

(See table of contents for next steps: **sealing joints; doors & windows; interiors.**)

its back-to-the-land sloganeering, and, especially, its endorsement of savvy consumerism as a form of political activism. The publisher and sage Stewart Brand was the chief proponent of such views. "The consumer has more power for good or ill than the voter," he announced in the pages of his *Whole Earth Catalog*, which débuted in 1968 and was geared to communalists and others who sought to drop out of the mainstream.

Inspired by the technophilia of his intellectual hero Buckminster Fuller, Brand played a key role in celebrating the personal computer as the ultimate tool of emancipation. He convinced the consumers he celebrated that they were actually far more radical than the student rebels who were being beaten up by the police. At a recent conference, Brand drew a contrast between "what happened around Berkeley in the sixties and what happened around Stanford in the sixties," a contrast that captures the fate of activism in America more broadly:

> "Around Berkeley, it was Free Speech Movement, 'power to the people.' Around Stanford, it was 'Whole Earth Catalog,' Steve Wozniak, Steve Jobs, people like that, and they were just power to people. They just wanted to power anybody who was interested, not 'the people.' Well, it turns out there is no, probably, 'the people.' So the political blind alley that Berkeley went down was interesting, we were all taking the same drugs, the same length of hair, but the stuff came out of the Stanford area, I think because it took a Buckminster Fuller access-to-tools angle on things."

To convince consumers that they were rebels, Brand first convinced them that they were "hackers," a slang term that was already in use in places like MIT but that Brand went on to popularize and infuse with much wider meaning. In 1972, he published "Spacewar," a long and much read article in *Rolling Stone* about Stanford's Artificial Intelligence Laboratory. He distinguished the hackers from the planners, those rigid and unimaginative technocrats, noting that "when computers become available to everybody, the hackers take over." For Brand, hackers were "a mobile new-found elite." He seemed to have had a transcendental experience in that lab: "Those magnificent men with their flying machines, scouting a leading edge of technology which has an odd softness to it; outlaw country, where rules are not decree or routine so much as the starker demands of what's possible." Computers were the new drugs—without any of the side effects.

In a later edition of the *Whole Earth Catalog*, Brand reminisced about its mid-seventies heyday,

To convince consumers that they were rebels, Brand first convinced them that they were "hackers."

when it recommended two products: the Vermont Castings Defiant woodstove and the Apple personal computer. The odd juxtaposition made sense to Brand. "Both cost a few hundred dollars, both were made by and for revolutionaries who wanted to de-institutionalize society and empower the individual." Yet, while the Defiant woodstove ran into trouble, Apple prospered—because it was in the business of manipulating information, not heat. With information now intruding into every field, Brand held, there was considerably more scope for hacking. And the country was ready for it. His subscribers were more likely to be office workers than factory workers; few were forced to be mill operatives, as in Dennett's day. But the transition to "cognitive capitalism" (as some labor theorists would put it) didn't make the workplace less alienating. Brand's remedy was hacking of a particular kind: "With over half of the American workforce now managing information for a living, any apparent drone drudging away on mainstream information chores might be recruited, via some handy outlaw techniques or tool, into the holy disorder of hackerdom. A hacker takes nothing as given, everything as worth creatively fiddling with, and the variety which proceeds from that enricheth the adaptivity, resilience, and delight of us all."

For all the talk of the "de-institutionalization of society" enabled by the personal computer, Brand was brutally honest about the kinds of emancipation that he had to offer. The way to join the holy disorder of hackerdom was by, say, playing Tetris—and, on weekends, going home and hacking rubber stamps, postcards, and whatever else one had ordered from the *Whole Earth Catalog*.

Is Brand's hacking revolutionary, or counter-revolutionary? The plentiful recent books that preach hacking as a way of life—*Reality Hacking*, *Hacking Your Education*, *Hacking Happiness*—express devotion at least to the rhetoric of revolt. *Hacking Work*, a business book published in 2010, announces that "you were born to hack" and suggests ways in which one could "hack" work to achieve "*morebetterfaster* results." As in most of these books, our hackers aren't smashing the system; they're fiddling with it

From *Domebook 2*, 1971

Hunger Strike

'Liferaft Earth

Sinks--50 Fle

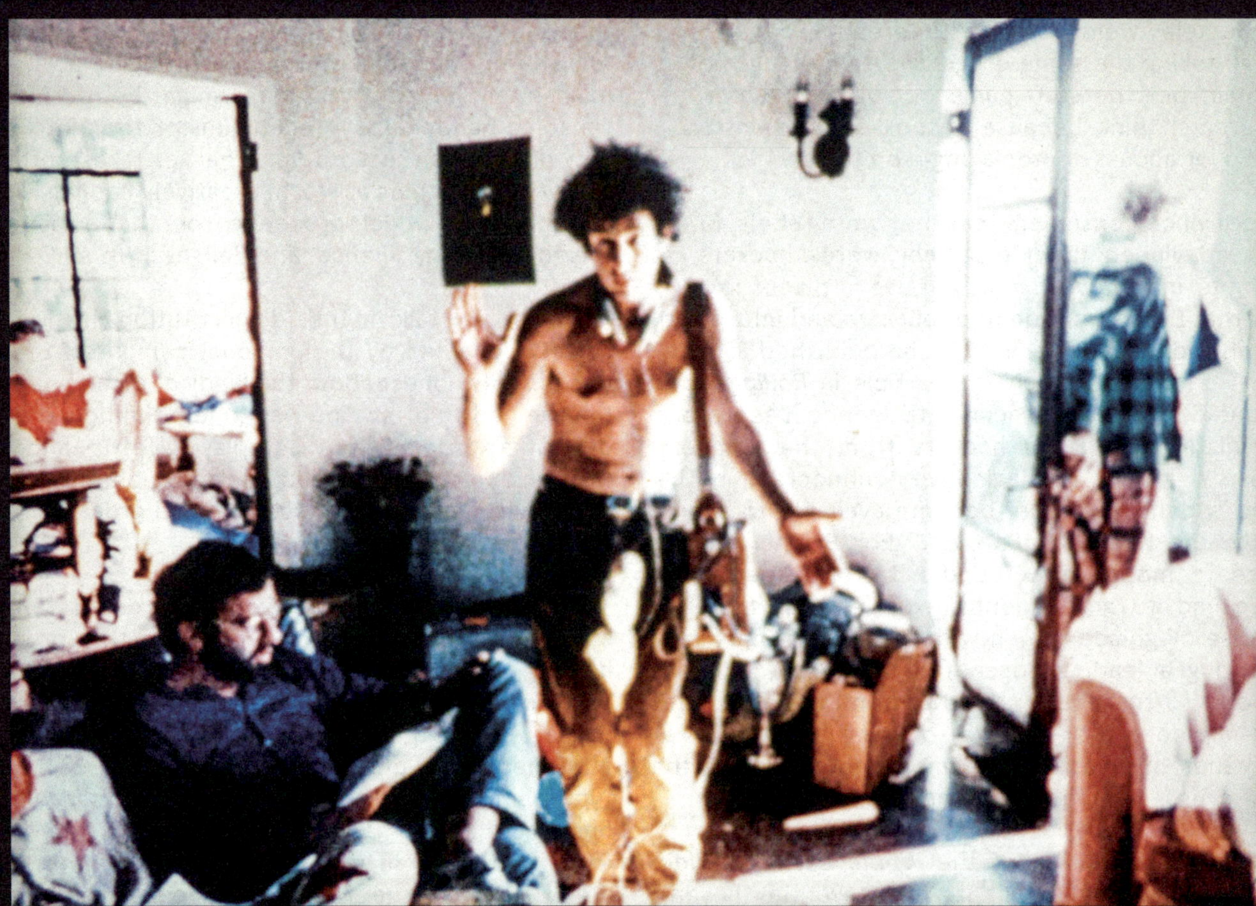

Robert Frank, from *Liferaft Earth*, 1969

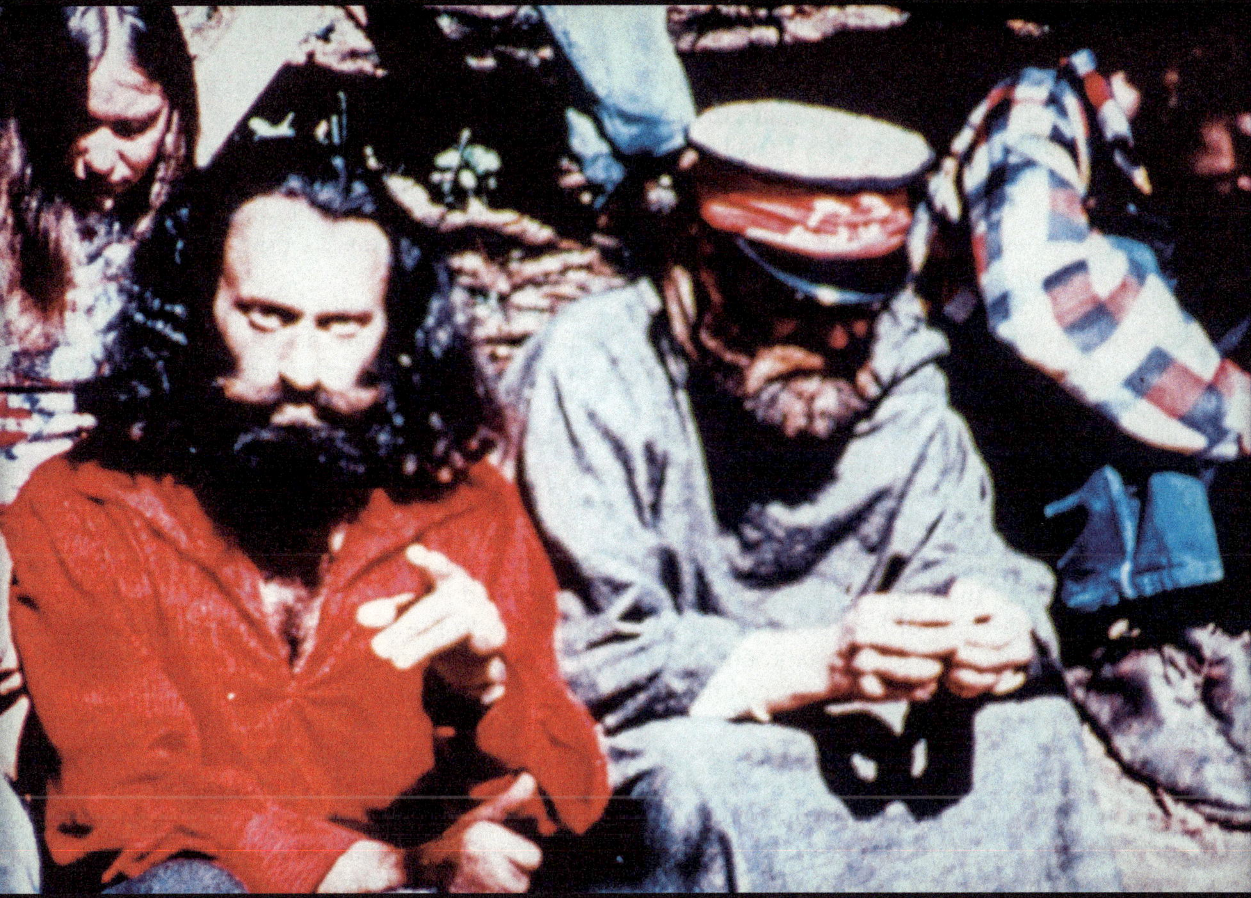

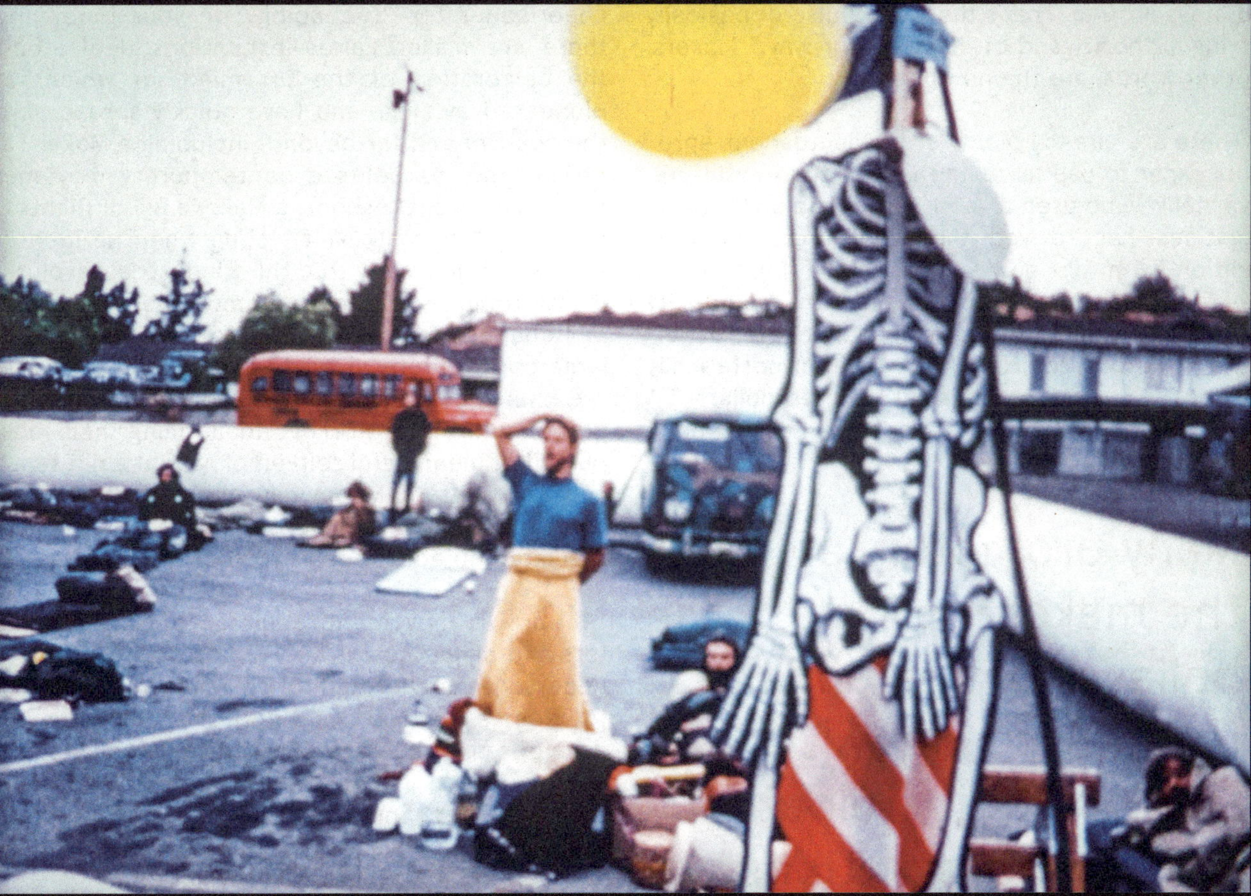

so that they can get more work done. In this vision, it's up to individuals to accommodate themselves to the system rather than to try to reform it. The shrinking of political imagination that accompanies such attempts at doing more with less usually goes unremarked.

That hacking has come to mean two very different aspirations became evident when Barack Obama belittled Edward Snowden as "a twenty-nine-year-old hacker" only a few weeks after the White House endorsed the first National Day of Civic Hacking. In Britain, the Metropolitan Police might be busy finding hackers like Snowden, but in April it helped organize "Hack the Police!"—a so-called "hackathon," where software developers and designers were encouraged to bring their "unique talents to the fight against crime." In contrast to jabbering, feckless politicians, hackers offer hope for the most hopeless endeavors. "I'd like to see the spirit of hackerdom improve peace in the Middle East," the influential technology publisher and investor Tim O'Reilly proclaimed a couple of years ago.

Inevitably, hacking itself had to get hacked. When, in November, Brand was asked about who carries the flag of counterculture today, he pointed to the maker movement. The makers, Brand said, "take whatever we're not supposed to take the back off of, rip the back off and get our fingers in there and mess around. That's the old impulse of basically defying authority and of doing it your way." Makers, in other words, are the new hackers.

There are already plenty of intellectual entrepreneurs eager to capitalize on the new counterculture. Kevin Kelly—who used to work with Brand on his many magazines—has revived the *Whole Earth Catalog* tradition with his new catalogue-like publication, *Cool Tools*. It features product tips for the true reality hacker—from "quick-refreshing underwear for travel" to the "luxurious, squirting WC seat" (thermostatically warmed, and yours for just eight hundred dollars). "A third industrial revolution is stirring—the Maker era," Kelly writes in the introduction to *Cool Tools*. "The skills for this accelerated era lean toward the agile and decentralized. Therefore tools recommended here are aimed at small groups, decentralized communities, the do-it-yourselfer, and the self-educated. ... These possibilities cataloged here will help makers become better makers." In his world, the main thing it takes to be a maker is a credit card.

> Many promoters of the maker movement believe that personal manufacturing will undermine the clout of large corporations.

The maker era might not be upon us yet, but the maker movement has arrived. Just who are these people? Like the Arts and Crafts movement—a mélange of back-to-the-land simplifiers, socialists, anarchists, and tweedy art connoisseurs—the makers are a diverse bunch. They include 3-D-printing enthusiasts who like making their own toys, instruments, and weapons; tinkerers and mechanics who like to customize household objects by outfitting them with sensors and Internet connectivity; and appreciators of craft who prefer to design their own objects and then have them manufactured on demand.

Each of these subgroups has its own history. What turns them into a movement is the intellectual infrastructure that allows makers to reflect on what it means to be a maker. Makers interested in honing their skills can take classes in well-equipped "makerspaces," where they can also design and manufacture their wares. Makers have their own widely read publication—the magazine *Make*—a cheerleader for "technology on your time." Then there are Maker Faires—exhibitions dedicated to the celebration of the DIY mind-set which were pioneered by *Make* and have quickly spread across the country and far beyond, including a Maker Faire Africa. And, as befits a contemporary movement, the makers want respect: a Maker's Bill of Rights has been drafted. Kelly isn't jesting when he identifies the rise of makers with a third industrial revolution: many promoters of the maker movement believe that personal manufacturing will undermine the clout of large corporations. It might even liberate labor in a way that the Arts and Crafts radicals hadn't anticipated, with office workers abandoning their jobs in pursuit of meaningful self-employment amid sensors and 3-D printers. Meanwhile, the prospect of being able to print guns, drug paraphernalia, and other regulated objects appeals to libertarians.

A proper movement requires more than newsletters and magazines; it also needs manifestos. Chris Anderson, the *Wired* editor-in-chief who quit his job to become the CEO of 3D Robotics, a company that develops personal drones, published one such manifesto, *Makers*, in 2012. More recently, Mark Hatch, the CEO of TechShop, a chain of makerspaces across the country, published *The Maker Movement Manifesto*. Both books promise a revolution.

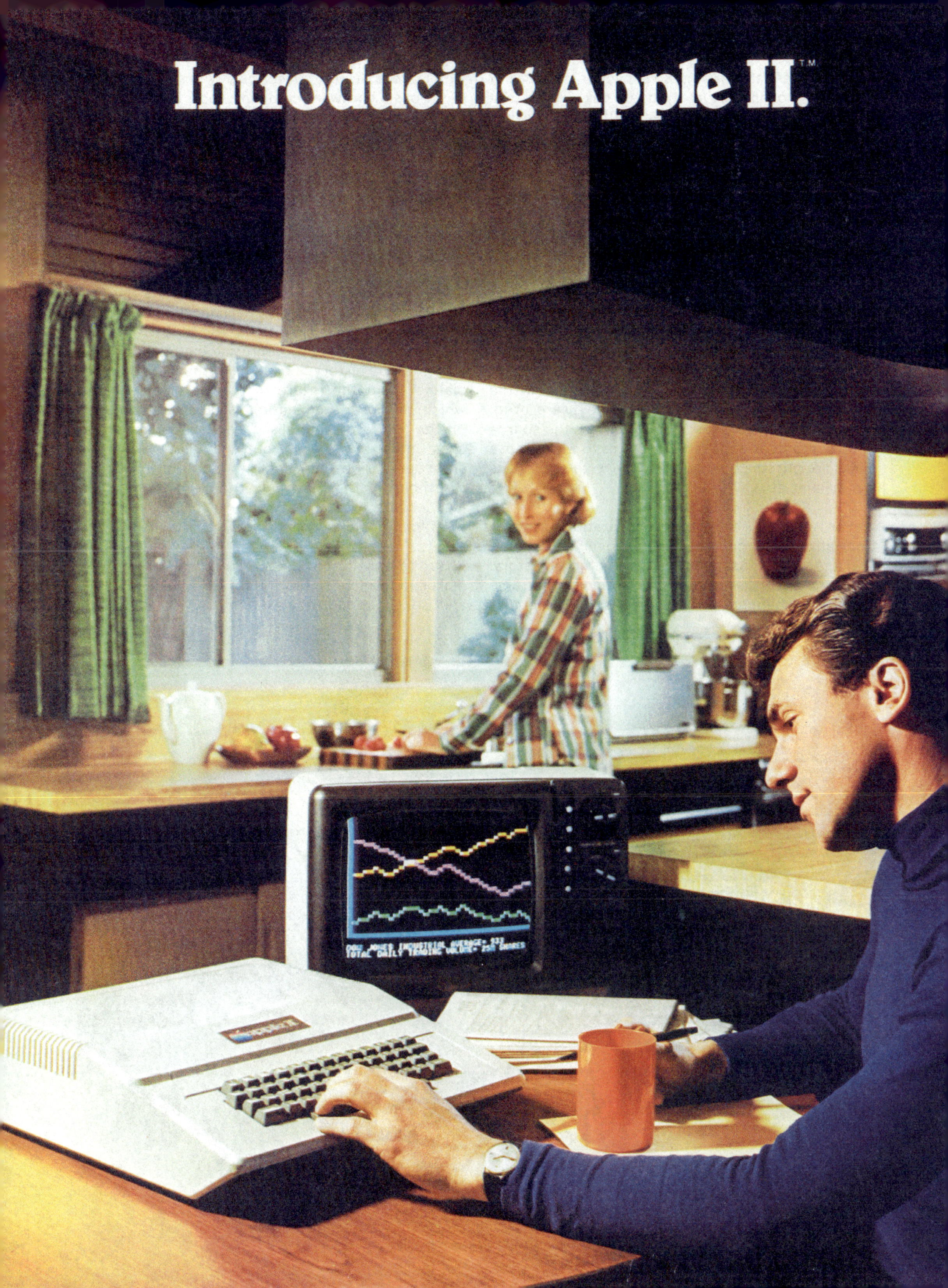
Introducing Apple II.™

Anderson defines "making" so expansively that all of us seem to qualify, at least once a day. "If you love to plant, you're a garden Maker. Knitting and sewing, scrap-booking, beading, and cross-stitching—all Making." There's nothing in this book about myth-making, but that surely qualifies as well. For someone who spent more than a decade at the helm of *Wired*, Anderson sounds surprisingly unhappy with the virtual turn that our lives have taken. He repeatedly blames screens and personal computers for our lack of contact with physical objects. "The digital natives are starting to hunger for life beyond the screen," he writes. "Making something that starts virtual but quickly becomes tactile and usable in the everyday world is satisfying in a way that pure pixels are not." Many aesthetes in the early Arts and Crafts debates complained about machines, rather than about the economic conditions under which they were used. Anderson, likewise, sees "pure pixels" as the source of discontent, as opposed to the uses to which those pixels are put (the boring spreadsheet, the senseless PowerPoint deck).

For Anderson, it's the democratization of invention—anyone can become an app mogul these days—that defines the past two decades of Internet history. Owing to the maker movement, he thinks, the same thing might happen to manufacturing: "'Three guys with laptops' used to describe a Web startup. Now it describes a hardware company, too." Every inventor can become an entrepreneur. Indeed, he anticipates a Web-like future for the maker movement: "ever-accelerating entrepreneurship and innovation with ever-dropping barriers to entry."

The kind of Internet metaphysics that informs Anderson's account sees ingrained traits of technology where others might see a cascade of decisions made by businessmen and policymakers. (Would "the history of the Web" be the same if the National Science Foundation hadn't relinquished control of the Internet to the private sector in 1995?) This is why Anderson starts by confusing the history of the Web with the history of capitalism and ends by speculating about the future of the maker movement, which, on closer examination, is actually speculation on the future of capitalism. What Anderson envisages—more of the same but with greater diversity and competition—may come to pass. But to set the threshold for the third industrial revolution so low just because someone somewhere forgot to regulate AT&T (or Google) seems rather unambitious.

In the absence of a savvy political strategy, the maker movement could have even weaker political and social impact than Anderson foresees. One

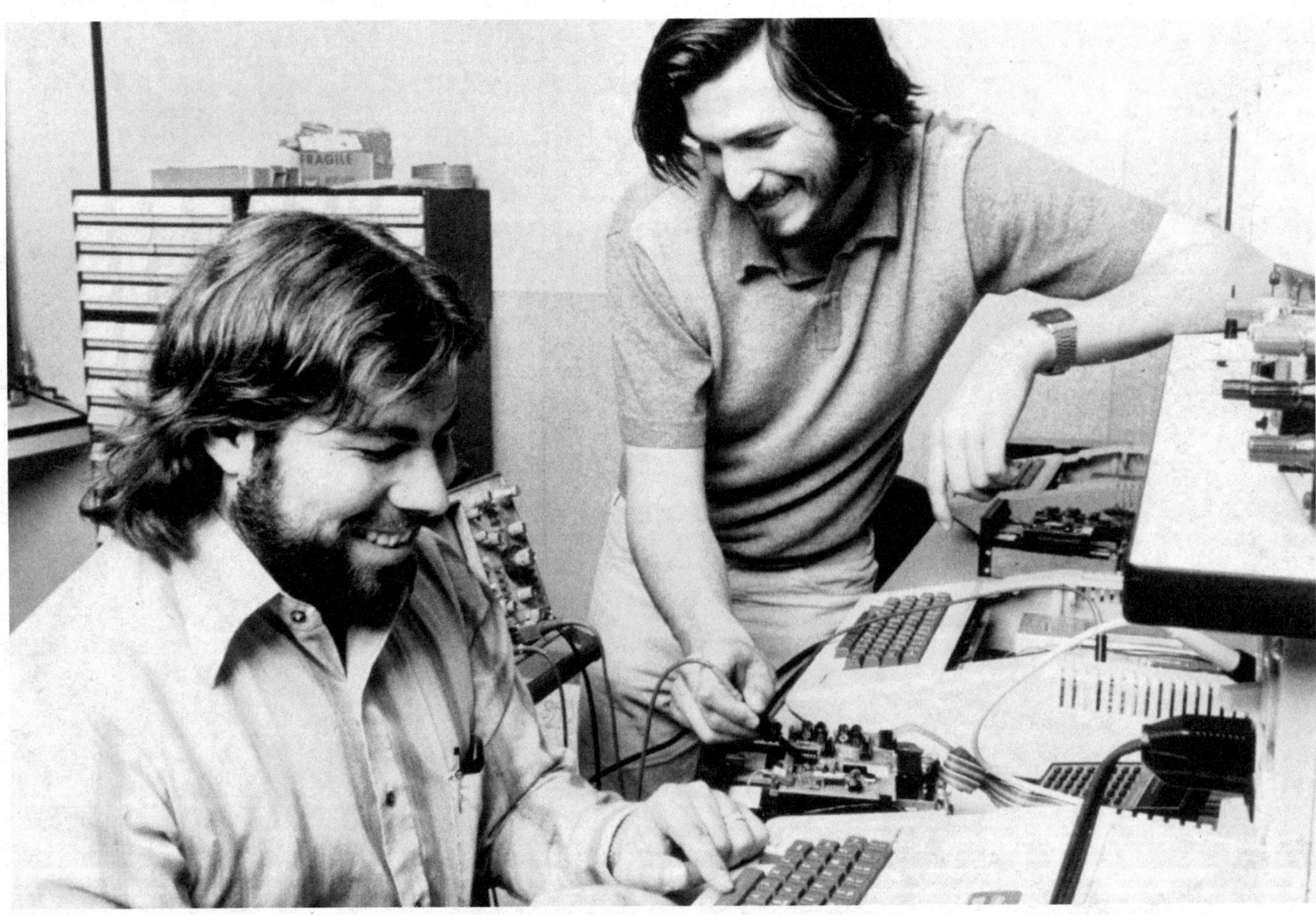

Anonymous, Steve Wozniak and Steve Jobs, 1970s

worrying sign appeared in the fall of 2012, when MakerBot, a pioneer in open-source 3-D printing, embraced a controlled, closed model. Then MakerBot was acquired by Stratasys, a big, established manufacturer of 3-D printers—a company that is the opposite of what MakerBot once aspired to be. 3-D printing is raising challenges with respect to copyright and trademark law, and regulatory backlash is inevitable. Some corporations will target the many intermediaries involved in the process, from the manufacturers of 3-D printers to sites hosting the files that users download in order to print an object. Other companies are developing software that would prevent printers from creating components that could be used to assemble a gun. Such a mechanism might control the printing of other artifacts, like the ones that litigious, patent-holding corporations claim a property interest in.

Then there are the temptations facing the movement. Two years ago, DARPA—the research arm of the Department of Defense—announced a ten-million-dollar grant to promote the maker movement among high-school students. DARPA also gave three and a half million dollars to TechShop to establish new makerspaces that could help the agency with its "innovation agenda." As a senior DARPA official told *Bloomberg BusinessWeek*, "We are pretty in tune with the maker movement. We want to reach out to a much broader section of society, a much broader collection of brains." The Chinese government, too, seems to have embraced the makers with open arms. Authorities in Shanghai have announced plans to launch a hundred makerspaces, while the Communist Youth League has been active in recruiting visitors to Maker Faires—or Maker Carnivals, as they are known in China. One of the co-founders of MakerBot has left New York for Shenzhen. Makers, it appears, are not necessarily troublemakers.

Mark Hatch, for one, shows no concern that proximity to power might compromise his movement's revolutionary potential. "Now, with the tools available at a makerspace, anyone can change the world," he writes in *The Maker Movement Manifesto*. "Every revolution needs an army. ... My objective with this book is to *radicalize* you and get you to become a soldier in this army." How radical is Hatch's project? At the start of the acknowledgments that open the book, he thanks Autodesk, Ford, DARPA, the V.A., Lowe's, and G.E. His talk of becoming an army soldier may not be a metaphor.

TechShop charges a monthly membership fee, which provides access to facilities equipped with everything from oxyacetylene welders to the latest design software. TechShop's support staffers are called Dream Consultants, and the book is peppered

Seeking salvation through tools alone is no more viable as a political strategy than addressing the ills of capitalism by cultivating a public appreciation of arts and crafts.

with yarns about desperate souls—laid off, poor, depressed, sleeping in their cars right next to the makerspace—who have been transformed by the experience of making. (Describing a woman who became a vender on Etsy after visiting TechShop, Hatch writes, "An accidental entrepreneur was born. And what was Tina's background? She was a labor organizer.") Like Anderson, Hatch emphasizes how we are all born makers but are everywhere in ready-made chains. We must abandon the virtual and embrace the physical—preferably at Hatch's TechShop.

Hatch and Anderson alike invoke Marx and argue that the success of the maker movement shows that the means of production can be made affordable to workers even under capitalism. Now that money can be raised on sites such as Kickstarter, even large-scale investors have become unnecessary. But both overlook one key development: in a world where everyone is an entrepreneur, it's hard work getting others excited about funding your project. Money goes to those who know how to attract attention.

Simply put, if you need to raise money on Kickstarter, it helps to have fifty thousand Twitter followers, not fifty. It helps enormously if Google puts your product on the first page of search results, and making sure it stays there might require an investment in search-engine optimization. Some would view this new kind of immaterial labor as 'virtual craftsmanship'; others as vulgar hustling. The good news is that now you don't have to worry about getting fired; the bad news is that you have to worry about getting downgraded by Google.

Hatch assumes that online platforms are ruled by equality of opportunity. But they aren't. Inequality here is not just a matter of who owns and runs the means of physical production but also of who owns and runs the means of intellectual production—the

February 3, 1976

An Open Letter to Hobbyists

To me, the most critical thing in the hobby market right now is the lack of good software courses, books and software itself. Without good software and an owner who understands programming, a hobby computer is wasted. Will quality software be written for the hobby market?

Almost a year ago, Paul Allen and myself, expecting the hobby market to expand, hired Monte Davidoff and developed Altair BASIC. Though the initial work took only two months, the three of us have spent most of the last year documenting, improving and adding features to BASIC. Now we have 4K, 8K, EXTENDED, ROM and DISK BASIC. The value of the computer time we have used exceeds $40,000.

The feedback we have gotten from the hundreds of people who say they are using BASIC has all been positive. Two surprising things are apparent, however. 1) Most of these "users" never bought BASIC (less than 10% of all Altair owners have bought BASIC), and 2) The amount of royalties we have received from sales to hobbyists makes the time spent of Altair BASIC worth less than $2 an hour.

Why is this? As the majority of hobbyists must be aware, most of you steal your software. Hardware must be paid for, but software is something to share. Who cares if the people who worked on it get paid?

Is this fair? One thing you don't do by stealing software is get back at MITS for some problem you may have had. MITS doesn't make money selling software. The royalty paid to us, the manual, the tape and the overhead make it a break-even operation. One thing you do do is prevent good software from being written. Who can afford to do professional work for nothing? What hobbyist can put 3-man years into programming, finding all bugs, documenting his product and distribute for free? The fact is, no one besides us has invested a lot of money in hobby software. We have written 6800 BASIC, and are writing 8080 APL and 6800 APL, but there is very little incentive to make this software available to hobbyists. Most directly, the thing you do is theft.

What about the guys who re-sell Altair BASIC, aren't they making money on hobby software? Yes, but those who have been reported to us may lose in the end. They are the ones who give hobbyists a bad name, and should be kicked out of any club meeting they show up at.

I would appreciate letters from any one who wants to pay up, or has a suggestion or comment. Just write me at 1180 Alvarado SE, #114, Albuquerque, New Mexico, 87108. Nothing would please me more than being able to hire ten programmers and deluge the hobby market with good software.

Bill Gates

Bill Gates
General Partner, Micro-Soft

so-called "attention economy" (or what the German writer Hans Magnus Enzensberger, in the early sixties, called the "consciousness industry"). All of this suggests that there's more politicking—and politics—to be done here than enthusiasts like Anderson or Hatch are willing to acknowledge.

A comparison to the world of original hackers—the folks that Brand profiled in his *Rolling Stone* article, not the 'reality hackers' of later decades—may be illuminating. It's a comparison that the makers are fond of. The subtitle of Hatch's book, tellingly, is *Rules for Innovation in the New World of Crafters, Hackers, and Tinkerers*. Anderson pays homage to the Homebrew Computer Club—a small hobbyist group that, starting in 1975, brought together computer enthusiasts from the Bay Area, including Steve Wozniak and Steve Jobs. For Anderson, such innovation is the prelude to a great business: when hobbyists cluster together to work on obscure technologies, someone eventually gets rich. But it's misleading to view the Homebrew Computer Club solely through the prism of innovation and entrepreneurship. It also had, at least at first, a political vision.

One of the leaders of the Homebrew Computer Club was Lee Felsenstein. A veteran of the Free Speech Movement in Berkeley, he wanted to build communication infrastructure that would allow citizens to swap information in a decentralized manner, bypassing the mistrusted traditional media. In the early nineteen-seventies, he helped launch Community Memory—a handful of computer terminals installed in public spaces in Berkeley and San Francisco which allowed local residents to communicate anonymously. It was the first true 'social media.'

Felsenstein got his inspiration from reading Ivan Illich's *Tools for Conviviality*, which called for devices and machines that would be easy to understand, learn, and repair, thus making experts and institutions unnecessary. "Convivial tools rule out certain levels of power, compulsion, and programming, which are precisely those features that now tend to make all governments look more or less alike," Illich wrote. He had little faith in traditional politics. Whereas Stewart Brand wanted citizens to replace politics with savvy shopping, Illich wanted to "retool" society so that traditional politics, with its penchant for endless talk, becomes unnecessary.

Felsenstein took Illich's advice to heart, not least because it resembled his own experience with ham radios, which were easy to understand and fiddle with. If the computer were to assist ordinary folks in their political struggles, the computer needed a ham-radio-like community of hobbyists. Such a club would help counter the power of IBM, then the dominant manufacturer of large and expensive computers, and make computers smaller, cheaper, and more useful in political struggles.

The hackers won their fight against IBM—only to lose it to Facebook and Google.

Then Steve Jobs showed up. Felsenstein's political project, of building computers that would undermine institutions and allow citizens to share information and organize, was recast as an aesthetic project of self-reliance and personal empowerment. For Jobs, who saw computers as "a bicycle for our minds," it was of only secondary importance whether one could peek inside or program them.

Jobs had his share of sins, but the naïveté of Illich and his followers shouldn't be underestimated. Seeking salvation through tools alone is no more viable as a political strategy than addressing the ills of capitalism by cultivating a public appreciation of arts and crafts. Society is always in flux, and the designer can't predict how various political, social, and economic systems will come to blunt, augment, or redirect the power of the tool that is being designed. Instead of deinstitutionalizing society, the radicals would have done better to advocate reinstitutionalizing it: pushing for political and legal reforms to secure the transparency and decentralization of power they associated with their favorite technology.

One thinker who saw through the naïveté of Illich, the Homebrewers, and the Whole Earthers was the libertarian socialist Murray Bookchin. Back in the late sixties, he published a fiery essay called "Towards a Liberatory Technology," arguing that technology is not an enemy of craftsmanship and personal freedom. Unlike Brand, though, Bookchin never thought that such liberation could occur just by getting more technology into everyone's hands; the nature of the political community mattered. In his book *The Ecology of Freedom* (1982), he couldn't hide his frustration with the 'access-to-tools' mentality. Bookchin's critique of the counterculture's turn to tools parallels Dennett's critique of the aesthetes' turn to education eighty years earlier. It didn't make sense to speak of "convivial tools," he argued, without taking a close look at the political and social structures in which they were embedded.

From *Homebrew Computer Club Newsletter*, 2, 2, 1976

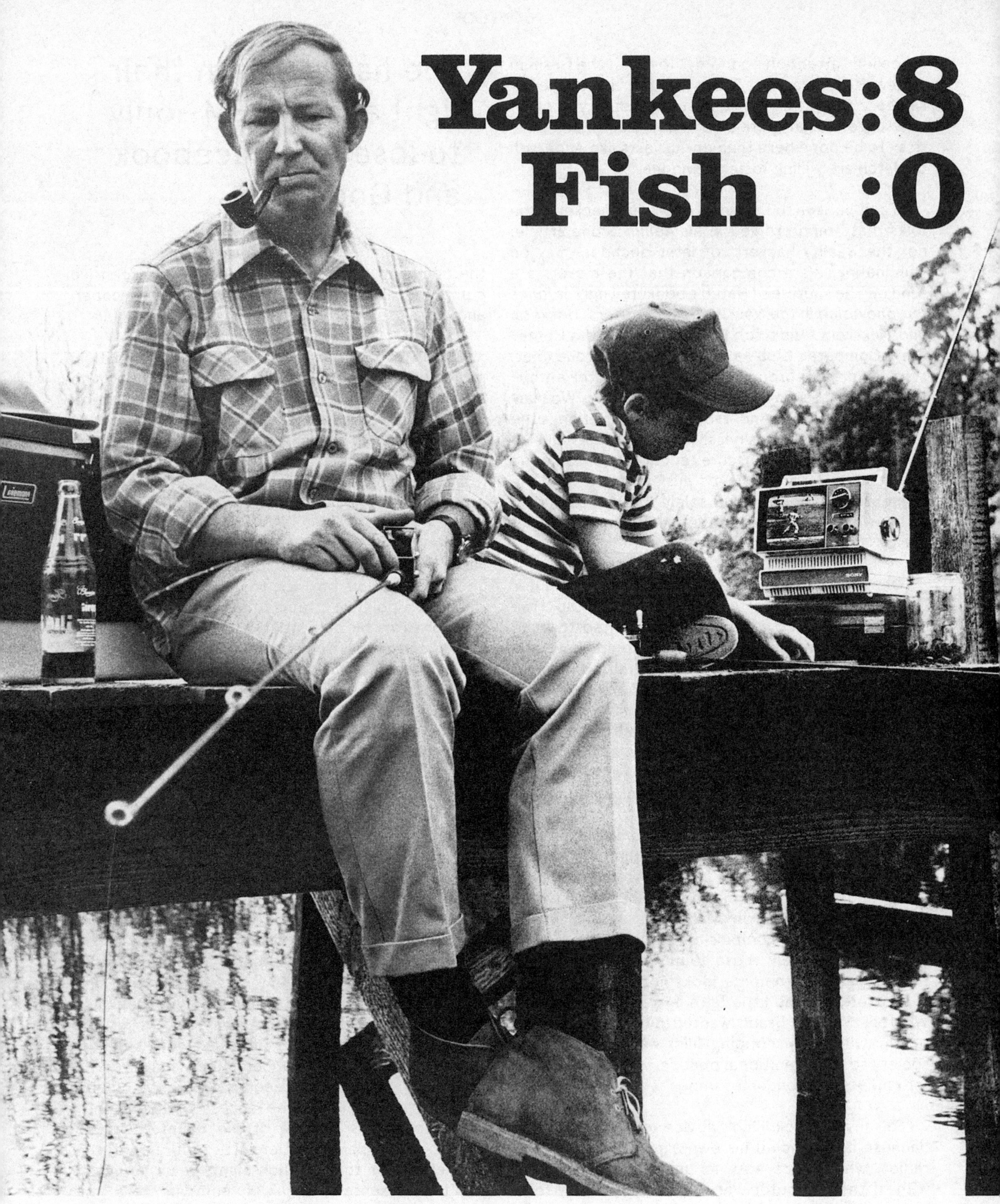

Fishing is great—when you catch fish.

But when you don't? The kid whines. The sun burns. And the time drags.

That's why it's nice to own a Sony portable. Like the little 5 inch* 7½ pound model in the picture. It's so light you can take it anywhere. And with its optional, snap-on battery-pack you can watch your favorite program even if you're not near a socket.

And no matter how strong the sun, you can still see every hit. Because every Sony portable has a sun screen.

So what if the fish don't bite. The kid won't mind. He'll watch the Sony.

Our Motto: If you can't catch a fish, at least catch a game.

The SONY® 5″ Lightweight T.V

*Picture measured diagonally. TV picture simulated.

A reluctance to talk about institutions and political change doomed the Arts and Crafts movement, channelling the spirit of labor reform into consumerism and DIY tinkering. The same thing is happening to the movement's successors. Our tech imagination, to judge from catalogues like *Cool Tools*, is at its zenith. (Never before have so many had access to thermostatically warmed toilet seats.) But our institutional imagination has stalled, and with it the democratizing potential of radical technologies. We carry personal computers in our pockets—nothing could be more decentralized than this!—but have surrendered control of our data, which is stored on centralized servers, far away from our pockets. The hackers won their fight against IBM—only to lose it to Facebook and Google. And the spooks at the National Security Agency must be surprised to learn that gadgets were supposed to usher in the "de-institutionalization of society."

The lure of the technological sublime has ruined more than one social movement, and, in this respect, even Mary Dennett fared no better than Felsenstein. For all her sensitivity to questions of inequality, she also believed that, once "cheap electric power" is "at every village door," the "emancipation of the craftsman and the unchaining of art" would naturally follow. What electric company would disagree?

Reprint from:
The New Yorker, January 13, 2014.

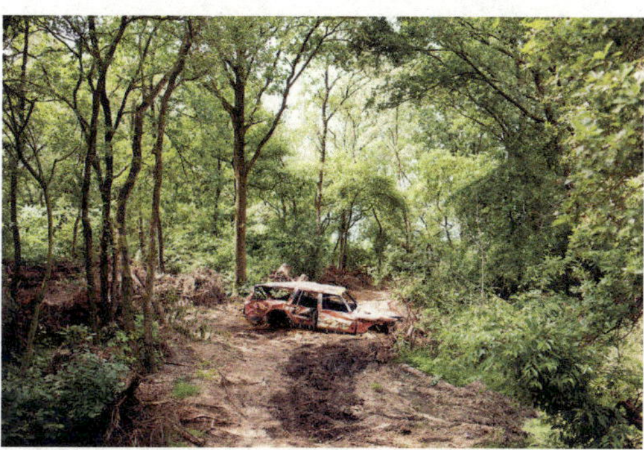

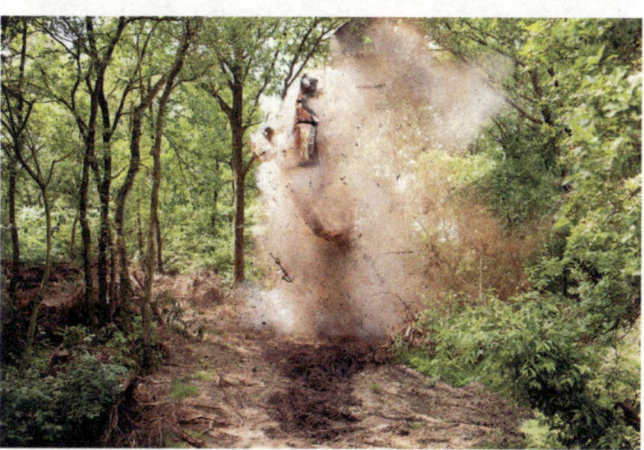

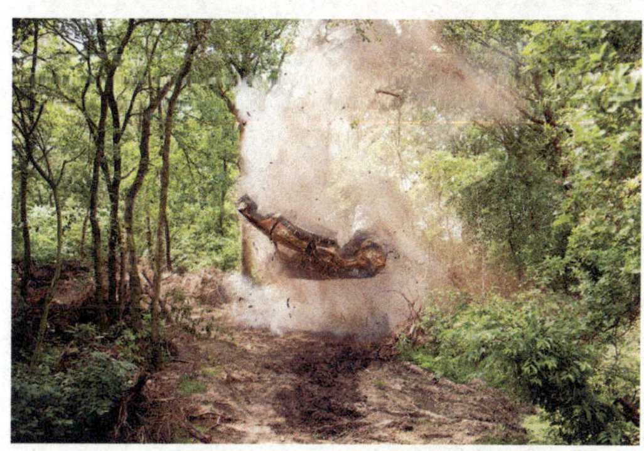

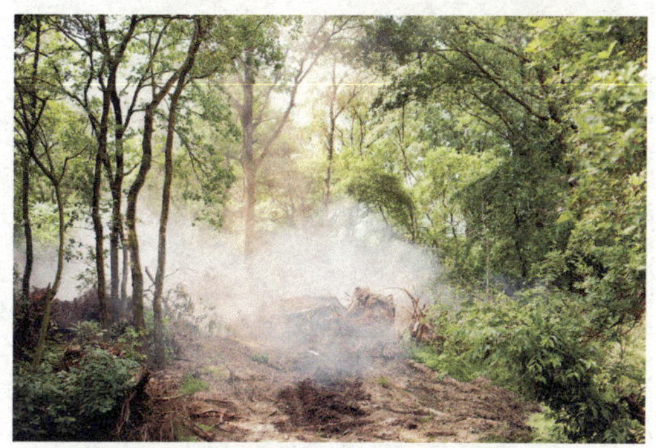

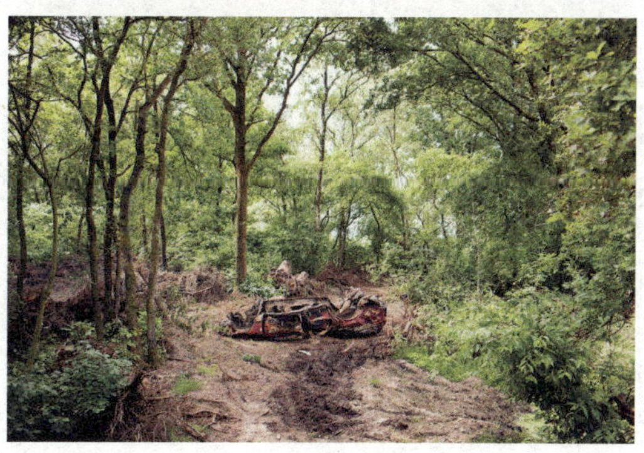

David De Beyter, *Auto Sculpture IV – Sequence*, 2016

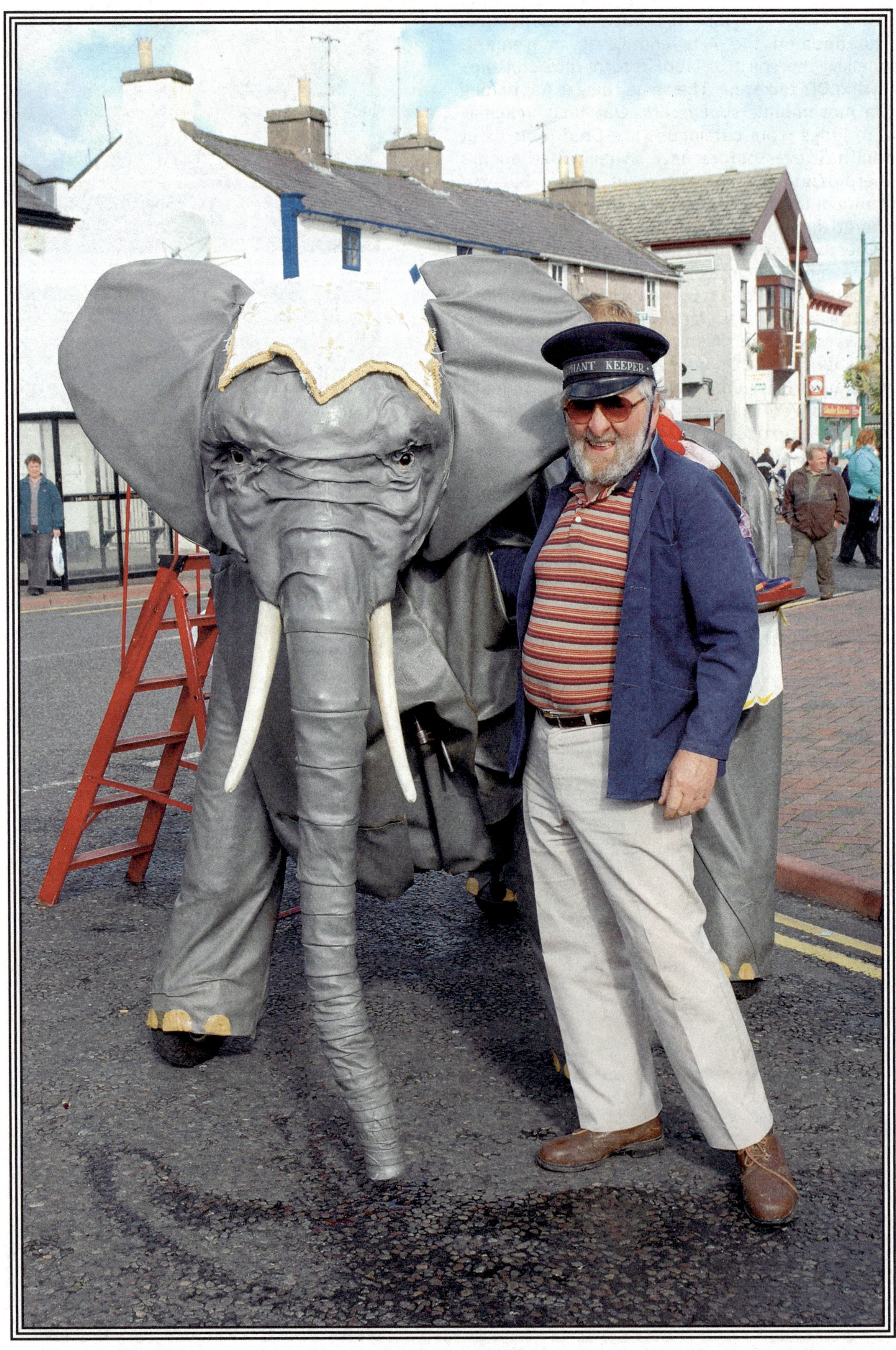

Snowdrop the Mechanical Elephant by the Clare Family, Egremont, Cumbria, 2004

A RATHER NAUGHTY AND SLIGHTLY MISCHIEVOUS VERSION OF BRITISH CULTURE

A Conversation with Jeremy Deller and Alan Kane about *Folk Archive*

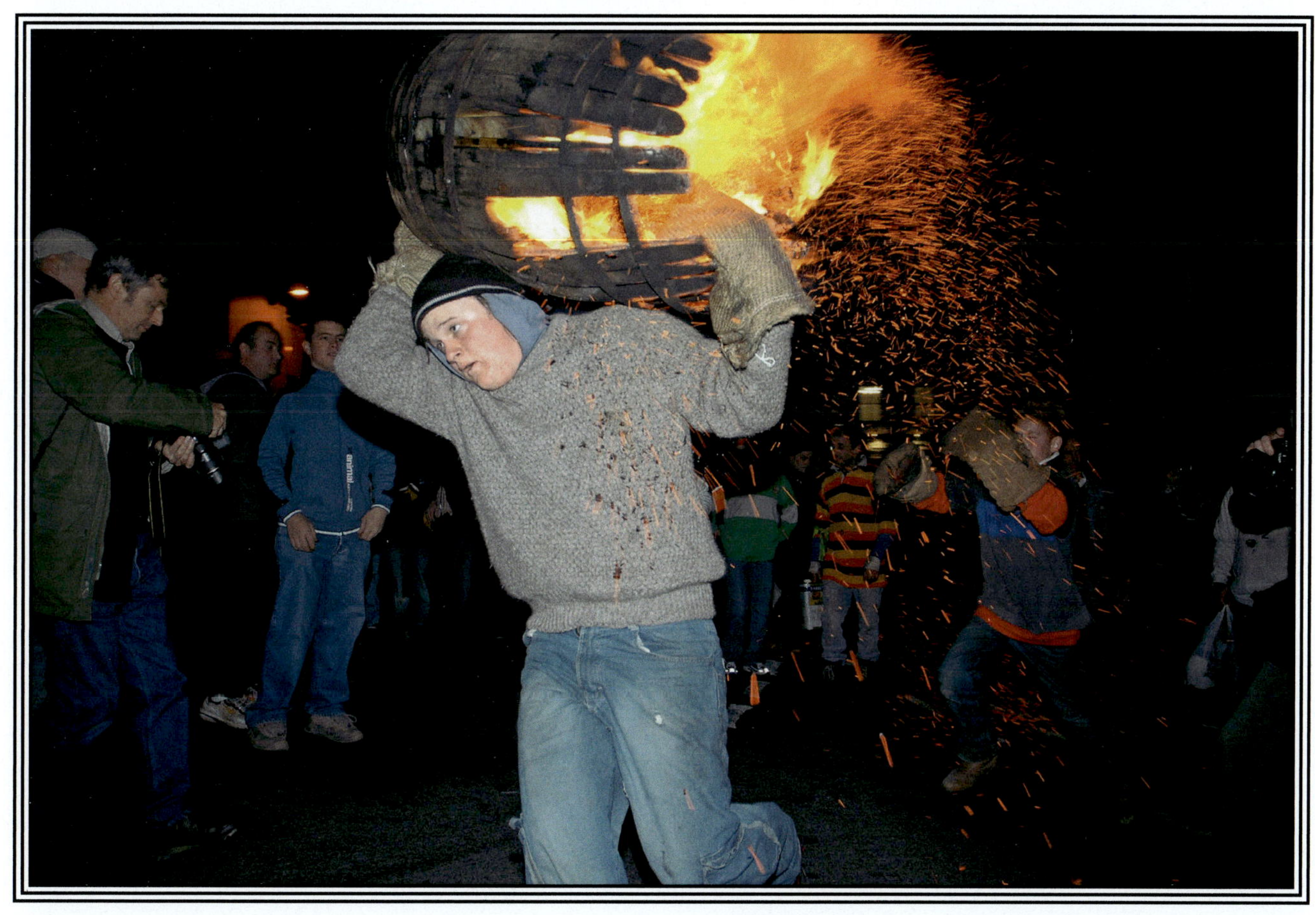

Boy's Barrel, Tar Barrel Rolling, Ottery St. Mary, Devon, 2004. Photo: Jessica Mallock

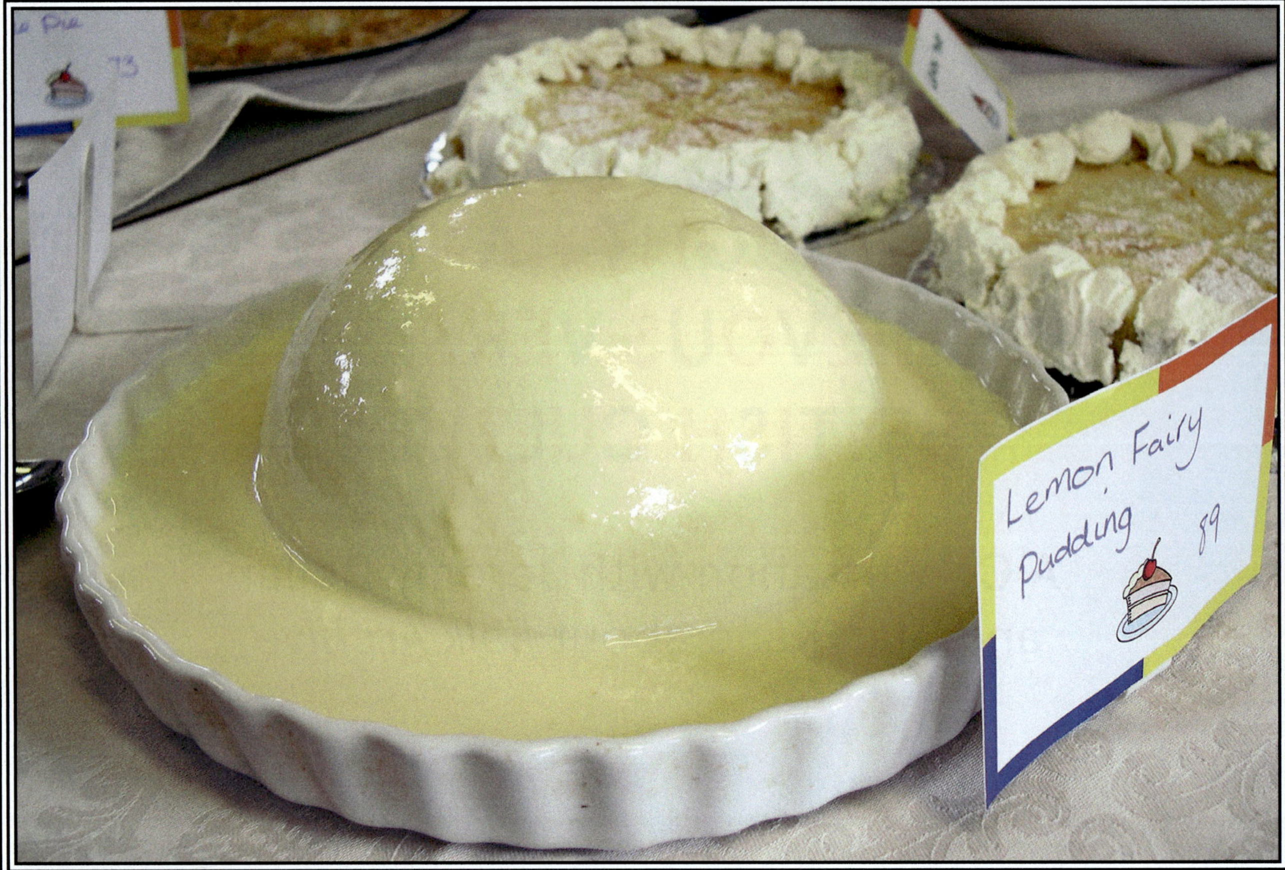

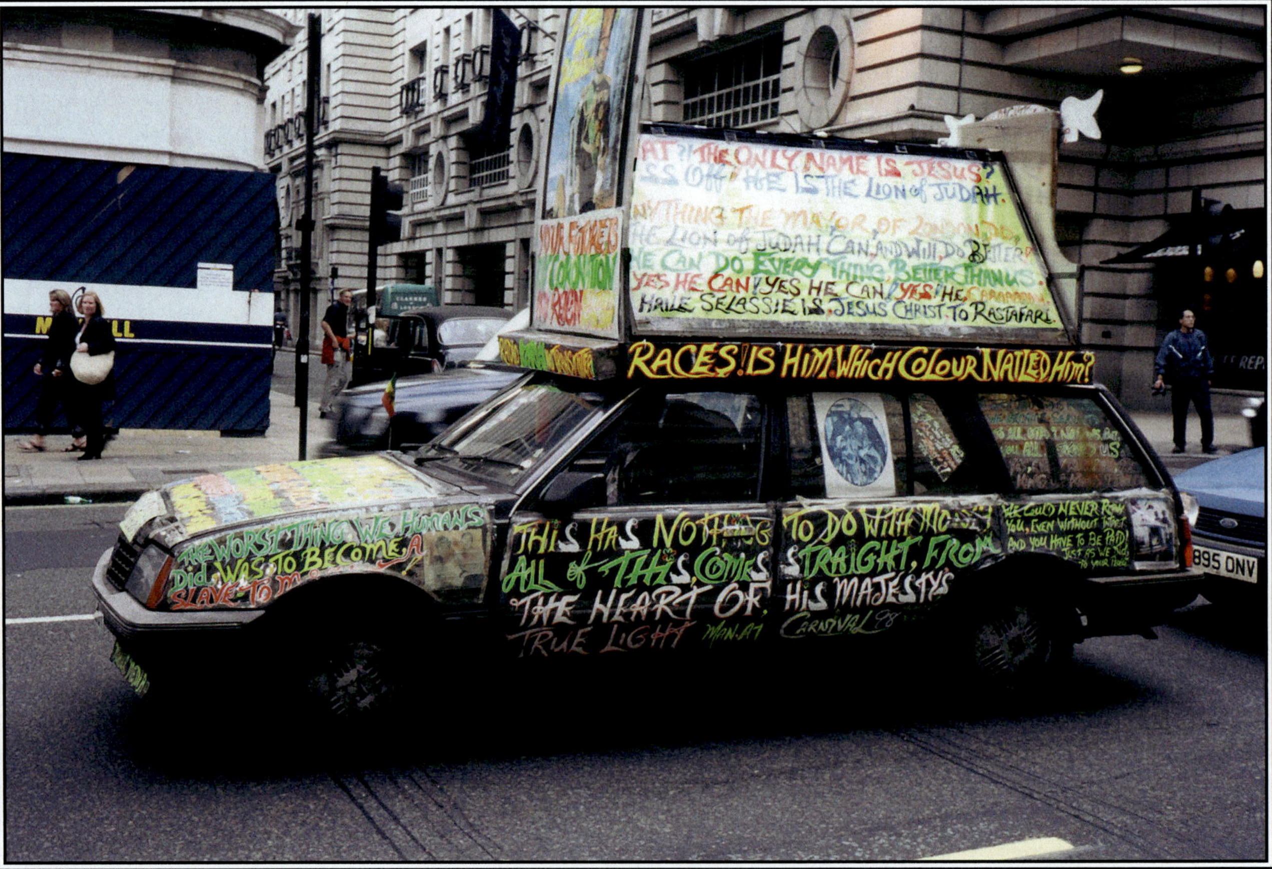

Cakes and Puddings from Braithwaite School, Pudding Festival, Cumbria, 2005

Painted Car Promoting Rastafarianism, Piccadilly, London, 2002

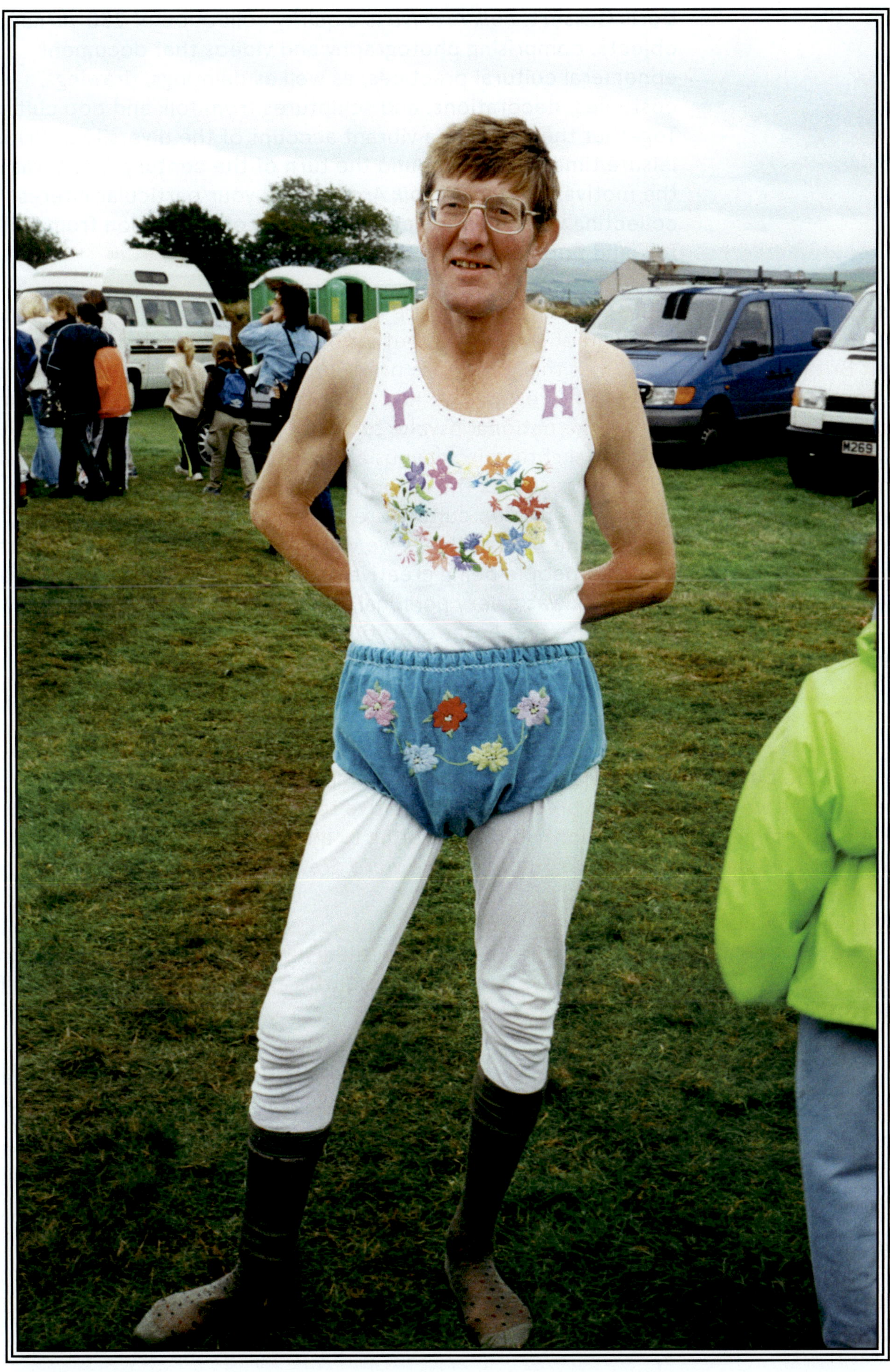

Tom Harrington MBE, Cumberland and Westmoreland Wrestling, Egremont, Cumbria, 1999

Doris Gassert: *Folk Archive* is a quirky collection of 280 vernacular objects, comprising photography and videos that document ephemeral cultural practices, as well as paintings, drawings, costumes, decorations, and sculptures from folk and pop culture. Together they provide a vibrant account of the diversity of British leisure time pursuits around the turn of the century. What was the motivation behind *Folk Archive* and your particular interest in collecting vernacular objects and forms of expression from British folk and popular culture?

Alan Kane: At the end of the last century we were talking about the government's plans for the Millennium Dome, a kind of gathering together of what's supposed to be great about Britain. We suspected that this corporate presentation wouldn't include the kind of things that we thought were interesting. We had it in the back of our minds to try and bring an alternative version of the national psyche to public display. Our version of British culture was rather naughty and slightly mischievous and it's quite interesting to see that, with time, it's becoming in some respects the authorized version.

Jeremy Deller: Folk art practices and pop culture are the things we grew up with and liked, as kids and young adults, the kind of things we were at ease with. We had a shared love in folk and pop culture and people being creative on an everyday basis and the way we engaged with these practices was a very personal, random, and chaotic process. We weren't trying to be exhaustive and cover everything that happened in Britain or go to every place.

DG: What principles did you base your selection on?

AK: From the beginning the project was conceived to be an exhibition rather than a collection. As we were trying to present an alternative to art, we were bringing to the problem the same sort of questions you would bring to any art—most of all we were looking for stimulation, I suppose. The things we were drawn to were the things that surprised us.

JD: And amused us.

AK: It became uninteresting to us when people saw themselves in any way as attempting to be professional artists. *Folk Archive* is about people who are amusing themselves off their own back and not taking any of it too seriously.

DG: How did you interact with the people you encountered and engage with their practices and what was your understanding of your role as artists treading a somewhat anthropological path?

JD: The relationships ranged from anonymity to very close working relationships. We approached people or something we didn't know and they all liked the idea and approved of being part of it.

AK: We are artists and were clear about the fact that that's where our interest lies, in visual culture and visual practices. We weren't doing any in-depth socio-anthropological studies, we're not anthropologists, and we were quite aware from the beginning that

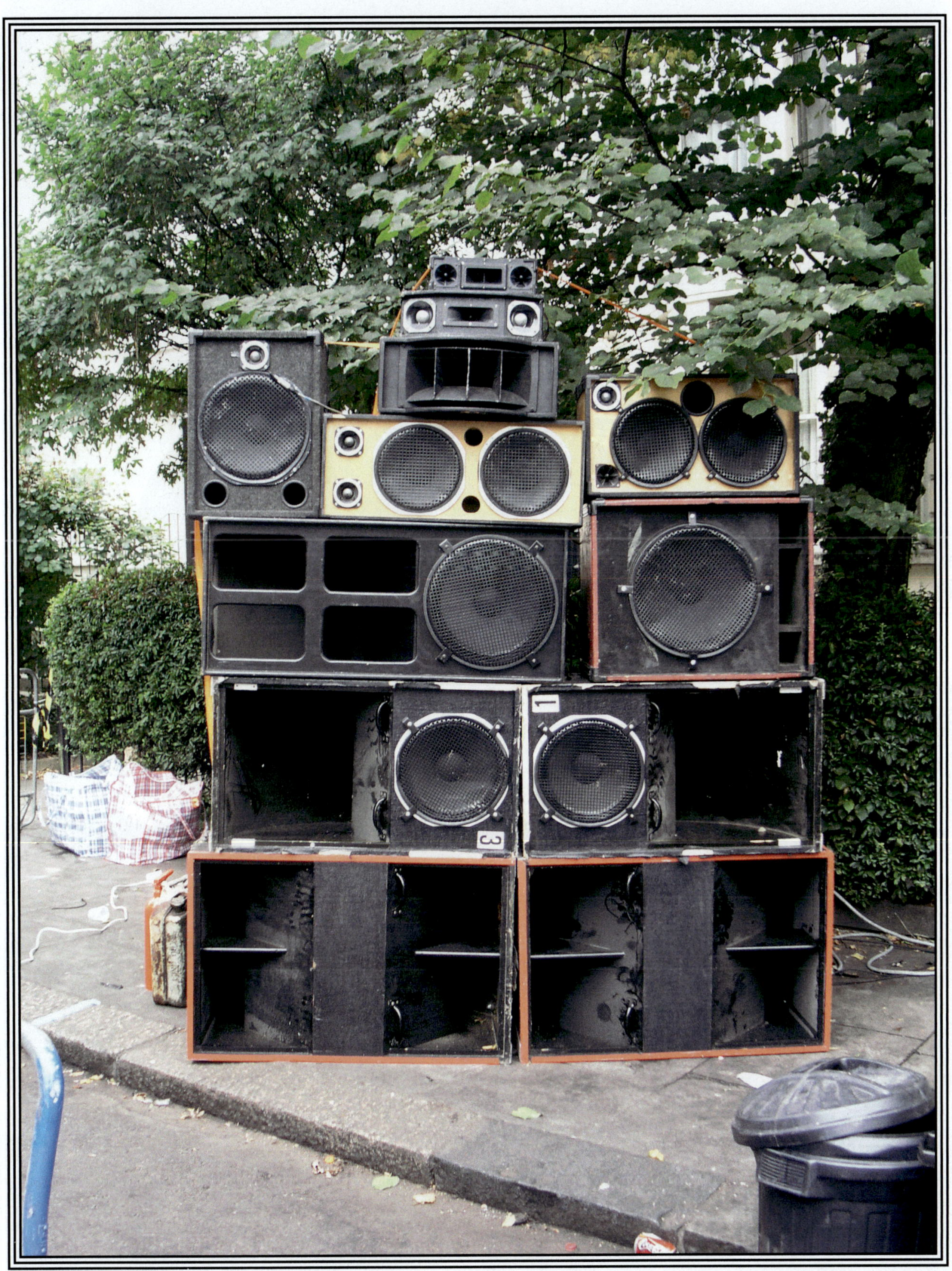

Sound System Speaker Stack, Notting Hill Carnival, London, 2003

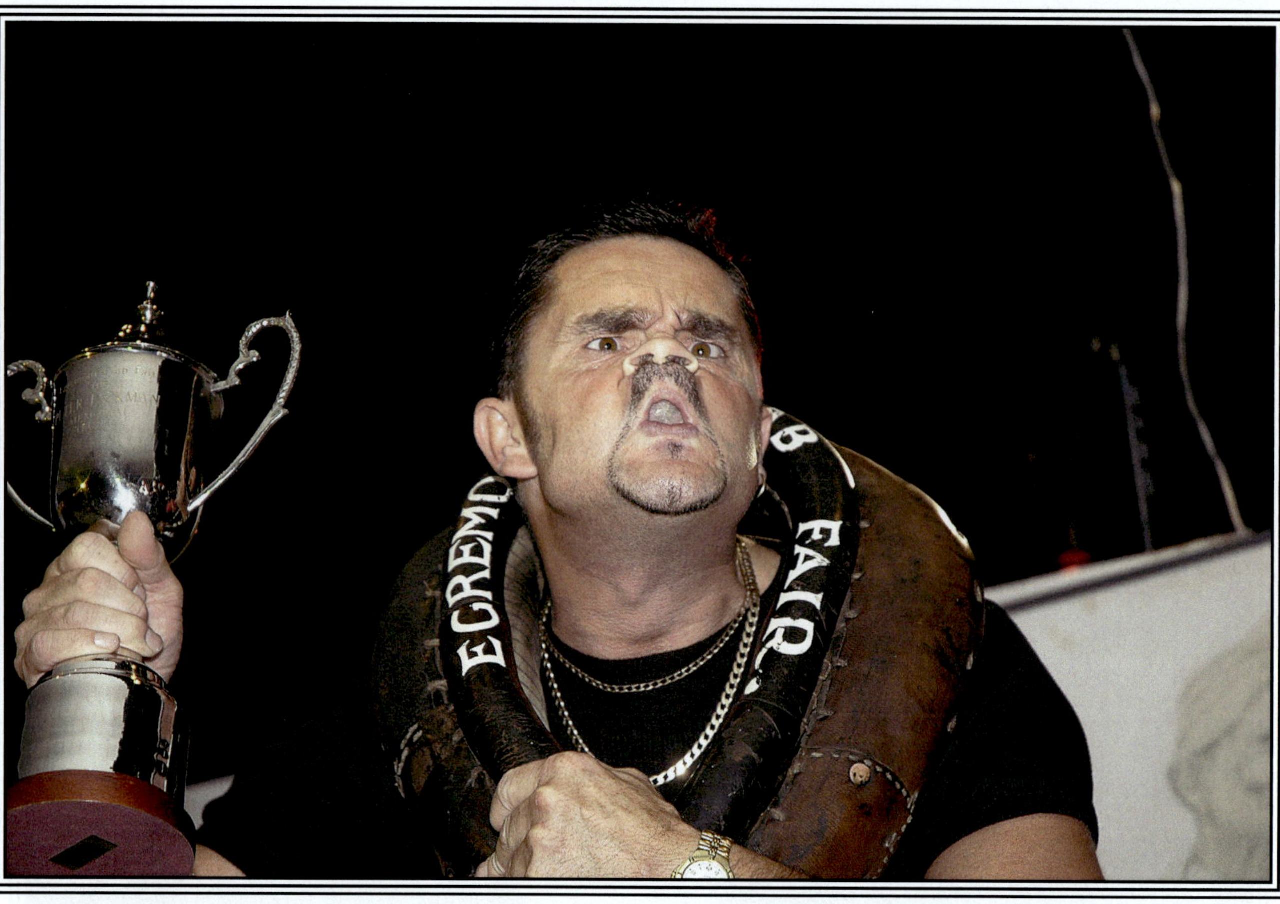

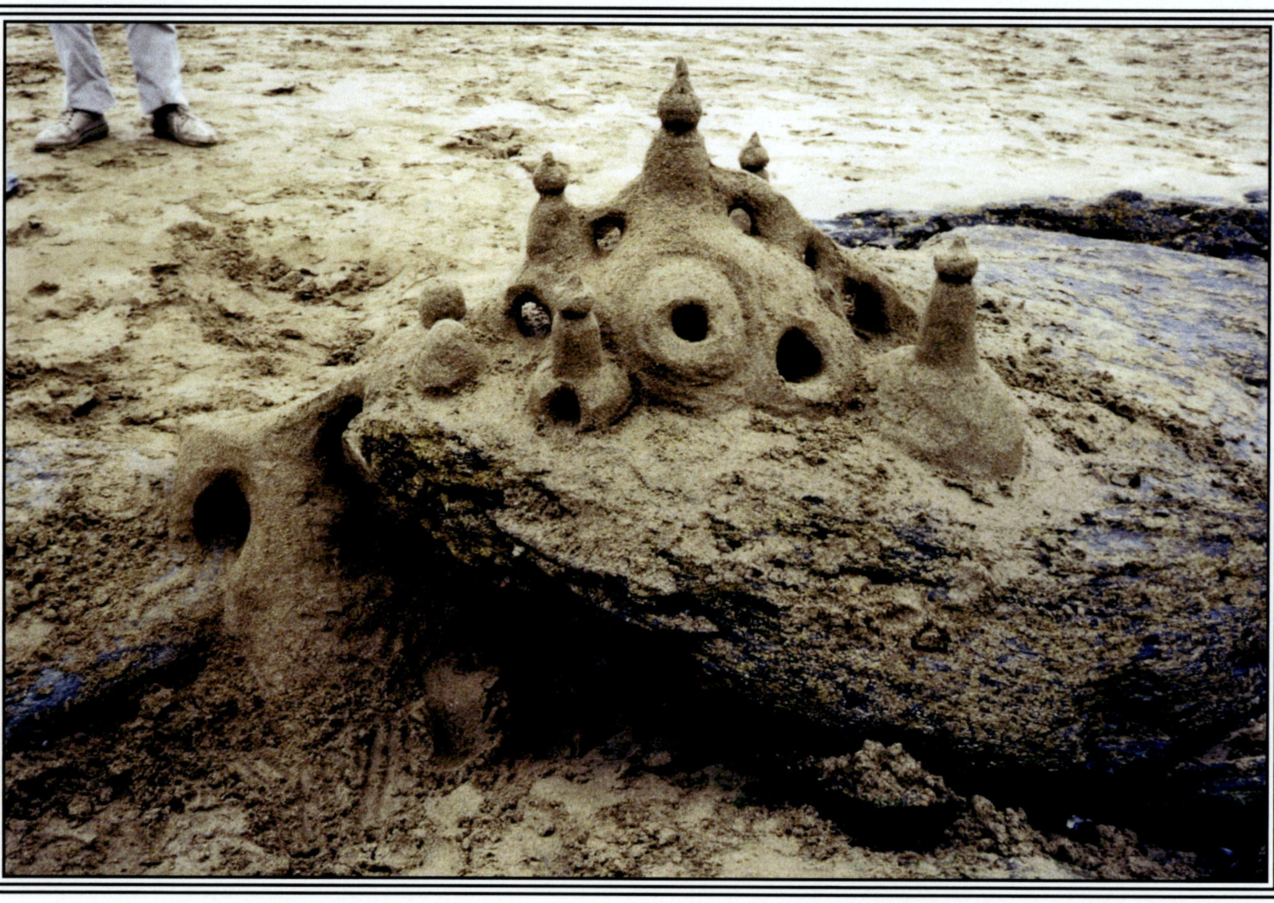

Tommy Mattinson, World Gurning Champion, Egremont, Cumbria, 2004

Sand Sculpture by N.R. Worrall, Trebarwith Strand, Cornwall, 2001

we would be getting a lot from the project personally. In this respect we were quite conscious that we wanted to show things that people were already showing, that were already there for public consumption. We knew that we were looking at our own world and our own lives as much as anything else which, in a way, excluded us from being scientific about it. And in some respect, as with most artists I suppose, the journey is an important part of the main work. With *Folk Archive* we were very clearly looking at ourselves and modifying ourselves along the way.

DG: Photography holds an ambivalent status between folk, hobbyist, common practice, and art form, between creative amateurism and artistic professionalism—this is one of the aspects that is explored in *The Hobbyist*. What role does photography play in *Folk Archive*?

JD: The photographs and the films are all of events and performances, so it's a documentation of ephemeral practices or of things that couldn't be shown in an art gallery because it was impossible to be in the exhibition physically. Our photographs are snaps really; I wouldn't call them great pieces of photography.
AK: What we were doing was looking at what other people were doing and we tried as hard as we could to give a very flat or as unmediated a version of it as possible in the gallery. For us the material was paramount, not our artistry with the lens.

DG: The presence of the lens—was this crucial to the folk art practices you encountered?

JD: *Folk Archive* is pre-YouTube; it was a different age back then. In the beginning no one had cameras on their phones and the Internet really wasn't as developed as it is now. If you would go to one of the performances or events now, three quarter of people would probably be filming and taking pictures with their phones—that's the change in life since the last century. Back then maybe ten percent of people had cameras, now it would be ninety percent. Everything we filmed and photographed you can now find online, only better and sharper, because it's shot with a camera that we could only have dreamt of having fifteen years ago that is now our phone. Nowadays you don't have to get an art gallery to look at this material anymore because you can put everything online, so what we did has become unnecessary in a way.

DG: Apart from the dramatic technological changes that have had a strong impact on photographic culture, Britain has also seen a dramatic political shift. How do you evaluate *Folk Archive* post-Brexit?

AK: At the time there was already a sort of sneaking suspicion or sense from the media, especially the right-wing press, that the British working class is lazy and passive, and we suspected that that wasn't the case and that instead people we're up to stuff that was interesting. We were very conscious about not trying to promote a particularly political position.

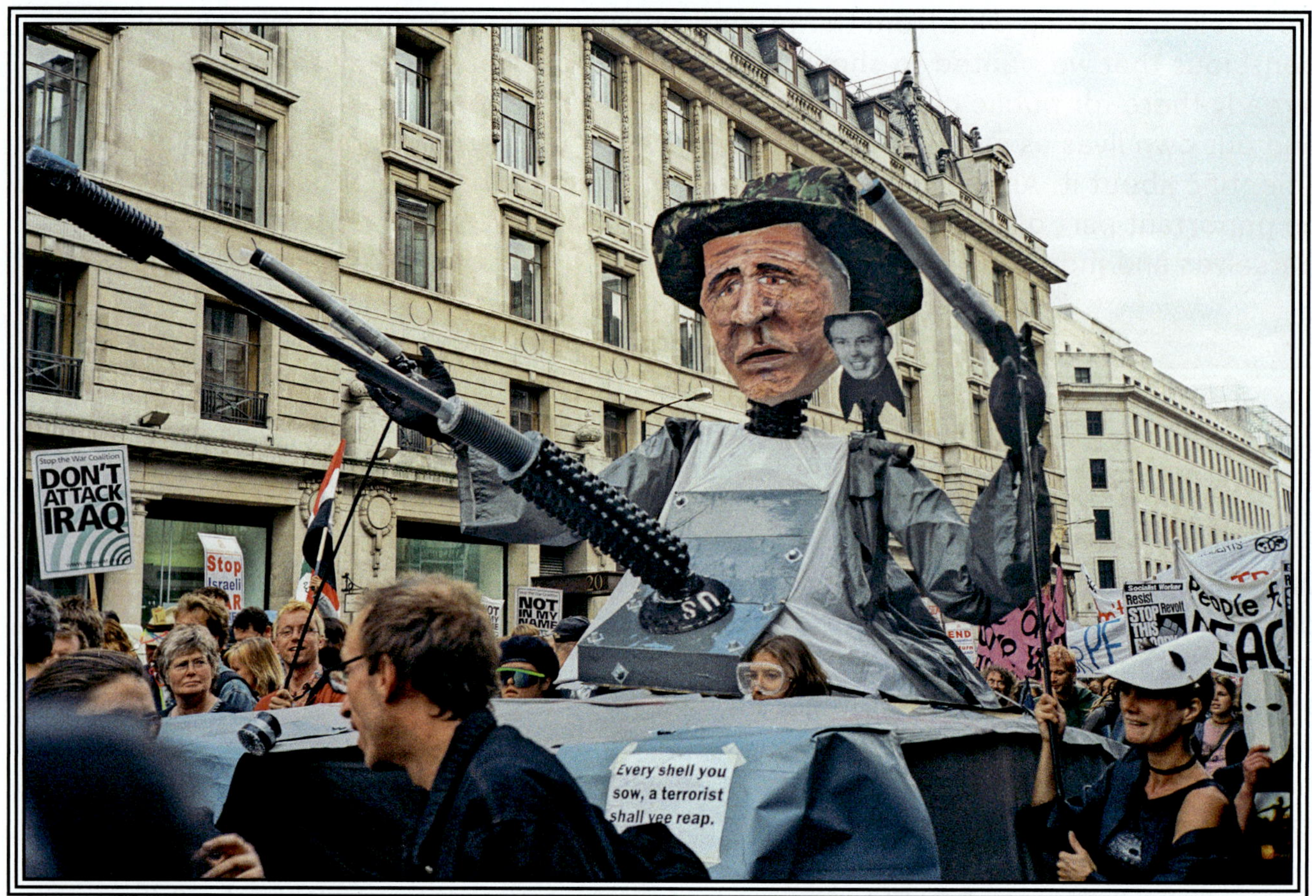

We were trying to make a reflection of the prescribed art industry from the world outside and, in that way, I suppose most of the material from that scene would be hard to pin down politically.

JD: The rift between the city and the country was already obvious back then. If you leave London and you go to the countryside it tends to be quite white, so this show reflects that. In *Folk Archive* we were also looking at areas between country and city, suburbs and fringes of towns. A lot of it is about chaos and anarchy for a day or inverting power structures, about behaving badly. Rather than being a re-enactment of social structures, they are very often inverted, put on their head, so the people who are poorest can be in charge for the day or get to do what they want. They're not solidifying established structures so much as playing with them. It's about chaos, not about order.

AK: The question of Brexit is really interesting and I'm thinking if we had done *Folk Archive* last year, there'd be far more interesting material generally by the Brexit camp than there would've been from the remainers.

JD: I guess there's more passion from the Brexit camp, but I don't think you would've seen much creativity when it comes to making things. For *Folk Archive,* we documented left-wing and overtly right-wing political causes when they included artworks that were made for those events, and it seemed on the whole that the left is better at making things when it comes to processions or demonstrations.

AK: One way or the other, I think as committed Europeans we would've had a problem going about the countryside in the last two years to take photographs of some of the things that probably would've been worrying us before—knowing of the potential political impact.

George Bush and Tony Blair Tank Sculpture, Stop the War March, London, 2003

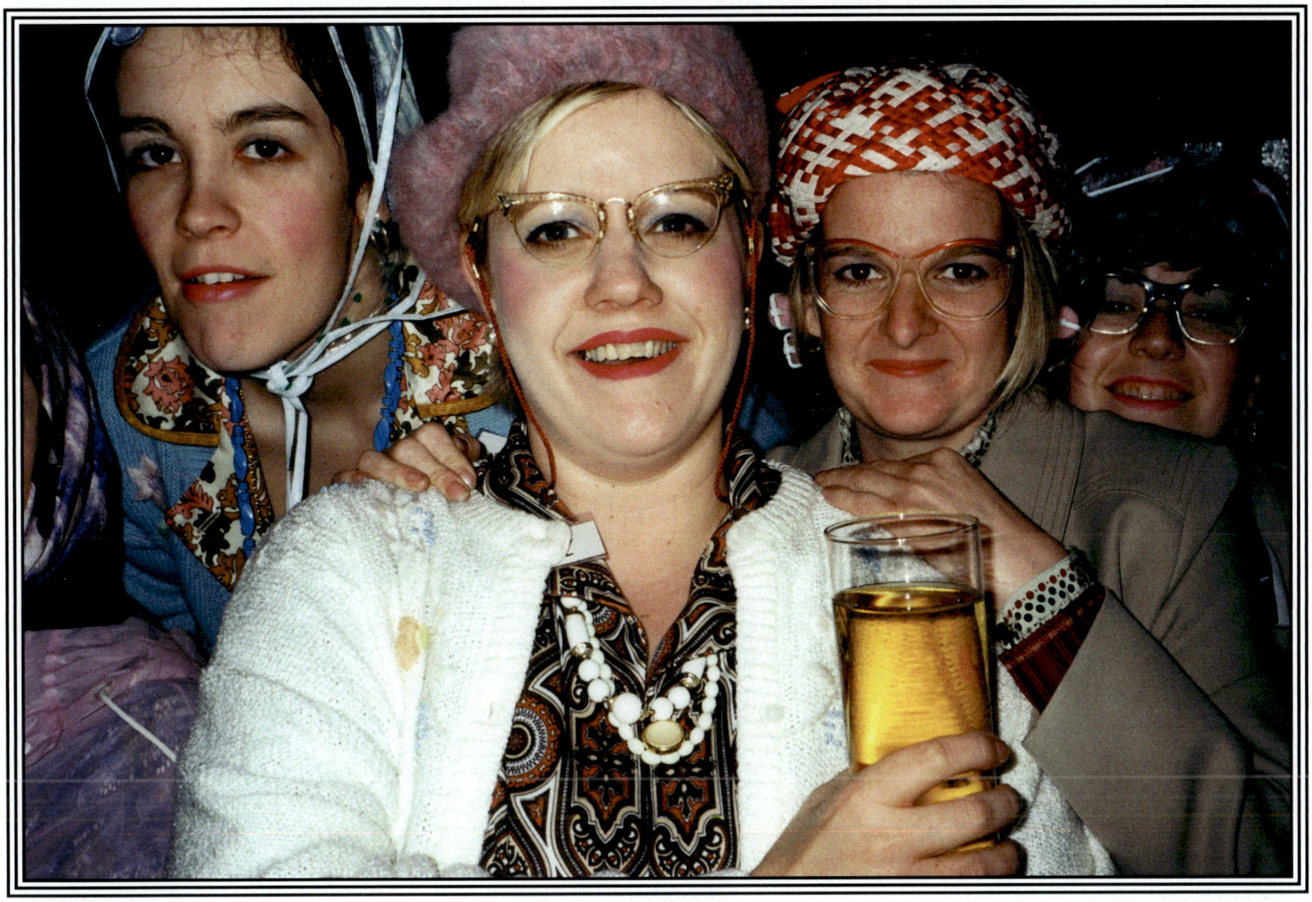

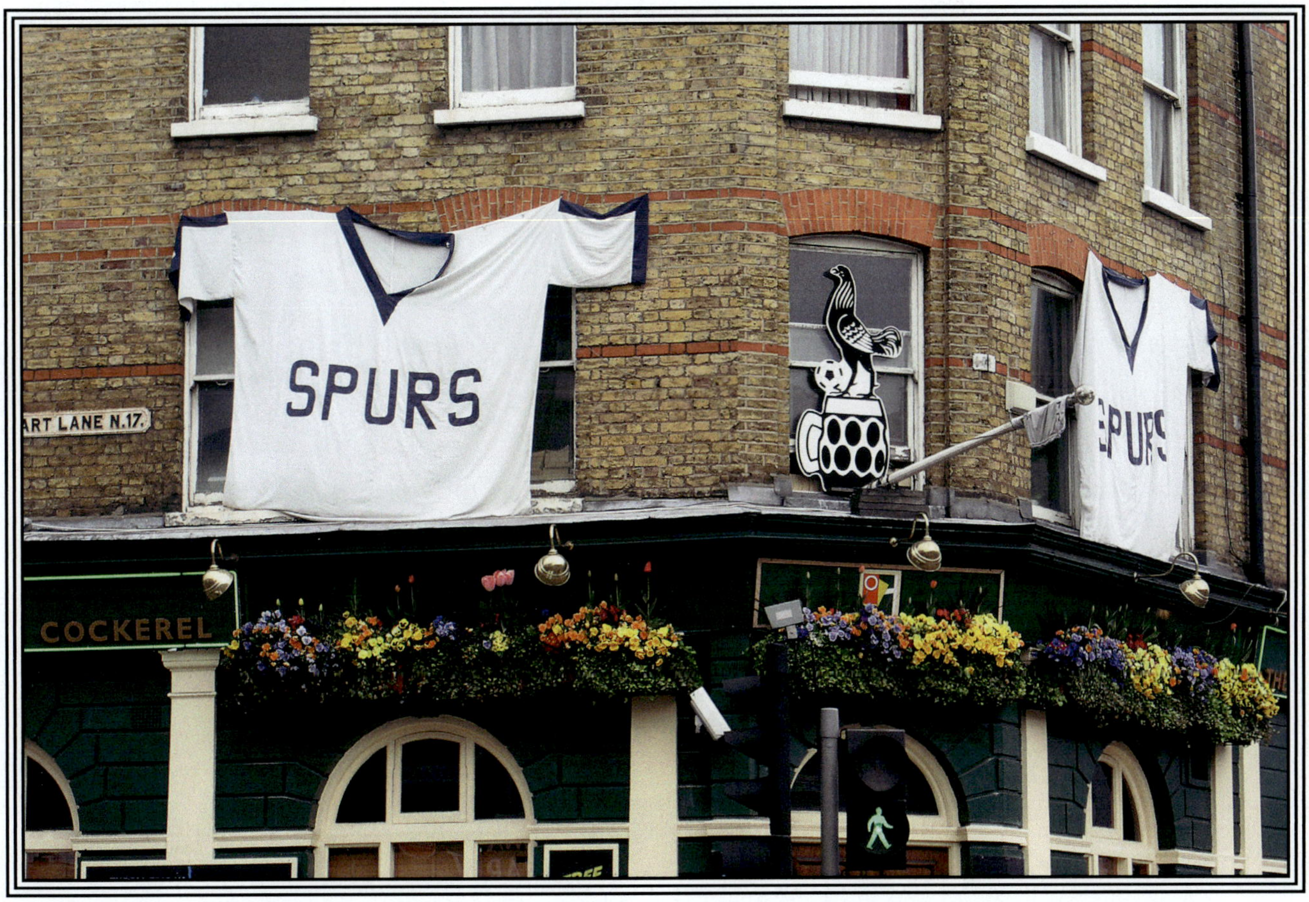

Young Women Dressed as Old Ladies,
Blackpool, 2000

Pub Decoration, Tottenham,
London, 2003

HOBBIES AND THEIR REPRESENTATION

Is Gender an Issue?

Therese Steffen

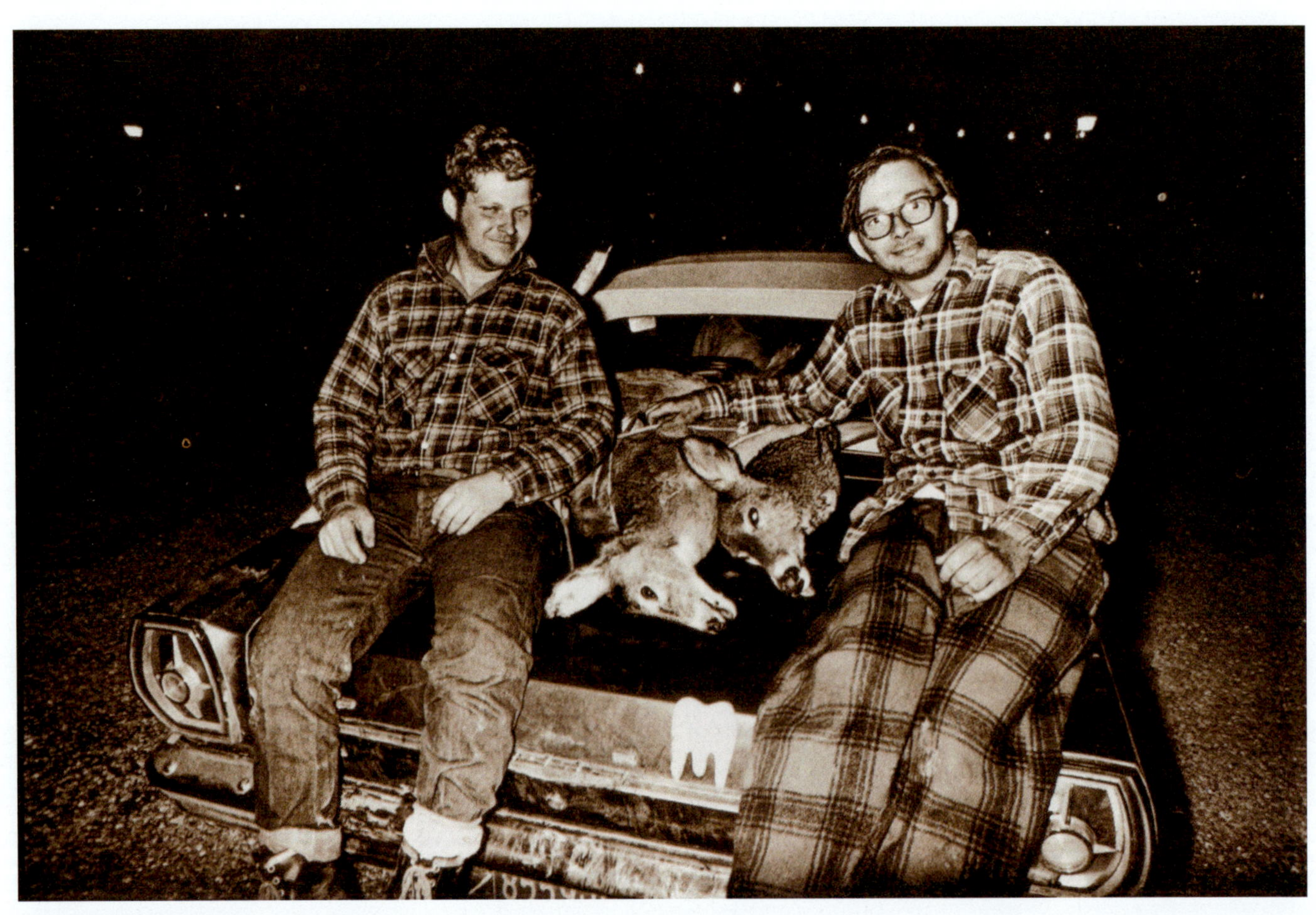

Les Krims, from *The Deerslayers*, 1972

Fishing, shooting, hunting, polo, architecture, ballet, classical music, painting, agriculture, history books—the list of Prince Charles' hobbies is seemingly endless. And Princess Anne? Why, that's simple: horses, horses, and more horses! At first glance, the leisure pursuits of the British royals fit with the usual clichés. Girls are as happy as can be on horseback, and statistics bear this out: according to Beatrix Fricke, some forty percent of German equestrians are under eighteen—and "more than ninety percent of them are female." Horses make for strong partners. A horse is an animal you can lean on, rely on; it understands you without a word, carries you where you want, lets you lavish care and attention on it. Yet even the British heir to the throne, for all his hobbies associated primarily with masculinity such as fishing, shooting, and hunting, also likes polo ponies. Incidentally, "hobby" is derived from the English term "hobby horse," which evokes a child's toy as much as a pastime.

In short: the gender-specific boundaries of career choices and leisure pursuits that have grown over the centuries have now become blurred, no matter how enduring the age-old clichés might be. In her essay on the distribution of family roles and tasks, Andrea Maihofer explores this complex correlation between change, continuity, and persistence in terms of "grasping the unquestioned given." This includes contemporary lifestyles premised on career goals and leisure pursuits that reflect the male and female work-life balance.

That said, this essay looks at the question of gender-specific choices when it comes to hobbies, and the way these are represented in photography and film. Gender-specific tendencies still exist in various activities, whether they are practiced professionally or as a hobby. Cooking tends to be a woman's thing in everyday life, while professional chefs are more likely to be men, especially when it comes to barbecues. The same can be said of the amateur seamstress—professional tailors are generally men. Just to define the terms here: "sex" is a biological definition, and "gender" a socio-cultural one, determining the female or male characteristics of a person. In everyday language, these terms are often used as synonyms.

The exhibition *The Hobbyist* presents thirty-six works created between the early 1960s and the present day. Twenty-six of those works are by male and eight by female photographers. Two of the works are by a mixed duo of artists. Nobody expects equal gender distribution in the presentation of photographic works in any exhibition, given the tenacious gender disparity that has so long existed in the realms of art, though this is broken down in favor of a more balanced ratio among the more contemporary works presented in *The Hobbyist*. As a visual artistic process and a means of documentation, photography is gender neutral. And yet, especially in the selection and interpretation of the works, "gender is always present" (Dietz/Hagemann-White) and it is indeed quite remarkable: some two thirds of the hobbies showcased are associated primarily with men. A brief look at three selected exhibits illustrates the gender-specific nature of these works. The common factor is the body: both as a car body and as a fetish, as a slain animal and hunting trophy, and as the physical cult of bodybuilding.

The stereotypical female-related alliteration in German—"*Kinder, Küche, Kirche*" (Kids, Kitchen, Church)—that imbues the social role of the woman with conservative values, meets its thoroughly male counterpart in the work of the US-American underground and avantgarde filmmaker Kenneth Anger: ***Kustom Kar Kommandos*** (1965). A hot rod (Kustom Kar) is a vintage car with a long engine for all to see without a hood, tuned for superfast starts (Kom-

Gender-specific tendencies still exist in various activities, whether they are practiced professionally or as a hobby. Cooking tends to be a woman's thing in everyday life, while professional chefs are more likely to be men, especially when it comes to barbecues. The same can be said of the amateur seamstress—professional tailors are generally men.

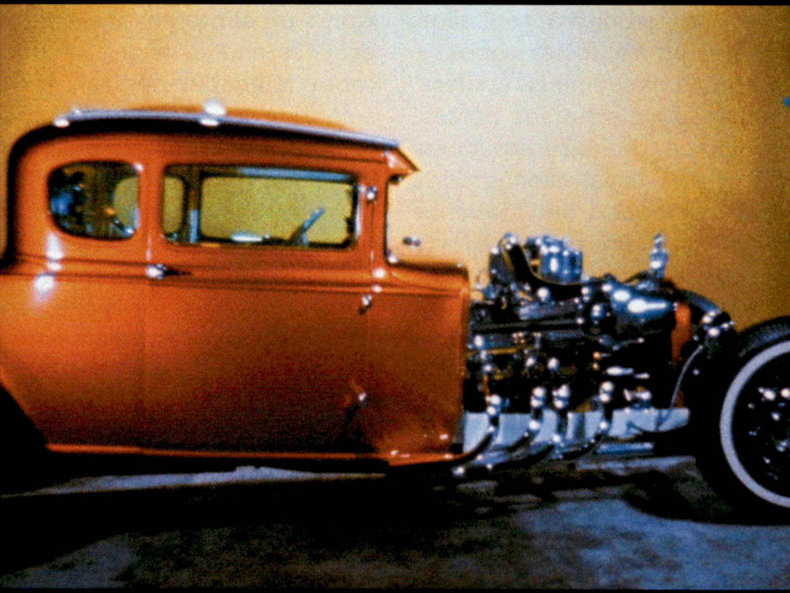

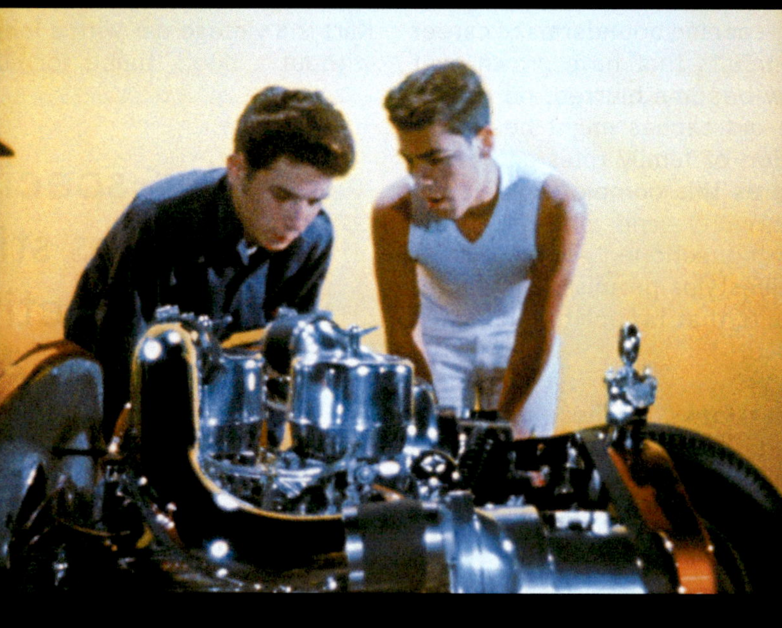

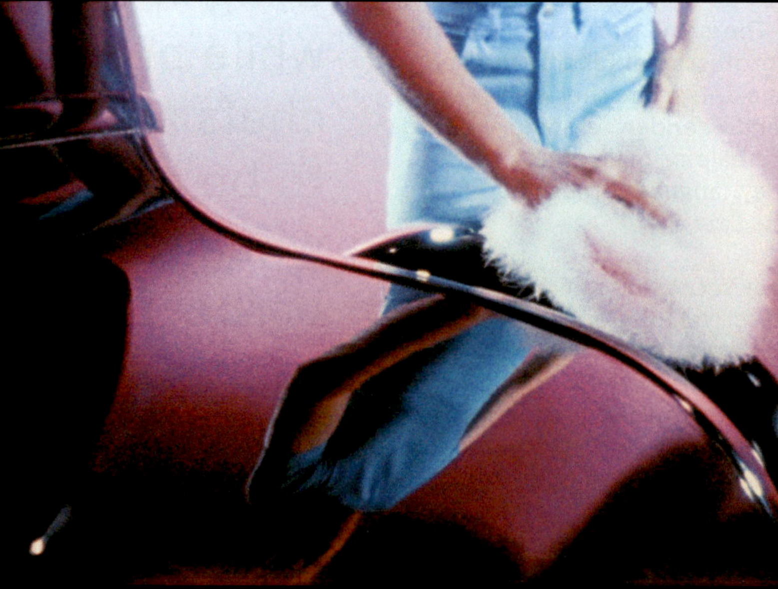

Kenneth Anger, from *Kustom Kar Kommandos*, 1965

mandos). Tom Wolfe, in his book *The Kandy-Kolored Tangerine-Flake Streamline Baby* (1965), was one of the first to pinpoint the significance of hot-rodding in popular culture. Kenneth Anger's aesthetically dizzying three-minute experimental film, commissioned by the Ford Foundation, uses camera pans to show a young man dressed in pale blue burnishing the amorphous bright pink and gleaming chrome parts of the car. With his pink feather duster, he polishes and tickles the lascivious curves of the automobile's shining surface, to the tune of *Dream Lover* by the Paris Sisters. The high-gloss paintwork, together with the melody, are like a siren song, or foreplay for the Kommandos. Then, the boy in blue takes his place on one of the three pink, oval-vaginal upholstered seats and starts up the hot rod. This representation of highly eroticized male/female union could hardly be more explicit. From the color coding (pale blue and pink) to the pimped-up hot rod as a fetish and sexually arousing object, to the 1960 song *Dream Lover* (originally performed by Bobby Darin, and five years later, by the Paris Sisters): Kenneth Anger's brilliant mise en scène of the car as young male fetish does not leave anything to coincidence, effortlessly spanning the divide between smouldering eroticism and coolly suggestive irony.

The slaughtered bodies of animals as hunting trophies are the focus of Les Krims's *The Deerslayers* (1972). This series of twenty-four black-and-white photographs also inspired the poems of the same name by the Welsh poet Tony Curtis which describe the senseless destruction of wildlife. The poems make a shift from the male-centered world of hunting towards critique and receptiveness, or, as noted in *The Cambridge History of Twentieth Century English History*, "... neither the One, nor the Other, but something else besides which contests the terms and the territories of both." This critique is not evident in Les Krims's photographs. Each one is like a brief poem or a fleeting snapshot. Yet all are carefully arranged, structurally simple images that focus on three elements: the vehicle, the hunter, the prey. The dead animal displayed on the vehicle only momentarily interrupts the bringing home of the quarry. It is the emotion, or rather the absence of any sympathy for the animal, that is the formulaic determinant of the image.

The first photograph in the book is also the cover picture and the symbol of the series: a hunter whose jacket bears the emblem of a deer, his totemic wild animal, is standing next to the prey. Does the emblem double his hunting success, or is it a sign of his group identity? Another 'hunter,' the photographer, takes up the invisible fourth position and, with him, the viewers. Hunting, which is still associated with masculinity, remains the preserve of men. The only female hunter here seems to be the exception that proves the rule. As Steven M. Gelber writes in his comprehensive study of American hobby culture: "For men in particular, the image of the hunt as both a search for game and a form of game imbued collecting with an air of masculinity that legitimized it as an expression of superiority in a Darwinian world. The underlying aggression common to both hunting and competitive games is also, of course, an integral element in marketplace dealings."

With his pink feather duster, he polishes and tickles the lascivious curves of the automobile's shining surface, to the tune of *Dream Lover* by the Paris Sisters.

However, the primal image of the hunt as a quest for food is relativized by current research, for the clear-cut division of labor into male hunters and female gatherers is one of those outmoded notions that has stubbornly endured. In her book *Jagende Sammlerinnen und Sammelnde Jägerinnen* (*Women as Hunting Gatherers and Gathering Hunters*), the anthropologist Sibylle Kästner shows that both men and women are hunters as well as gatherers. It is only the size of the prey that determines the gender of the hunter. And the prehistorian Brigitte Röder outlines how the bourgeois ideals of the nuclear family, which did not take hold until the nineteenth century, are unthinkingly projected onto prehistoric finds. In such retro-projections, not only in pseudo-scientific books, but even in academic writings, assumptions are stated about prehistoric gender and family roles which are no longer credible. That is particularly true of reconstructive drawings illustrating supposed 'everyday life' in prehistoric times. An analysis of such drawings has shown that their portrayal of human society is extremely stereotyped—men hunt, women gather—while at the same time insinuating that these roles have remained unchanged for some two and a half million years. Today, at least, this stubbornly entrenched view has been fundamentally challenged by findings of female skeletons with evidence of hunting injuries.

Kirill Golovchenko, from *KACHALKA—Muscle Beach*, 2012

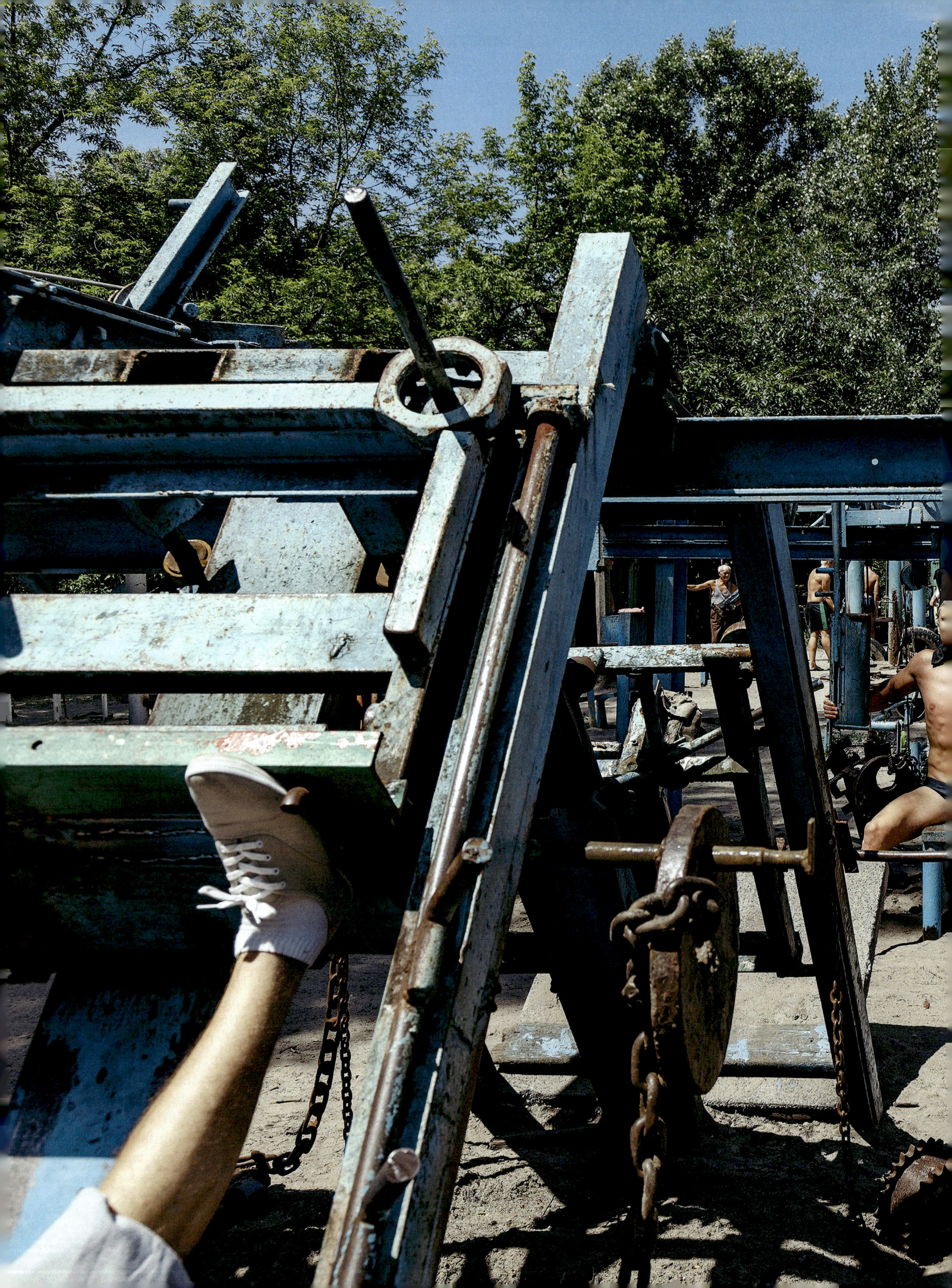

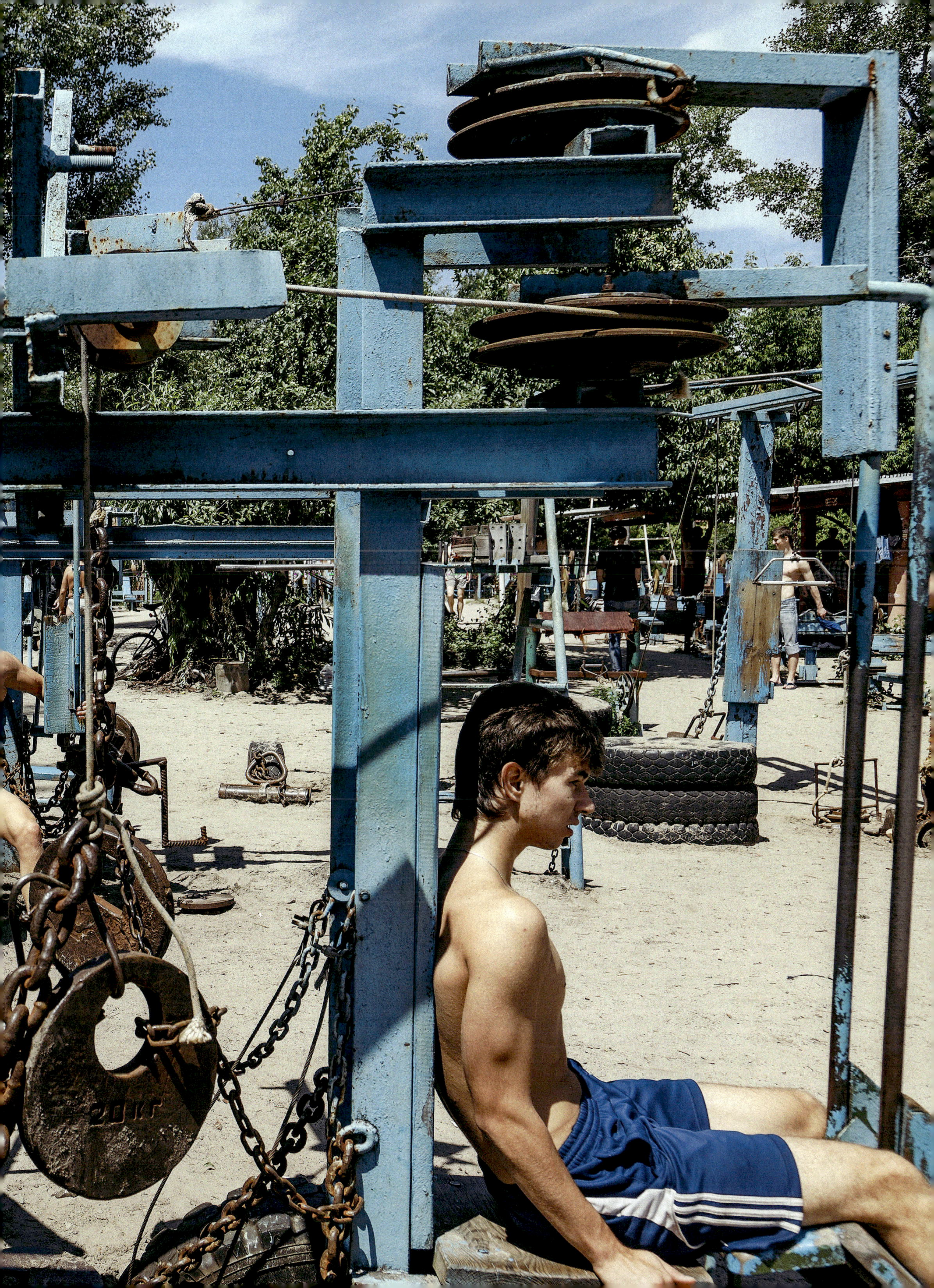
20 кг

Clichés of masculinity and femininity still endure in the works of Kenneth Anger, Les Krims, and Kirill Golovchenko, though they have been broken at times with more than a hint of irony, or have almost disappeared, as in Golovchenko's work.

In *KACHALKA–Muscle Beach* (2010–12) by the Ukrainian photographer Kirill Golovchenko the focus is on the body cult (bodybuilding) as a source of self-empowerment and self-optimization. For his book of color photographs, Golovchenko has created a portrait of Kachalka—a ten square kilometer outdoor fitness facility in the center of Kiev. Founded in the early 1970s by the Polish gymnast Kasimir Jagelsky and the Kiev mathematics professor Jurij Kuk, this huge open-air terrain for athletic enhancement has always been freely available to all, and, as such, is a legacy of the Communist era: collective strength training in the fresh air is—at least for Golovchenko—also associated with aspirations to emulate Arnold Schwarzenegger. "Kachat" means "to pump," and the training machines made up of turquoise-painted wood and rusty iron looks somewhat the worse for wear, like relics of a bygone age. Yet at the time, these pieces of apparatus were quite unconventional. The materials used consist of scrap metal and surplus metal from depots and closed-down factories. Parts of tracked vehicles serve as weights or as footrests for the rowing bench. From sections of tank tracks to bars and tires: a use has been found for everything in this green oasis. And the men, for there are very few women, train together on an equal footing. Golovchenko gives this collective of bodybuilders an audience that can take stock of them and see their efforts. Bodies are also political instruments. Here, they encapsulate the irrepressible will of Ukrainians across all social strata for self-empowerment and self-optimization; even the sporting spirit of the former Soviet Union shines through.

KACHALKA—Muscle Beach, in spite of the evidently strenuous physical effort, nevertheless exudes the atmosphere of a relaxed public fitness park. For all the macho posturing and turquoise scrap metal, these seemingly archaic, cobbled-together devices add a certain levity to the otherwise deadly serious business of pumping muscle, and they also level out social differences. As a human-machine hybrid, everyone is equal here; powerful and ironic visual metaphors of an individual and collective effort.

Gender gaps? Yes, they do undoubtedly still persist, in many forms, both in hobbies and in the way they are represented, though the long-standing gender boundaries in career choices and leisure pursuits have actually been opened up. Clichés of masculinity and femininity still endure in the works of Kenneth Anger, Les Krims, and Kirill Golovchenko, though they have been broken at times with more than a hint of irony, or have almost disappeared, as in Golovchenko's work. Hobbies remain within the field of tension between change and persistence, between women and men, labor and leisure. As Gelber notes: "For most of the 19th century, public leisure was a man's world. Women's leisure, like women's work, remained in the home, but the leisure grew as the work shrank."

Beyond their gender- or class-specific differences, the definition of hobbies as 'productive free time' is a contradiction in terms. By turning work into free time and free time into work, hobbies occupy a liminal area that is no longer just play, but not quite paid work. Working at a hobby is a job that cannot be lost and, perhaps with that, something that ultimately lends meaning and pleasure to life.

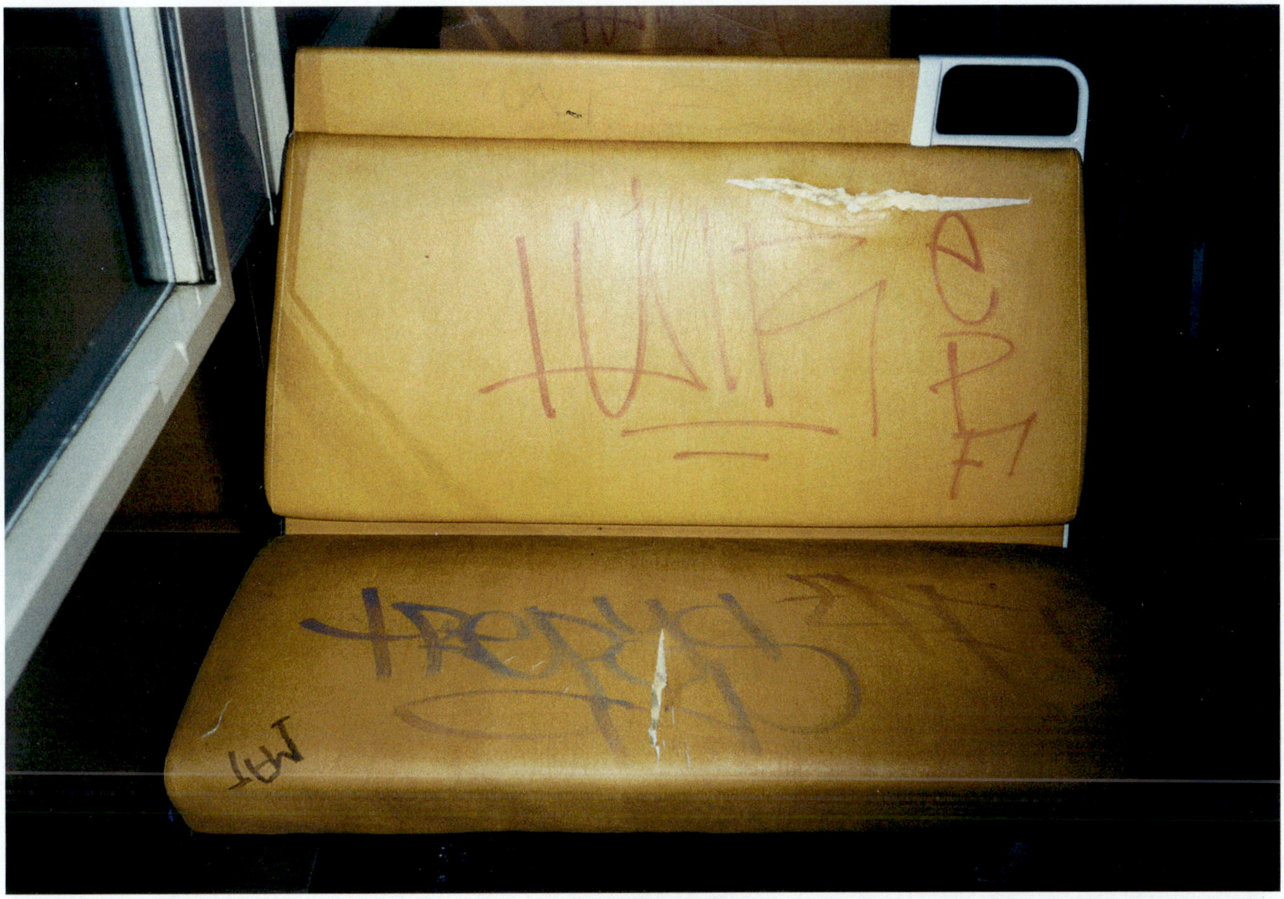

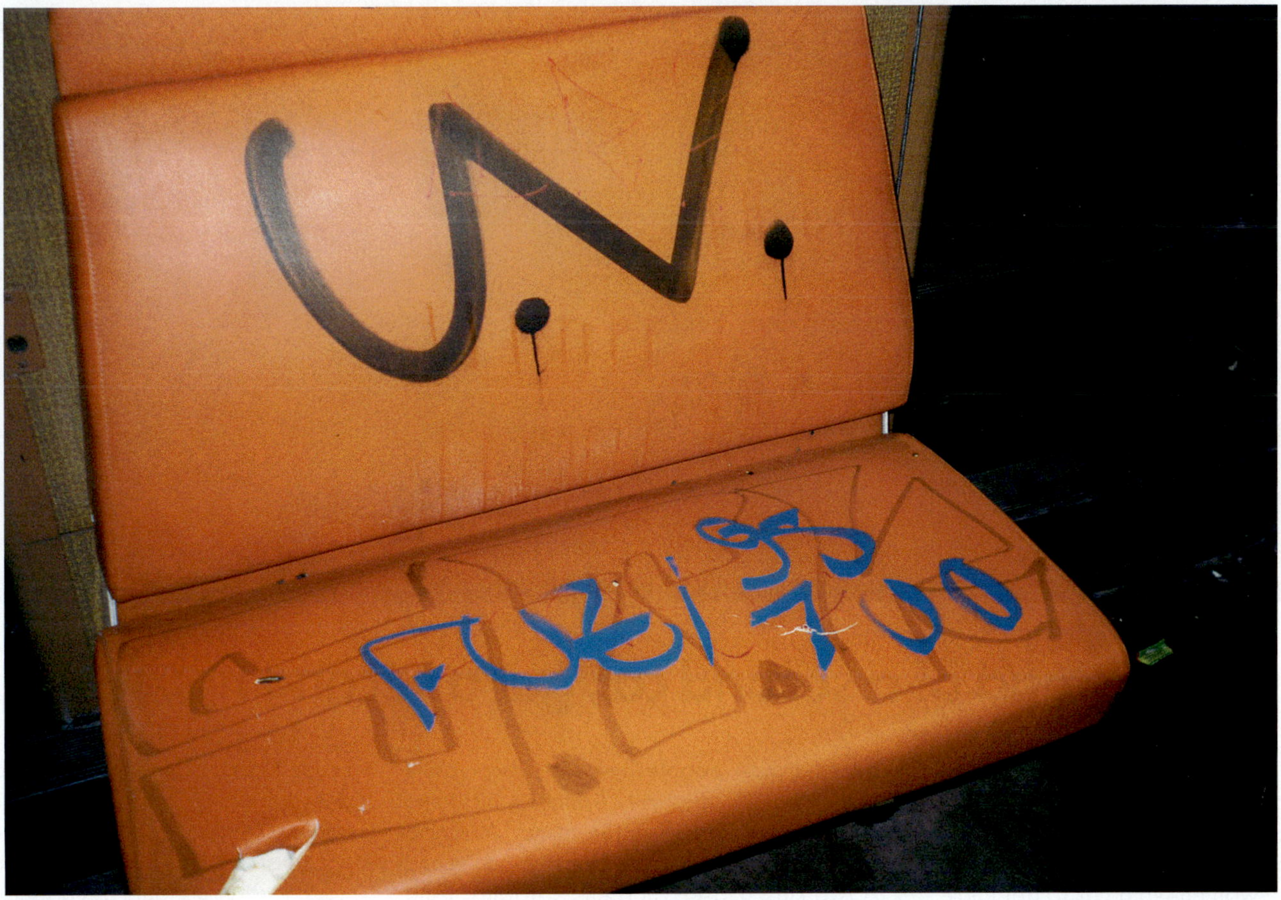

Fuzi, from *Ma Ligne*, 1996–2001

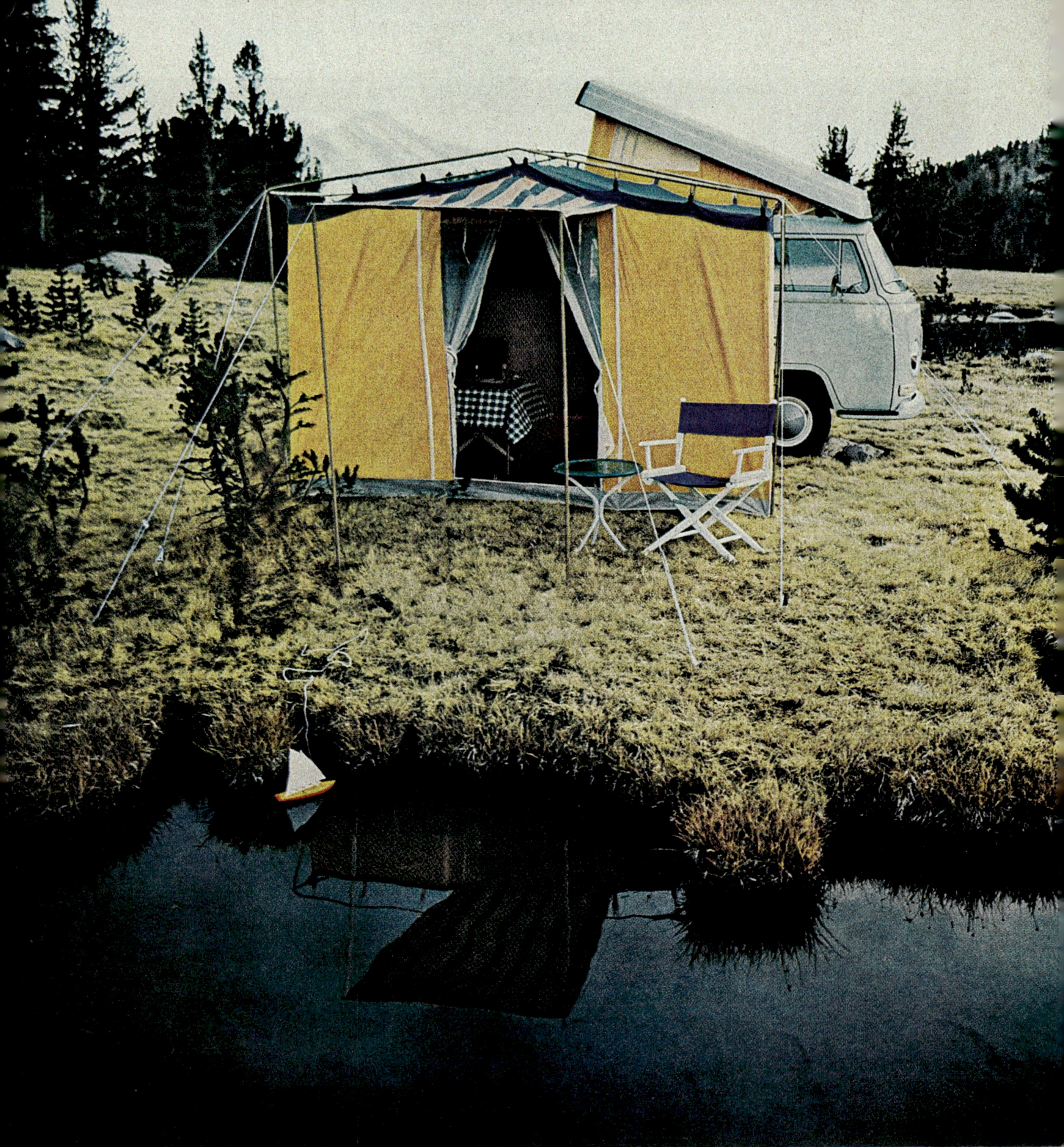

Instead of a second car, get a second house.

It's not as expensive as it sounds. There's no land to buy. No land taxes to pay. Yet you can own a hunting lodge in the mountains. Or a cottage at the beach. And you won't need a car to get there.

All you need is a Volkswagen Campmobile. Which, as houses go, is rather unusual. It goes.

But most people buy the Campmobile for what it comes with: A kitchen. Including sink, icebox and water pump. A dining table. Bedroom enough for two adults and two kids. Closets. Screens. Curtains. (And an optional pop-up top and tent.)

You can even run this second house a lot cheaper than you can run a lot of second cars. It gets about 23 mpg. Takes only 5 pints of oil. And its engine is air cooled, so it never needs antifreeze.

So instead of getting a second car, maybe you should get a second house.

And get the car that comes with it.

Free.

FREE TIME

Theodor W. Adorno

The question concerning free time, what people do with it and what opportunities could eventually evolve from it, must not be posed as an abstract generalisation. Incidentally the expression 'free time' or 'spare time' originated only recently – its precursor, the term 'leisure' (*Muße*) denoted the privilege of an unconstrained, comfortable life-style, hence something qualitatively different and far more auspicious – and it indicates a specific difference, that of time which is neither free nor spare, which is occupied by work, and which moreover one could designate as heteronomous. Free time is shackled to its opposite. Indeed the oppositional relation in which it stands imbues free time with certain essential characteristics. What is more, and far more importantly, free time depends on the totality of social conditions, which continues to hold people under its spell. Neither in their work nor in their consciousness do people dispose of genuine freedom over themselves. Even those conciliatory sociologies which use the term 'role' as a key recognize this fact, in so far as the term itself, borrowed from the domain of the theatre, suggests that the existence foisted upon people by society is identical neither with people as they are in themselves nor with all that they could be. Of course one should not attempt to make a simple distinction between people as they are in themselves and their so-called social roles. These roles affect the innermost articulation of human characteristics, to such an extent that in the age of truly unparalleled social integration, it is hard to ascertain anything in human beings which is not functionally determined. This is an important consideration for the question of free time. It means to say that even where the hold of the spell is relaxed, and people are at least subjectively convinced that they are acting of their own free will, this will itself is shaped by the very same forces which they are seeking to escape in their hours without work. The question which today would really do justice to the phenomenon of free time would be following: what becomes of free time, where productivity of labour continues to rise, under persisting conditions of unfreedom, that is, under relations of production into which people are born, and which prescribe the rules of human existence today just as they always have done? Free time has already expanded enormously in our day and age. And this expansion should increase still further, due to inventions in the fields of automation and atomic power, which have not yet been anywhere like fully exploited. If one were to try and answer the question without ideological preconceptions, one could not avoid the suspicion that 'free time' is tending toward its own opposite, and is becoming a parody of itself. Thus unfreedom is gradually annexing 'free time', and the majority of unfree people are as unaware of this process as they are of the unfreedom itself.

I should like to elucidate the problem with the help of a trivial experience of my own. Time and time again, when questioned or interviewed, one is asked about one's hobbies. When the illustrated weeklies report on the life of one of those giants of the culture industry, they rarely forego the opportunity to report, with varying degrees of intimacy, on the hobbies of the person in question. I am shocked by the question when I come up against it. I have no hobby. Not that I am the kind of workaholic, who is incapable of doing anything with his time but applying himself industriously to the required task. But, as far as my activities beyond the bounds of my recognised profession are concerned, I take them all, without exception, very seriously. So much so, that I should be horrified by the very idea that they had anything to do with hobbies – preoccupations with which I had become mindlessly infatuated merely in order to kill the time – had I not become hardened by experience to such examples of this now widespread, barbarous mentality. Making music, listening to music, reading with all my attention, these activities are part and parcel of my life; to call them hobbies would make a mockery of them. On the other hand I have been fortunate enough that my job, the production of philosophical and sociological works and university teaching, cannot be defined in terms of that strict opposition to free time, which is demanded by the current razor-sharp division of the two. I am however well aware that in this I enjoy a privilege, with both the element of fortune and of guilt which this involves: I speak as one who has had the rare opportunity to follow the path of his own intentions and to fashion his work accordingly. This is certainly one good reason why there is no hard and fast opposition between my work itself and what I do apart from it. If free time really was to become just that state of affairs in which everyone could enjoy what was once the prerogative of a few – and compared to feudal society bourgeois society has taken some steps in this direction – then I would picture it after my own experience of life outside work, although given different conditions, this model would in its turn necessarily alter.

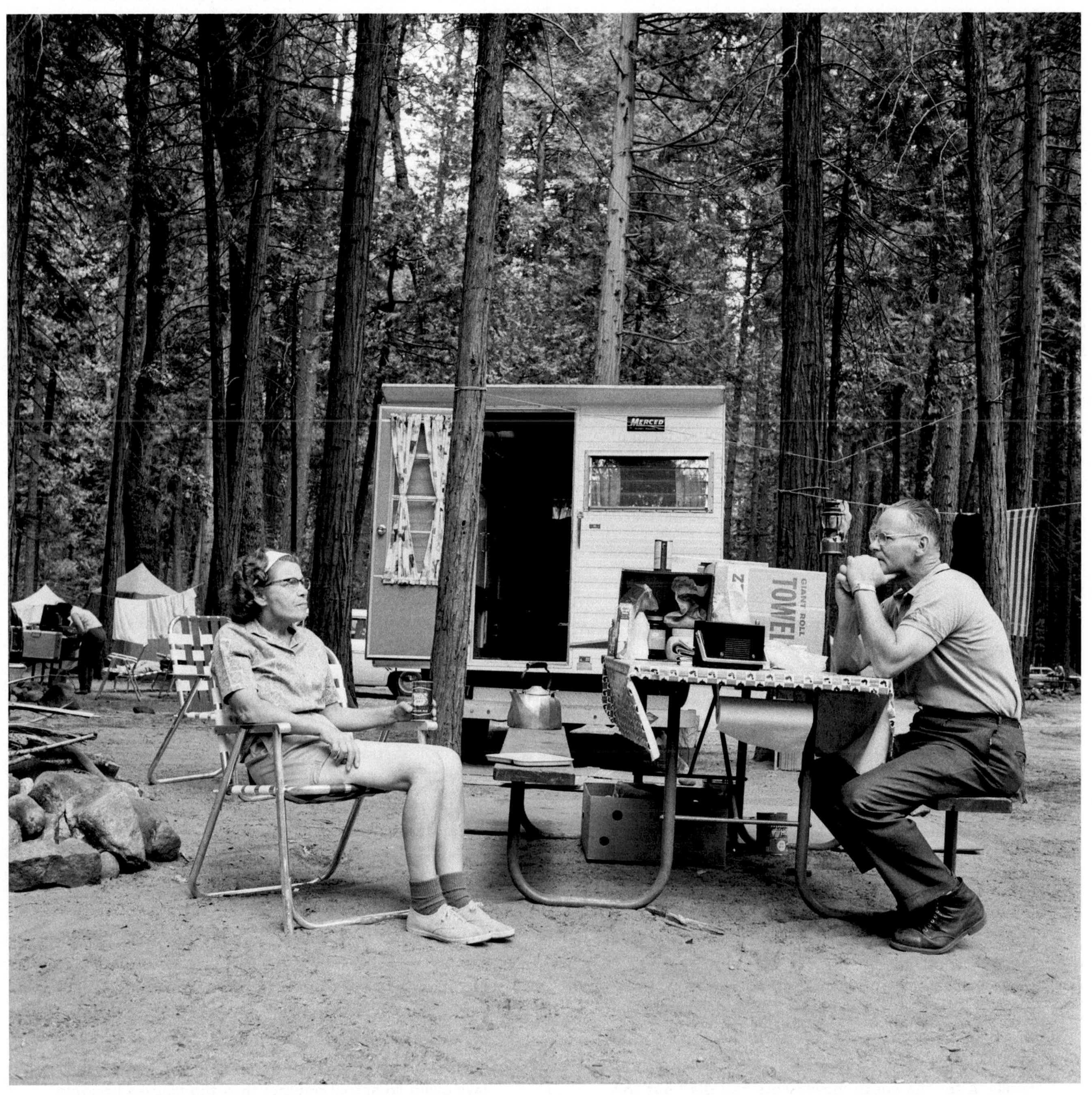

Bruce Davidson, from *USA. Ugly America*, 1965

If we suppose with Marx that in bourgeois society labour power has become a commodity in which labour is consequently reified, then the expression 'hobby' amounts to a paradox: that human condition which sees itself as the opposite of reification, the oasis of unmediated life within a completely mediated total system, has itself been reified just like the rigid distinction between labour and free time. The latter is a continuation of the forms of profit-oriented social life. Just as the term 'show business' is today taken utterly seriously, the irony in the expression 'leisure industry' has now been quite forgotten. It is widely known but no less true therefore that specific leisure activities like tourism and camping revolve around and are organised for the sake of profit. At the same time the difference between work and free time has been branded as a norm in the minds of people, at both the conscious and the unconscious level. Because, in accordance with the predominant work ethic, time free of work should be utilized for the recreation of expended labour power, then work-less time, precisely because it is a mere appendage of work, is severed from the latter with puritanical zeal. And here we come across a behavioural norm of the bourgeois character. On the one hand one should pay attention at work and not be distracted or lark about; wage labour is predicated on this assumption and its laws have been internalized. On the other hand free time must not resemble work in any way whatsoever, in order, presumably, that one can work all the more effectively afterwards. Hence the inanity of many leisure activities. And yet, in secret as it were, the contraband of modes of behaviour proper to the domain of work, which will not let people out of its power, is being smuggled into the realm of free time. In earlier times children were allotted marks for attentiveness in their school reports. This had its corollary in the subjective, perhaps even well-meaning worries of adults that the children should not overstrain themselves in their free time; not read too much and not stay awake too late in the evening. Secretly parents sensed a certain unruliness of mind which was incompatible with the efficient division of human life. Besides, the prevalent ethos is suspicious of anything which is miscellaneous, or heterogeneous, of anything which has not clearly and unambiguously been assigned to its place. The rigorous bifurcation of life enjoins the same reification, which has now almost completely subjugated free time.

This subjugation can be clearly seen at work in the hobby ideology. The naturalness of the question of what hobby you have, harbours the assumption that you must have one, or better still, that you should have a range of different hobbies, in accordance with what the 'leisure industry' can supply. Organized freedom is compulsory. Woe betide you if you have no hobby, no pastime; then you are a swot or an old-timer, an eccentric, and you will fall prey to ridicule in a society which foists upon you what your free time should be. Such compulsion is by no means merely external in character. It is linked to the inner needs of people in the functional system. Camping – an activity so popular amongst the old youth movements – was a protest against the tedium and convention of bourgeois life. People had to 'get out', in both senses of the phrase. Sleeping out beneath the stars meant that one had escaped from the house and from the family. After the youth movements had died out this need was then harnessed and institutionalized by the camping industry. The industry alone could not have forced people to purchase its tents and dormobiles, plus huge quantities of extra equipment, if there had not already been some longing in people themselves; but their own need for freedom gets functionalized, extended and reproduced by business; what they want is forced upon them once again. Hence the ease with which the free time is integrated; people are unaware of how utterly unfree they are, even where they feel most at liberty, because the rule of such unfreedom has been abstracted from them.

Taken in its strict sense, in contradistinction to work, as it at least used to apply in what would today be considered an out-dated ideology, there is something vacuous (Hegel would have said abstract) about the notion of free time. An archetypal instance is the behaviour of those who grill themselves brown in the sun merely for the sake of a sun-tan, although dozing in the blazing sunshine is not at all enjoyable, might very possibly be physically unpleasant, and certainly impoverishes the mind. In the sun-tan, which can be quite fetching, the fetish character of the commodity lays claim to actual people; they themselves become fetishes. The idea that a girl is more erotically attractive because of her brown skin is probably only another rationalization. The sun-tan is an end in itself, of more importance than the boy-friend it was perhaps supposed to entice. If employees return from their holidays without having acquired the mandatory skin tone, they can be quite sure their colleagues will ask them the pointed question, 'Haven't you been on holiday then?' The fetishism which thrives in free time, is subject to further social controls. It is obvious that the cosmetics industry with its overwhelming and ineluctable advertisements, is a contributory factor here, but people's willingness to ignore the obvious is just as great.

The act of dozing in the sun marks the culmination of a crucial element of free time under present conditions – boredom. The miracles which people expect from their holidays or from other special treats in their free time, are subject to endless spiteful ridicule, since even here they never get beyond the threshold of the eversame: distant places are no longer – as they still were for Baudelaire's *ennui* – different places. The victim's ridicule is automatically connected to the very mechanisms which victimize. At an early age Schopenhauer formulated a theory of boredom. True to his metaphysical pessimism he teaches that people either suffer from the unfulfilled desires of their blind will, or become bored as soon as these desires are satisfied. The theory well describes what becomes of people's free time under the sort of conditions of heteronomy, and which in new German tends to be termed *Fremdbestimmtheit* (external determination). In its cynicism Schopenhauer's arrogant remark that mankind is the factory product of nature also captures something of what the totality of the commodity character actually makes man into. Angry cynicism still does more honour to human beings than solemn protestations about man's irreducible essence. However, one should not hypostatize Schopenhauer's doctrine as something of universal validity or even as an insight into the primal character of the human species. Boredom is a function of life which is lived under the compulsion to work, and under the strict division of labour. It need not be so. Whenever behaviour in spare time is truly autonomous, determined by free people for themselves, boredom rarely figures; it need not figure in activities which cater merely for the desire for pleasure, any more than it does in those free time activities which are reasonable and meaningful in themselves. Even fooling about need not be crass, and can be enjoyed as a blessed release from the throes of self-control. If people were able to make their own decisions about themselves and their lives, if they were not caught up in the realm of the eversame, they would not have to be bored. Boredom is the reflection of objective dullness. As such it is in a similar position to political apathy. The most compelling reason for apathy is the by no means unjustified feeling of the masses that political participation within the sphere society grants them, and this holds true for all political systems in the world today, can alter their actual existence only minimally. Failing to discern the relevance of politics to their own interests, they retreat from all political activity. The well-founded or indeed neurotic feeling of powerlessness is intimately bound up with boredom: boredom is objective desperation. It is also, however, symptomatic of the deformations perpetrated upon man by the social totality, the most important of which is surely the defamation and atrophy of the imagination (*Phantasie*). Imagination is suspected of being only sexual curiosity and longing for the forbidden by the spirit (*Geist*) of a science which is no longer spirit. Those who want to adapt must learn increasingly to curb their imagination. For the most part the very development of the imagination is crippled by the experience of early childhood. The lack of imagination which is cultivated and inculcated by society renders people helpless in their free time. The impertinent question of what people should do with the vast amount of free time now at their disposal – as if it was a question of alms and not human rights – is based upon this very unimaginativeness. The reason why people can actually do so little with their free time is that the truncation of their imagination deprives them of the faculty which made the state of freedom pleasurable in the first place. People have been refused freedom, and its value belittled, for such a long time that now people no longer like it. They need the shallow entertainment, by means of which cultural conservatism patronizes and humiliates them, in order to summon up the strength for work, which is required of them under the arrangement of society which cultural conservatism defends. This is one good reason why people have remained chained to their work, and to a system which trains them for work, long after that system has ceased to require their labour.

Under prevailing conditions it would be erroneous and foolish to expect or to demand that people should be genuinely productive in their free time; for productivity – the ability to bring forth something that was not already there – is the very thing which has been eradicated from them. At best what they then produce in free time is scarcely better than the ominous hobby – the imitation of poems or pictures which, given the

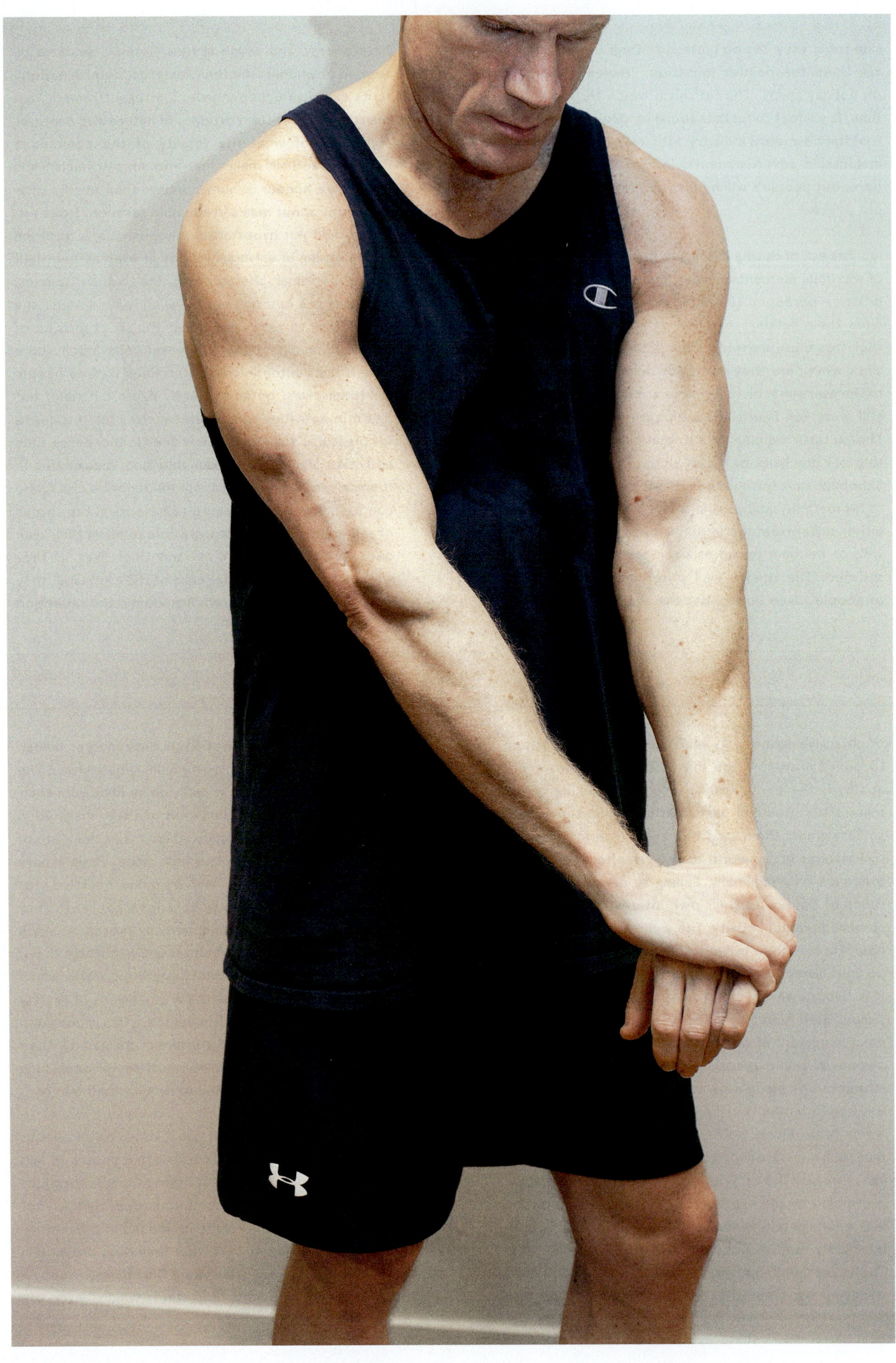

Stephanie Kiwitt, from *GYM*, 2012–2013

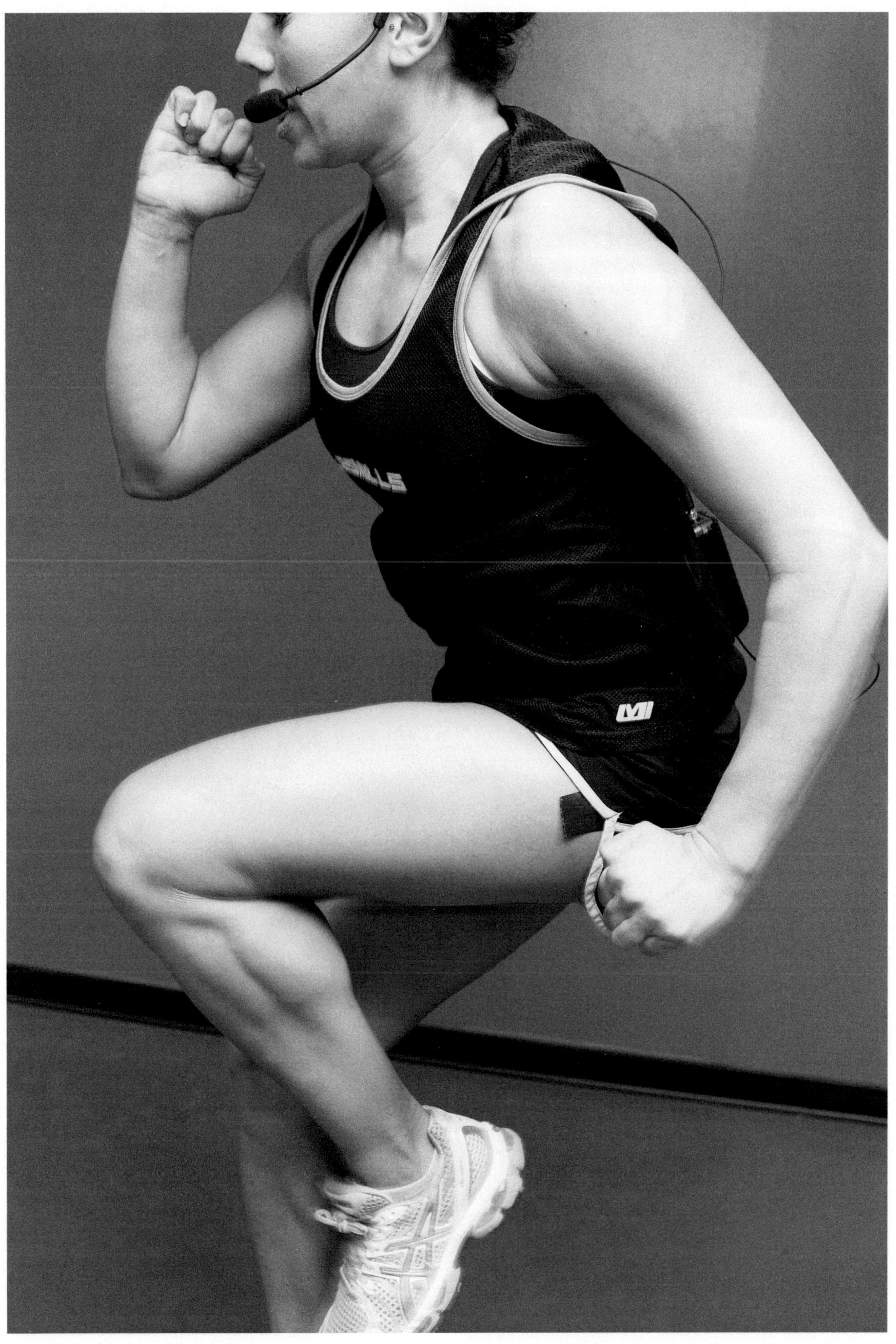

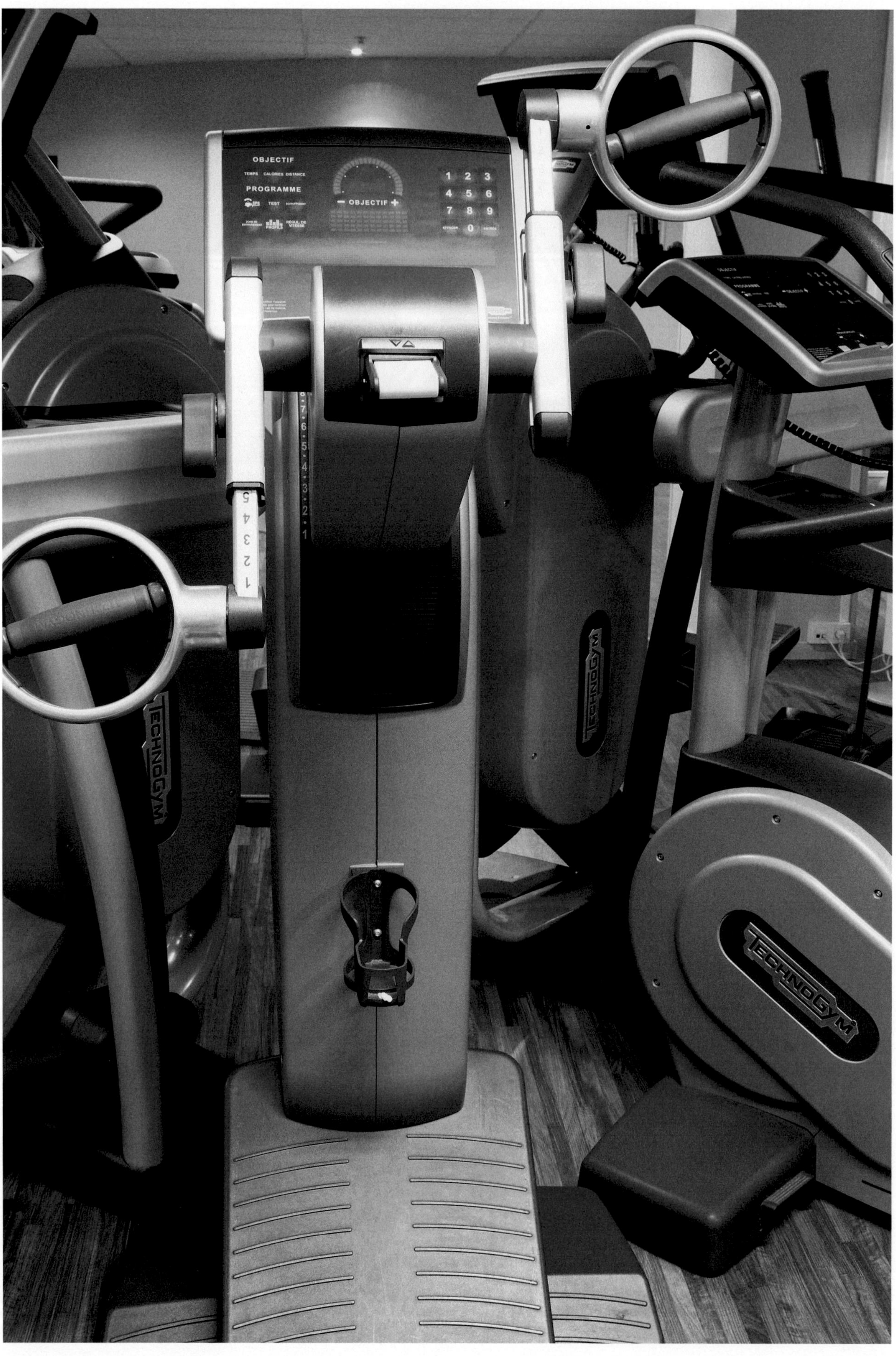

Stephanie Kiwitt, from *GYM*, 2012–2013

almost irrevocable division of labour, others could do better than these amateurs (*Freizeitler*). What they create has something superfluous about it. This superfluousness makes known the inferior quality of the product, which in turn vitiates any pleasure taken in its production.

Even the most superfluous and senseless activity undertaken in people's free time is integrated in society. Once again a social need is at work. Certain forms of service, in particular domestic servants, are dying out; demand is disproportionate to supply. In America only the really wealthy can afford to keep servants, and Europe is following close behind. This means that many people carry out activities which were formerly delegated. The slogan 'do it yourself' latches onto this as practical advice. However, it also latches on to the resentment which people feel towards mechanization, which unburdens people, without – and not the fact itself but only its current interpretation is a matter of dispute – their having any use for the newly acquired time. Thus, once again in the interests of certain specialized industries, people are encouraged to perform tasks, which others could do more simply and more proficiently for them, and which for this very reason, deep down, they must despise. Actually, the idea that one can save the money one spends on services, in a society based upon the division of labour, belongs to a very old level of bourgeois consciousness; it is an economy made from stubborn self-interest, an economy which flies in the face of the fact that it is only the exchange of specialized skills which keeps the whole mechanism going in the first place. William Tell, the obnoxious paradigm of absolute individuality, proclaimed that the household axe spared the need for the carpenter – indeed a whole ontology of bourgeois consciousness could be compiled from Schiller's maxims.

'Do it yourself', this contemporary type of spare time behaviour fits however into a much more far-reaching context. More than thirty years ago I described such behaviour as 'pseudo-activity'. Since then pseudo-activity has spread alarmingly, even (and especially) amongst those people who regard themselves as anti-establishment. Generally speaking there is good reason to assume that all forms of pseudo-activity contain a pent-up need to change the petrified relations of society. Pseudo-activity is misguided spontaneity. Misguided, but not accidentally so; because people do have a dim suspicion of how hard it would be to throw off the yoke that weighs upon them. They prefer to be distracted by spurious and illusory activities, by institutionalized vicarious satisfactions, than to face up to the awareness of how little access they have to the possibility of change today. Pseudo-activities are fictions and parodies of the same productivity which society on the one hand incessantly calls for, but on the other holds in check and, as far as the individual is concerned, does not really desire at all. Productive free time is only possible for people who have outgrown their tutelage, not for those who under conditions of heteronomy, have become heteronomous for themselves.

Free time then does not merely stand in opposition to labour. In a system where full employment itself has become the ideal, free time is nothing more than a shadowy continuation of labour. As yet we still lack an incisive sociology of sport, and particularly of the spectator. Nevertheless one hypothesis, amongst others, springs to mind; namely that, by dint of the physical exertion exacted by sport, by dint of the functionalization of the body in team-activity, which interestingly enough occurs in the most popular sports, people are unwittingly trained into modes of behaviour which, sublimated to a greater or lesser degree, are required of them by the work process. The accepted reason for playing sport is that it makes believe that fitness itself is the sole, independent end of sport: whereas fitness for work is certainly one of the covert ends of sport. Frequently it is in sport that people first inflict upon themselves (and celebrate as a triumph of their own freedom) precisely what society inflicts upon them and what they must learn to enjoy.

Let me say a little more on the relation of free time and the culture industry. Since Horkheimer and I coined the term more than thirty years ago, so much has been written about this means of domination and integration, that I should like to pick out a particular problem, which at the time we were not able to gain a proper perspective on. The ideology critic, dealing with the culture industry, and working on the premise that the standards of the culture industry are the ossified standards of what was formerly entertainment and low art, has the tendency to believe that the culture industry totally and utterly dominates and controls both the conscious and the unconscious of those people at whom it is directed – the same people out of whose taste during the liberal era the culture industry grew. Nevertheless there is reason to believe that production regulates consumption in the process of mental life, just as it does in that of material life, especially where the former has so closely approximated the latter, as it has in the culture industry. One would have thought the culture industry was perfectly adapted to its consumers. But since the culture industry has meanwhile become total – itself a phenomenon of the eversame, from which it promises temporarily to divert people – it is doubtful whether the culture industry and consumer-consciousness can be simply equated with one another. A few years ago at the Frankfurt Institute for Social Research we conducted a study devoted to this problem. Unfortunately, the full analysis of this material was postponed in favour of more pressing tasks. Nevertheless a passing inspection of it does reveal something which might well be relevant to the so-called problem of free time. The study concerned the wedding of Princess Beatrix of Holland with the junior German diplomat Claus von Amsberg. The objective was to assess the reactions of the German public to the wedding, which was broadcast by all the mass media, dwelt on incessantly by the illustrated weeklies, and so consumed by the public in their free time. Since the way in which the event was presented, like the articles written about it, accorded it an unusual degree of importance, we expected the spectators and readers to treat it just as seriously. In particular we expected to observe the operation of the characteristic contemporary ideology of personalization; through which, as a clear compensation for the functionalization of reality, the value of individual people and private relationships is immeasurably overestimated in comparison to actual social determinants. I should now like to say with due caution, that these expectations were too simplistic. In fact the study offers a virtually text book example of how critical-theoretical thought can both learn from and be corrected by empirical social research. It was possible to detect symptoms of a split consciousness. On the one hand people enjoyed it as a concrete event in the here and now quite unlike anything else in their everyday life: it was to be a 'unique experience' (*einmalig*) to use a cliché beloved of modern German. To this extent the reaction of the audience corresponded to the familiar pattern, according to which even the relevant, possibly political news was transformed into a consumer item by the way in which the information was transmitted. The format of our interview, however, was devised in such a way that the questions concerned with determining the immediate reactions of the viewers, were supplemented by control questions about the political significance that the interviewees ascribed to the grand event. Here it turned out that many of the people interviewed – we shall ignore the exact proportion – suddenly showed themselves to be thoroughly realistic, and proceeded to evaluate critically the political and social importance of the same event, the well publicized once-in-a-lifetime nature of which they had drooled over breathlessly in front of their television sets. What the culture industry presents people with in their free time, if my conclusions are not too hasty, is indeed consumed and accepted, but with a kind of reservation, in the same way that even the most naive theatre or filmgoers do not simply take what they behold there for real. Perhaps one can go even further and say that it is not quite believed in. It is obvious that the integration of consciousness and free time has not yet completely succeeded. The real interests of individuals are still strong enough to resist, within certain limits, total inclusion. That would concur with the social prediction that a society, whose inherent contradictions persist undiminished, cannot be totally integrated even in consciousness. Society cannot have it all its own way, especially not in free time, which does indeed lay claim to people, but by its very nature still cannot totally claim them without pushing them over the edge. I shall refrain from spelling out the consequences; but I think that we can here glimpse a chance of maturity (*Mündigkeit*), which might just eventually help to turn free time into freedom proper.

Reprint from:
Theodor W. Adorno, *The Culture Industry*, 2001 [1969]

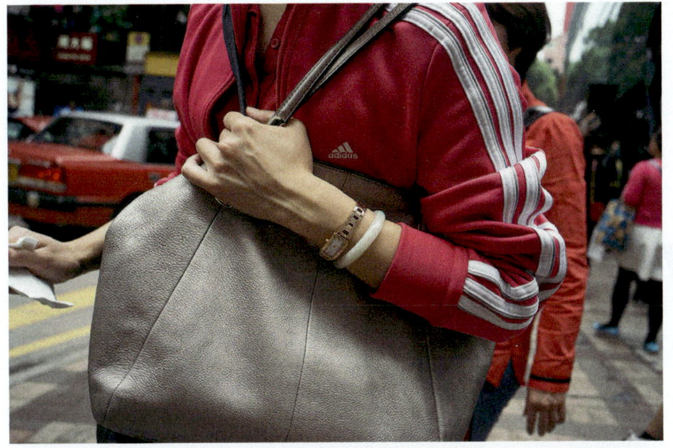

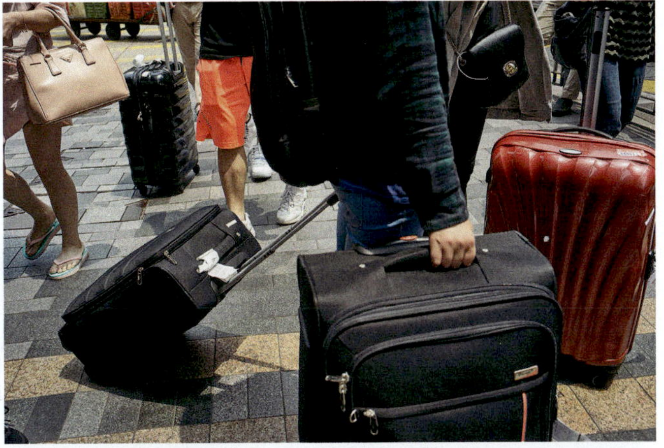

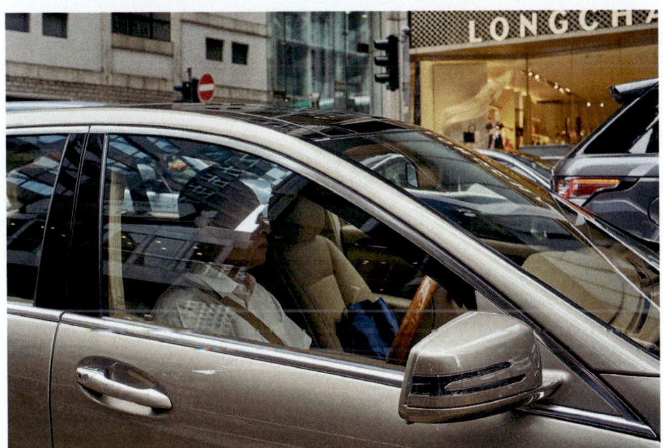

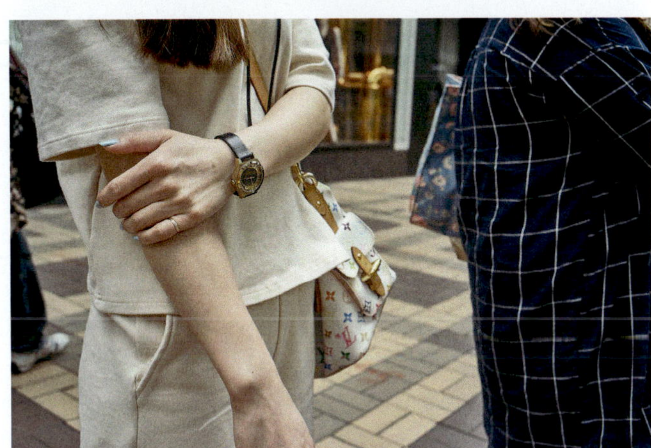

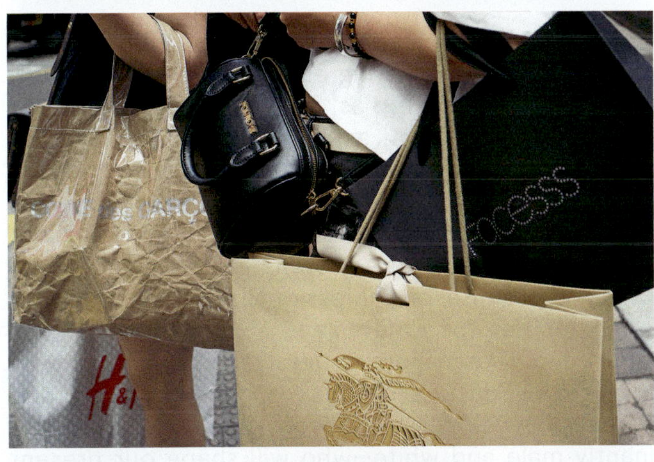

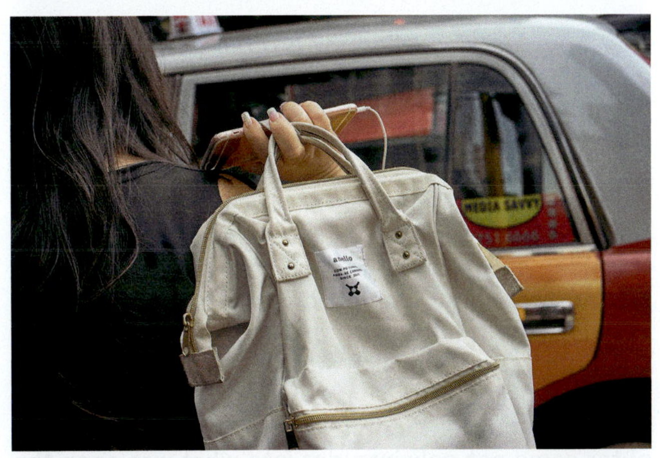

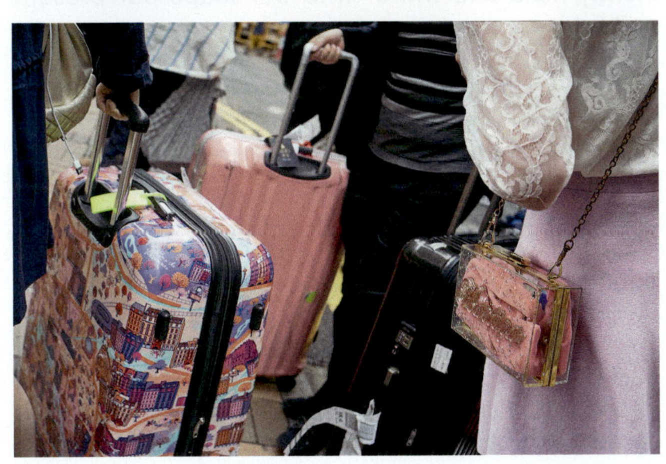

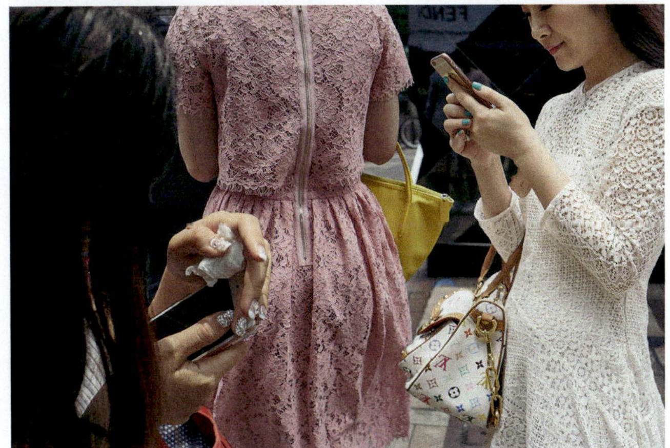

Volker Heinze, from *Mapping Hong Kong's Bet on Greed*, 2016

BETWEEN WORK, PLAY, AND ATTENTION

Hobbies/Images under Digital Conditions

Doris Gassert

"My mom just cancelled my brother's *World of Warcraft* account and he is freaking out—oh my God!" A young teenager with dental braces smirks gloatingly into the camera he is carrying as he leads us upstairs to the room where his brother is writhing on the bed like a wild animal fighting for survival, shrieking, and totally out of control. *My Generation* is the title of the video by Italian net art pioneers Eva and Franco Mattes, who have compiled sequences of footage showing the meltdowns and outbursts of young computer gamers, which was filmed and posted on YouTube. It is a work that plays right into the hands of the most ardent cultural pessimists: for the computer game not only intrudes into what was once the safe space of the 'innocent' child's room, but even infiltrates the minds of a new generation of gamers, governing their emotions to the point of complete self-abandonment. *My Generation* features volatile and psychologically unstable media junkies—only male and mostly white—whose hobby has become an addiction, and the game itself bitter reality.

Is gaming a hobby? Hobby and leisure pursuits in today's information age have certainly become increasingly media- and screen-based: computer games, television, and Internet are trending. Whereas, in the 1970s, gaming was mainly the preserve of a group of techie geeks and hobbyists, it has now become a mass phenomenon that has developed into a market-dominating entertainment and leisure industry. Long debated as, at best, a senseless waste of time and, at worst, as a damaging pursuit fueling aggressive and addictive behavior, the social acceptance of gaming as an eagerly practiced hobby has slowly but surely increased. This is not least due to the marketing machine of a growing games industry that drives a promise of professionalization and earning opportunities for a new generation of gamers. The freaked-out teenagers in *My Generation* might be tomorrow's YouTube millionaires, game designers, and software developers of Silicon Valley—also predominantly male and white—who will shape our present and future.

Against the backdrop of digital change, the computer game is perhaps the paradigmatic hobby of the transition to the twenty-first century: both a (child's) game and a leisure pursuit, it is also a genuine media product of our times. Games carry us off into a simulated, parallel world where (within certain regulated bounds) we act and make decisions. With mobile devices and faster connectivity, such immersion in mediatized parallel worlds has become an integral part of our experience of reality, which is increasingly informed by images and screens. The smartphone screen, in particular, draws us into other worlds

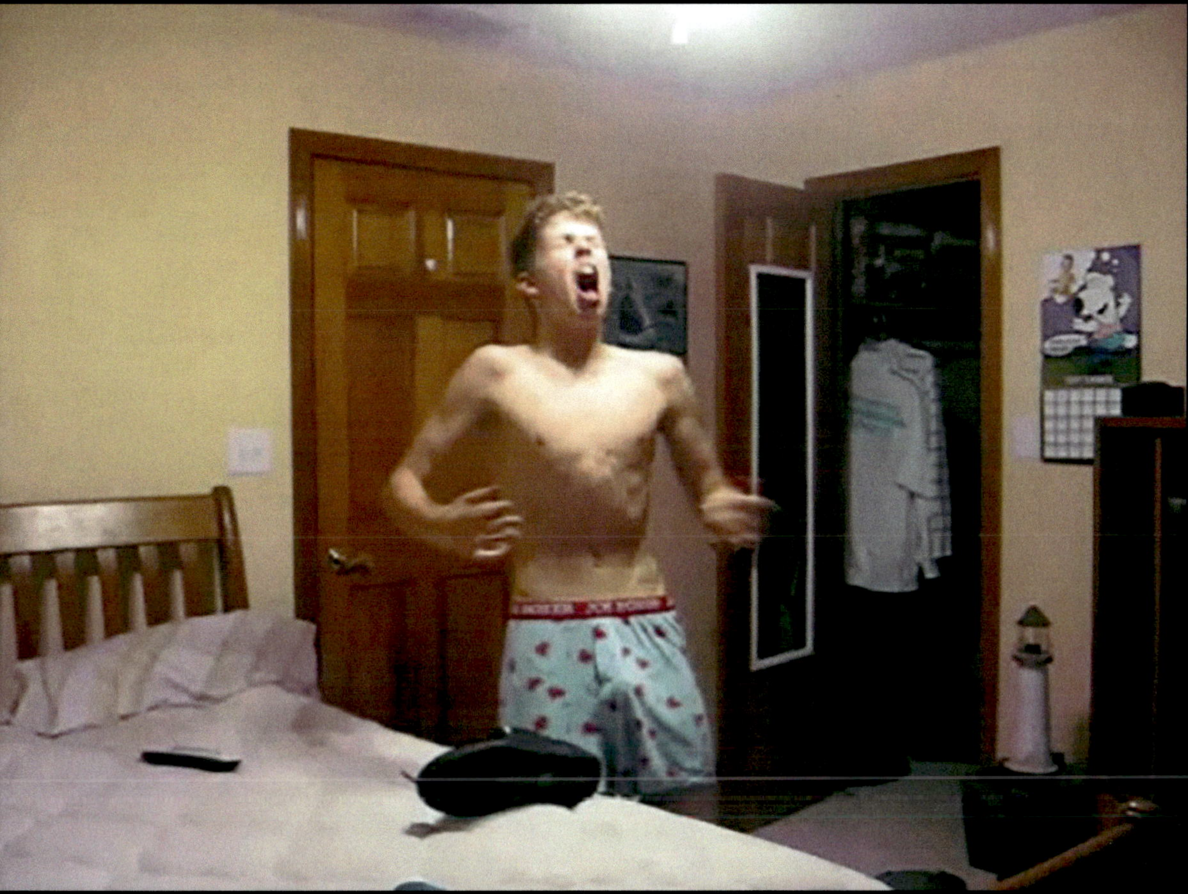

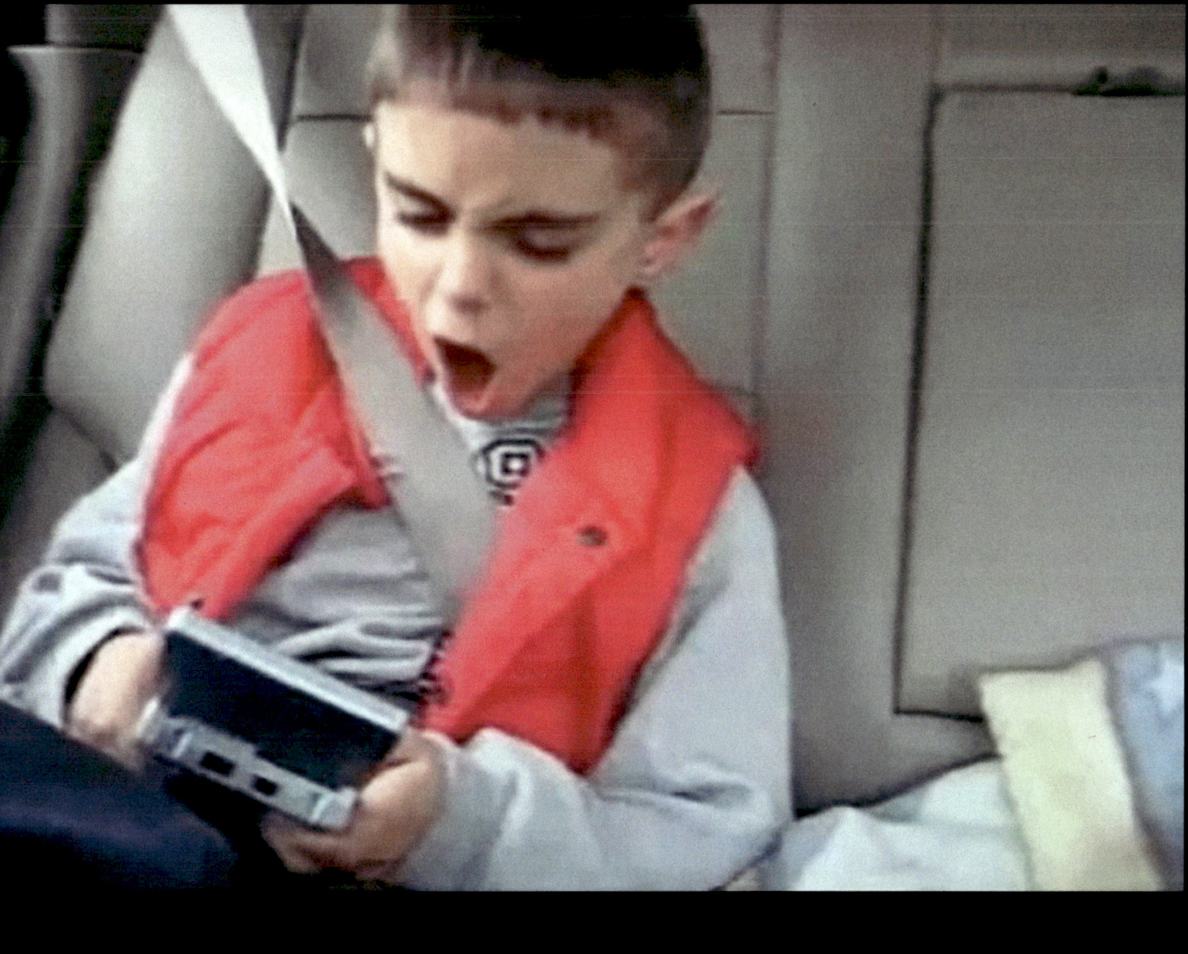

Eva & Franco Mattes, from *My Generation*, 2010

My Generation, 2010. Photo: Julian Abrams

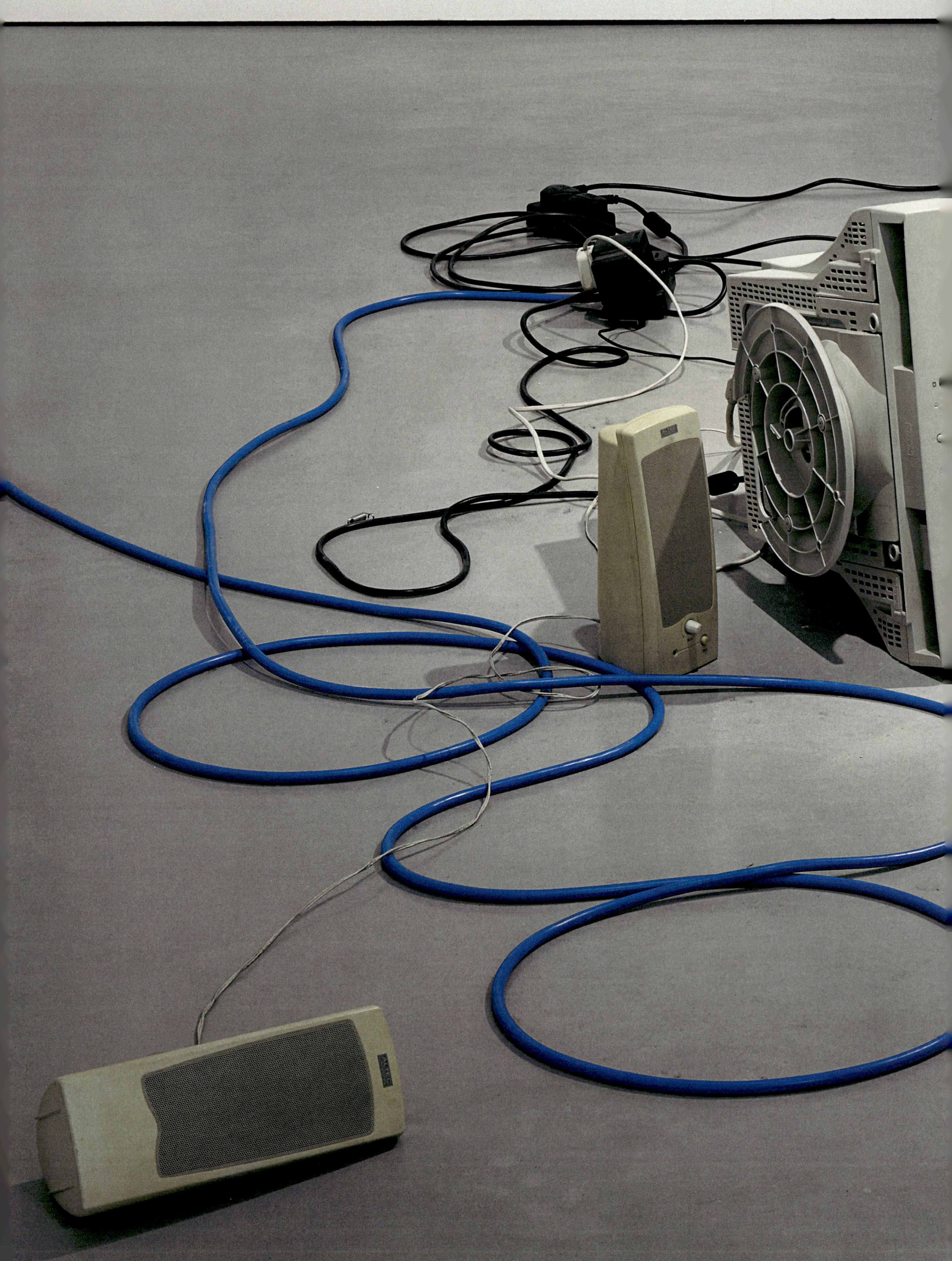

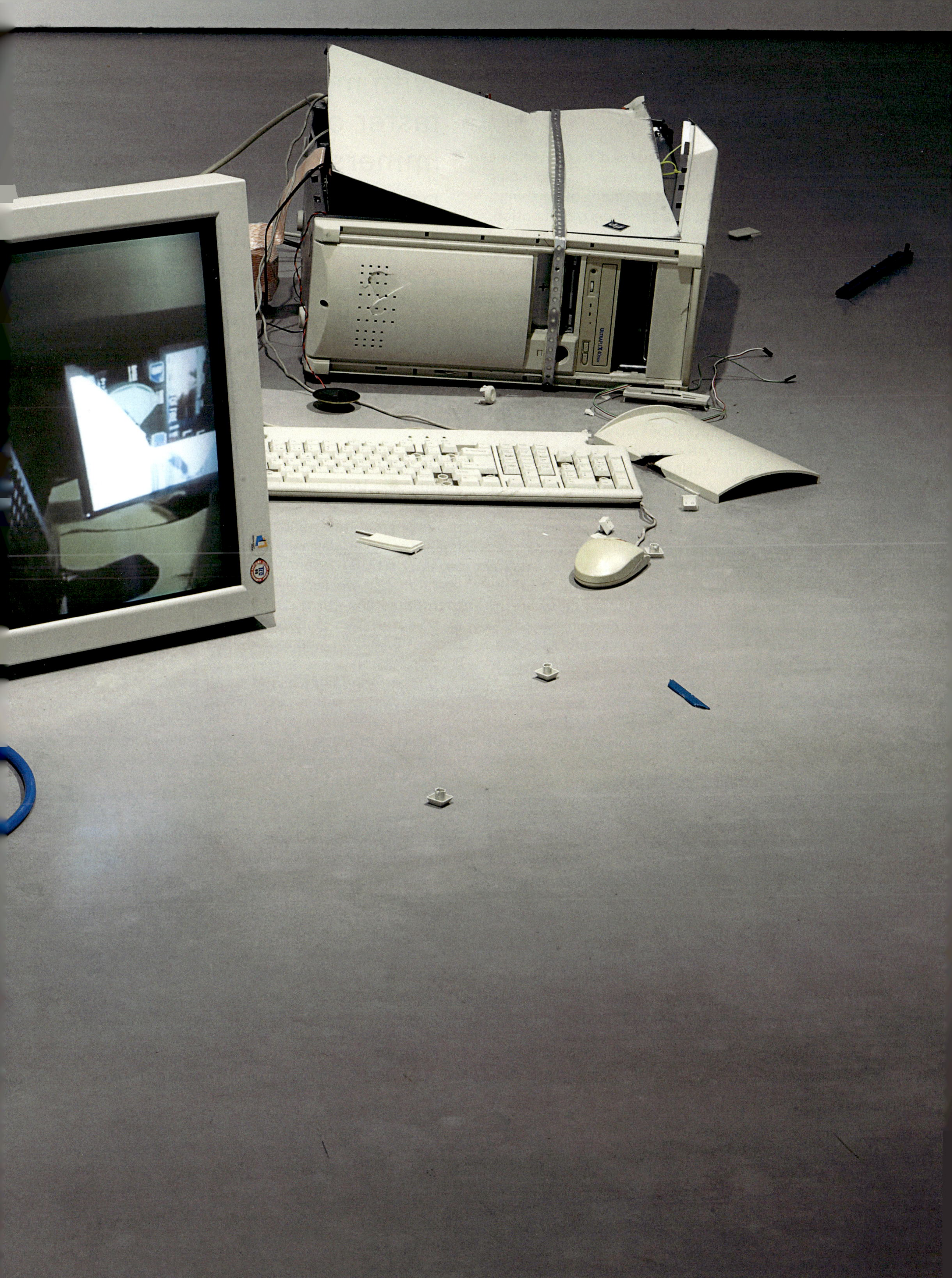

within seconds, and today we navigate between them as a matter of course. While in the early years of the twentieth century it was film, according to Walter Benjamin, that served "to train human beings in the apperceptions and reactions needed to deal with a vast apparatus whose role in their lives is expanding almost daily," a century later it is, among other things, the computer game that has taken on this function. Through play, it trains perception and our handling of the new digital devices. According to media theorist Marshall McLuhan, the tools we create in turn shape and in/form us: irrespective of their content, they affect us as media, influencing our sensory organs and altering our perception, our thinking, and our entire lifeworld.

In terms of the changing work and leisure behavior under these digital conditions, it is fundamentally the case that the classic categories of work and leisure, amateur culture and professionalism, production and consumption are increasingly disintegrating. Unlike the couch potatoes of the television era, the digital age has spawned such hybrids as 'prosumers' and 'produsers,' who are not just passive consumers or users, but who actively participate, produce, and distribute by means of their access to various digital tools, networks, and platforms. When the YouTube generation makes the Internet a hobby, they are no longer merely consuming, but are creating videos as well, distributing them online and in some cases even making a lot of money doing so.

For her work *People Younger Than Me Explaining How To Do Things* (2013–) the American Internet artist Jenny Odell compiled a selection of screenshots from 'how to' videos made by teenagers and posted on YouTube. Whether it is about how to apply your make-up properly, how to ditch your girlfriend, or how to enhance your cleavage—filmed for the most part in some kid's bedroom or within the home environment—it is the self that is communicating with the world, with the anonymous masses, and benevolently sharing a life experience. Three years after launching her project, Odell noted an entirely different visual aesthetic in these youth videos that heralded a shift from the amateur "unmediated" and "informal" home video to the "hyper-produced" video that appropriates professional advertising strategies right through to the "sponsored how-to" video including "corporate product placement." As such the ego goes far beyond merely putting itself in the spotlight and becomes part of a capitalist, neo-liberal, value-added chain in which life, lifestyle, hobbies, and (un)paid work converge.

These dynamics are inextricably linked with photography and the increasing visualization and mediatization of our lifeworld. The photographic image contributes to a hobby, transforming it into a visual and thus malleable, optimizable, marketable product. Today, we are all increasingly involved in (re-) producing capitalist and neo-liberal values in hobby images: as everyday snappers increasingly influenced by standardized forms of staging in advertising and social media, we ourselves become advertising photographers and our hobby images are no longer just an object of identification but also a status symbol, a promotional item, and a model we aspire to.

With mobile devices and faster connectivity, such immersion in mediatized parallel worlds has become an integral part of our experience of reality, which is increasingly informed by images and screens.

Digital technology allows us to snap a picture or record a video within seconds, share it with friends on social media, and send it around the world. The photographic image is a networked, shared, migrating image that is increasingly shaped by our own views and turns the picture of the world into a world as a picture. Catch a fish, snap a photo (choosing an angle that makes the fish look enormous), add a filter (a retro look suits this theme nicely), then post it on Instagram, where it is liked, commented on, and shared by friends—more and more, we're 'doing it for the 'gram.' Any hobby, no matter how classic, is increasingly becoming part and parcel of a visual chain of commercialization, integrated into the processes and (attention) economies of a digitally networked visual communication.

And then there are also those hobbies that are inextricably linked to the image itself, the very purpose and experience of which feeds off the photographic shoot and its distribution. When the Russian photographer Alexander Remnev scales the highest skyscrapers and cranes a city has to offer without any safety gear and equipped with only a smartphone and a selfie stick, then it is not just about capturing the breathtaking photographic views of the urban landscape, but above all about the spectacularly staged

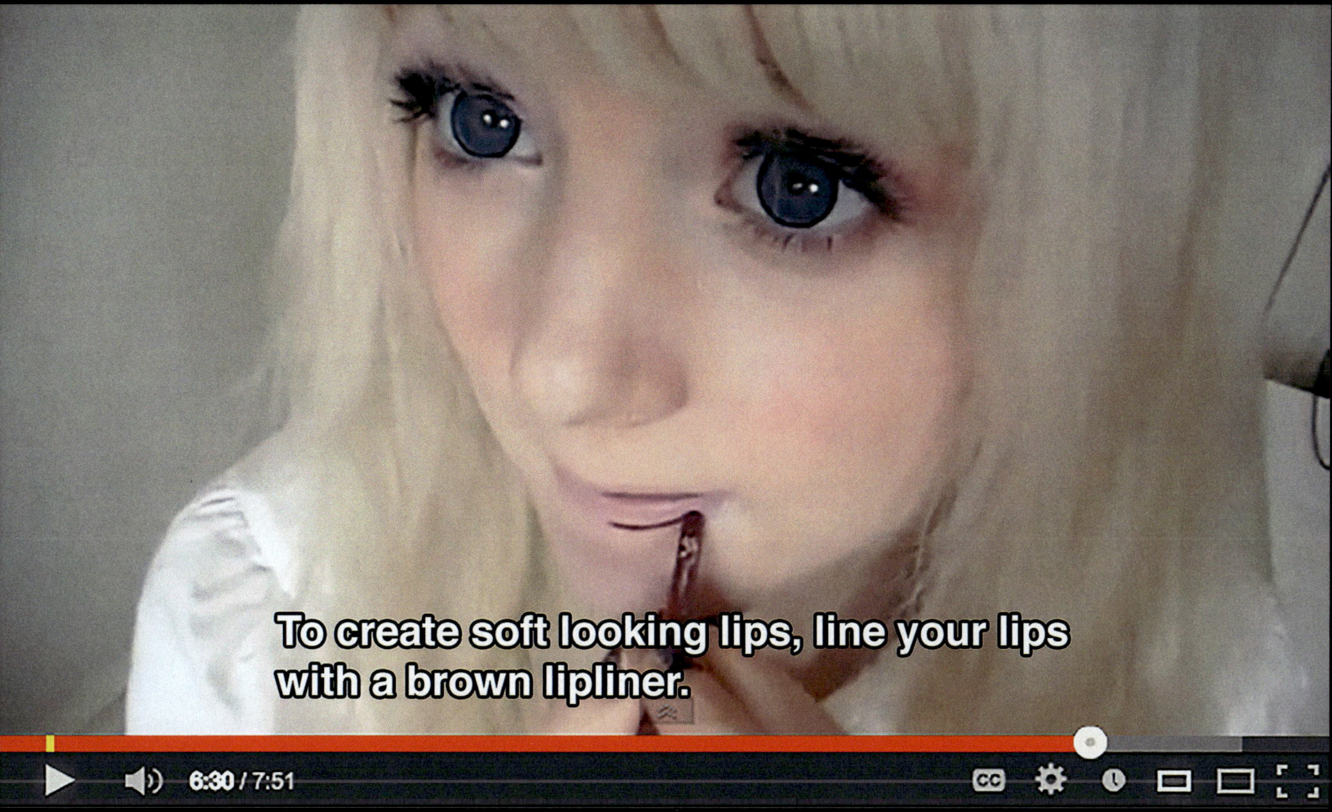

To create soft looking lips, line your lips with a brown lipliner.

6:30 / 7:51

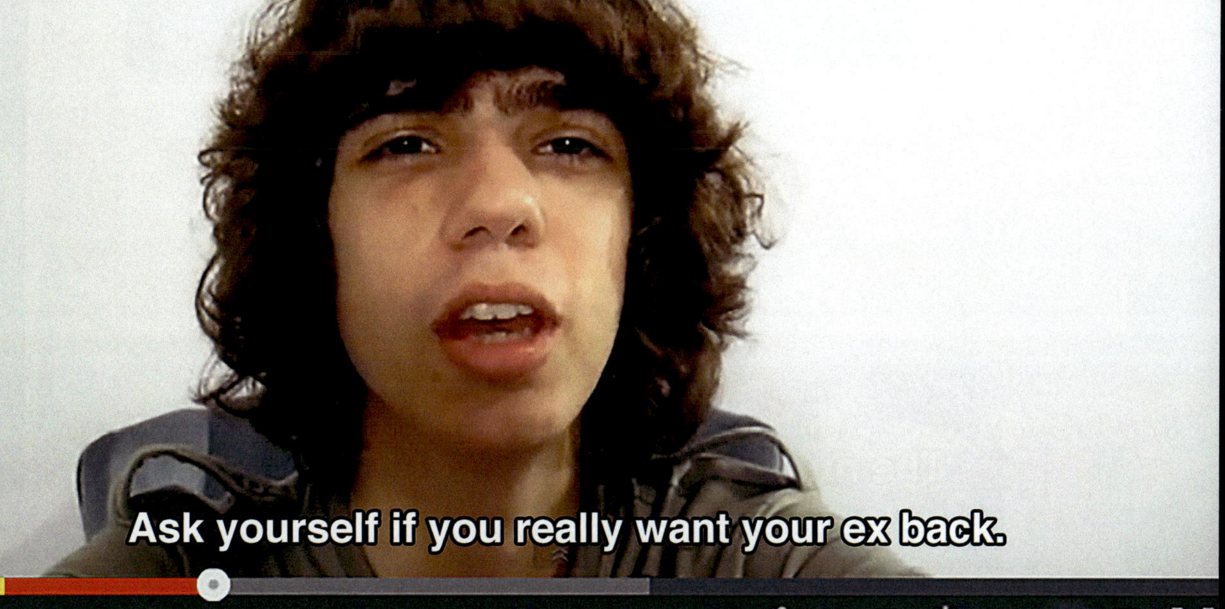

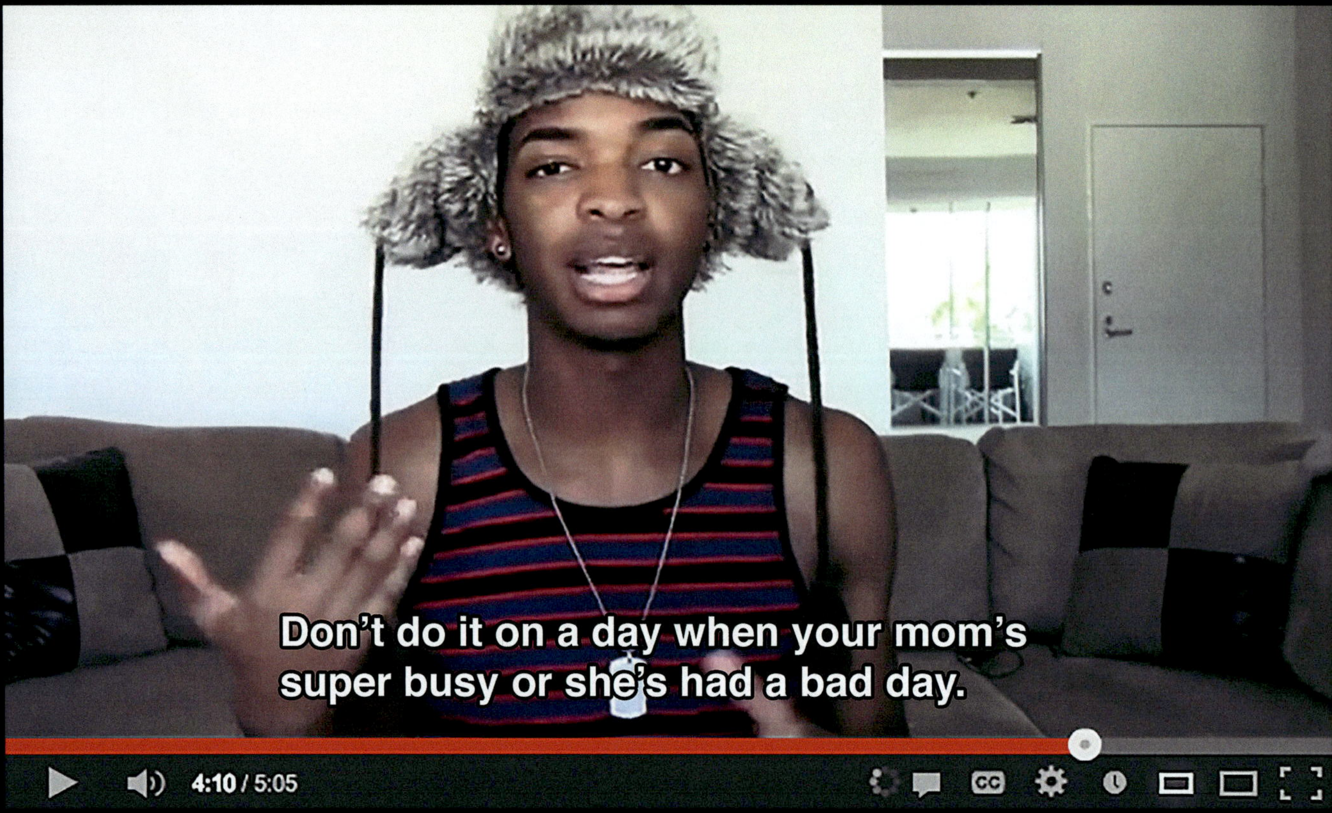

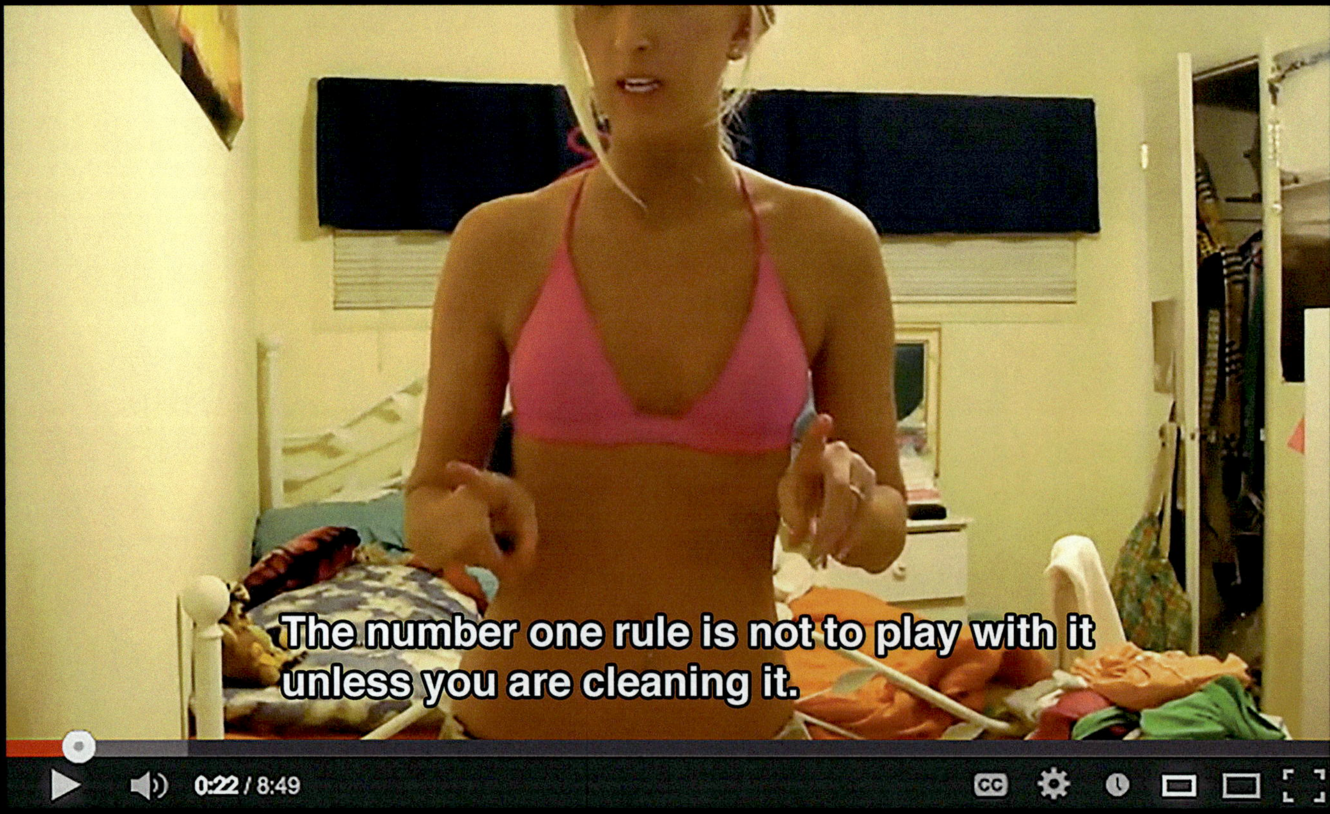

Don't do it on a day when your mom's super busy or she's had a bad day.

4:10 / 5:05

The number one rule is not to play with it unless you are cleaning it.

0:22 / 8:49

Jenny Odell, from *People Younger Than Me Explaining How to Do Things*, 2013–

The photographic image contributes to a hobby, transforming it into a visual and thus malleable, optimizable, marketable product.

demonstration of life and survival. Photographic and video recordings of his stunts on the edge aim to set his images apart from the current visual flood, and get them noticed. The presence of the camera spurs on the performance, which, in turn, becomes a distinguishing feature that creates a sense of identity for the lifestyle of the community. The thrill of 'roofing' or 'skywalking' lies not only in its life-threatening challenge and illegality, but also in the photographic image's promise of fame and media immortality. Lifestyle and life become one in the image. Just how strongly even this relationship can be commercialized is evident in Remnev's latest project: photographing slender models in classic poses on rugged rooftops with spectacular views into the cavernous city below. For 200 US dollars and just a touch of courage, anyone can have themselves photographed in this exceptional way without actually risking their lives. The real thrill is sure to lie in posting the photos and garnering the adulation of 'friends.' And just like that, the hobby of a Russian subculture deprived of future prospects has turned into a new trending hashtag.

Actions such as these blur the boundaries between work, leisure, play and lifestyle, serving in turn as a model for companies to exploit labor for financial gain by packaging it as a hobby and aspirational activity. The fact that this imbues both work and free time with a precarious status is highlighted by theoretical concepts such as 'free labor' (Tiziana Terranova) and 'precarious playbor' (Julian Kücklich). Using the gamer scene as an example, Kücklich elucidates the central role that identification as a hobbyist actually plays in carrying out unpaid creative work, and just how strongly the gaming industry shores up such ideological values as democratic access to tools and participative powers of creativity in order to profit from them.

"For companies it is very clear that the new source of added value in the digital economy is user participation," writes Trebor Scholz in his introduction to the anthology *Digital Labor. The Internet as Playground and Factory,* which "claims that the divide between leisure time and work has vanished so that every aspect of life drives the digital economy." Since the boundaries between work, leisure, and play also blur on a perceptual level in online environments, in particular, it is possible to tap into labor in an area that feels least like work and most like free time. Every 'like,' every click, every share, and every term put into a search engine is a form of unpaid labor that generates profits for Google, Facebook, and their ilk, because they evaluate our digital footprint and allow targeted advertising. And what is more: they also organize our attention, through which our perceptions and thinking is regulated. "This is the attention economy, built upon the premise becoming conviction, becoming fact, that human attention is productive of value," writes Jonathan Beller, who examines the links between attention, post-industrial production, and capital—and who denies that there is still any kind of free time in which we can escape all of that. Under digital conditions both *work* and *play* function according to capitalist, neo-liberal rules whose mechanisms we have yet to decipher.

Alexander Remnev, ***Need Adrenaline!*****, 2014**

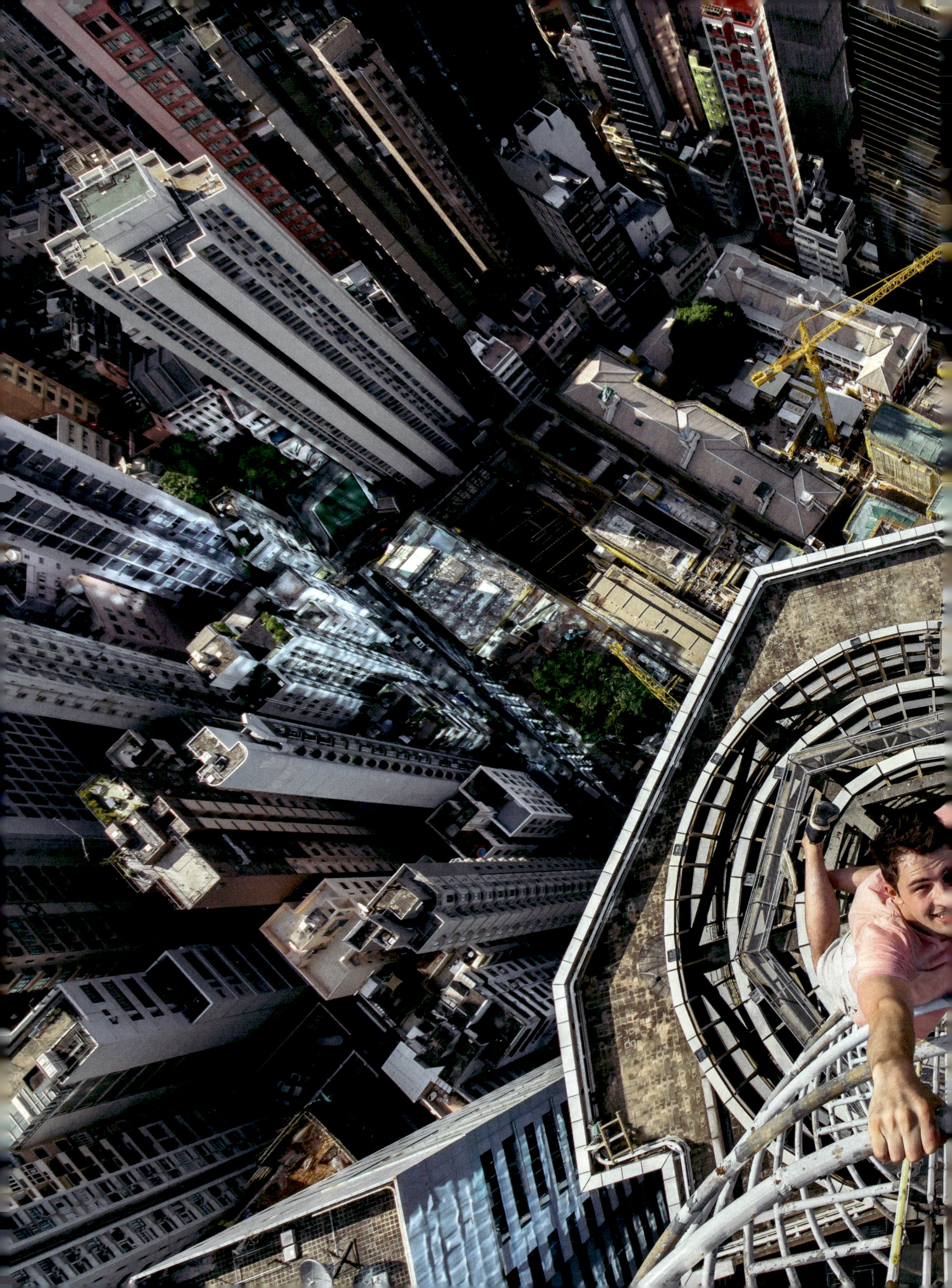

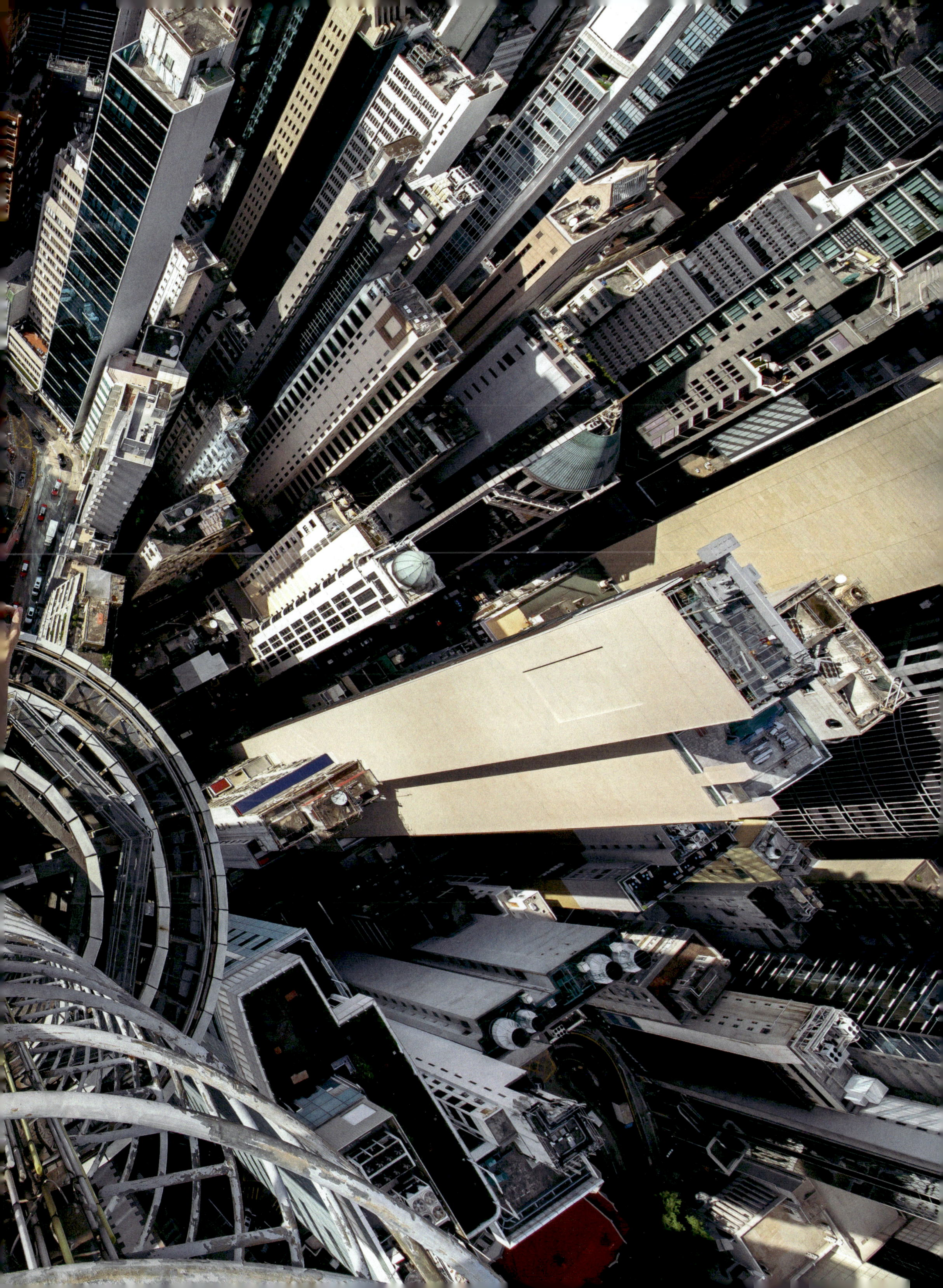

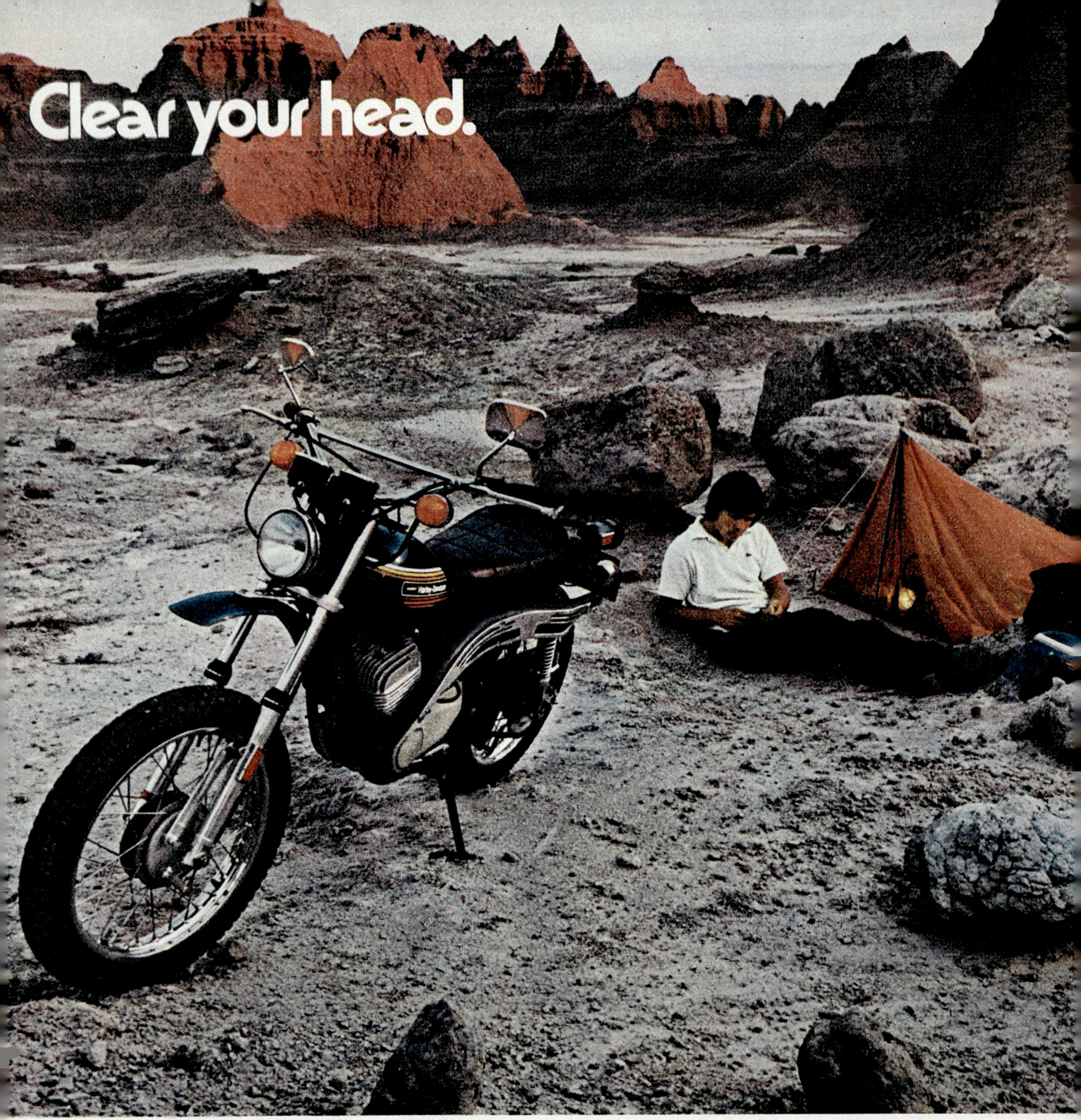

ALL NEW HARLEY-DAVIDSON SX-175

With a Harley-Davidson SX-175. A rugged on-road, off-road freedom machine.

It has a two-stroke, oil-injected, chrome bore, aluminum cylinder engine that'll move you out and away.

Plus breakerless CDI ignition, 5-way adjustable rear shocks, 5-speed trans, tachometer, speedometer, solid state rectifier and 12-volt alternator.

And more. I.S.D.T. quick, detachable rear wheel, primary kick start, cross-braced handlebars, oil tank integral with frame. Safety rim locks.

A hefty moto-cross type front fork with 6½" travel, labyrinth seal brake hubs, and full electrics are also part of the bargain. So when things hassle you, throw some stuff on your SX-175, kick her down, and move out to where you can get some freedom and solitude.

And clear your head.

The Great American Freedom Machine.

AMF Harley-Davidson

AMF Harley-Davidson • Milwaukee, Wisconsin 53201 • Member Motorcycle Industry Council